PYTHON 3

AND

MACHINE LEARNING
USING CHATGPT / GPT-4

Python 3
and
Machine Learning
Using ChatGPT / GPT-4

Oswald Campesato

Mercury Learning and Information
Boston, Massachusetts

Publisher: David Pallai
MERCURY LEARNING AND INFORMATION
121 High Street, 3rd Floor
Boston, MA 02110
info@merclearning.com
www.merclearning.com
800-232-0223

O. Campesato. *Python 3 and Machine Learning Using ChatGPT / GPT-4.*
ISBN: 978-1-50152-295-6

Library of Congress Control Number: 2024935754
242526321   This book is printed on acid-free paper in the United States of America.

Our titles are available for adoption, license, or bulk purchase by institutions, corporations, etc. For additional information, please contact the Customer Service Dept. at 800-232-0223(toll free).

I'd like to dedicate this book to my parents
– may this bring joy and happiness into their lives.

CONTENTS

*P*REFACE

This book is designed to bridge the gap between theoretical knowledge and practical application in the fields of Python programming, machine learning, and the innovative use of ChatGPT in data science. It aims to provide a comprehensive guide for those who aspire to deepen their understanding and enhance their skills in these rapidly evolving areas.

The motivation stems from a growing demand for practical, in-depth resources that cater to the needs of students, data scientists, and AI researchers looking to leverage advanced techniques and tools. As these fields continue to grow in importance and impact, the ability to adeptly manipulate data, understand machine learning algorithms, and apply the latest advancements in AI becomes critical.

This book is structured to facilitate a deep understanding of several core topics:

- *Introduction to Pandas*: We begin with a detailed introduction to Pandas, a cornerstone Python library for data manipulation and analysis. This section is tailored to help you master data frames and perform complex data cleaning and preparation tasks efficiently.
- *Machine Learning Classifiers*: Next, we explore a variety of machine learning classifiers, providing you with the knowledge to choose and implement the right algorithm for your projects. From kNN to SVMs, you will learn the intricacies of each method through practical examples.
- *GPT-4 and Linear Regression*: As we explore the capabilities of GPT-4, we discuss its application in enhancing traditional linear regression analysis. This section demonstrates how GPT-4 can be used to perform and interpret regression in ways that push the boundaries of conventional data analysis.

⬛ *Data Visualization with ChatGPT*: Finally, the book covers the innovative use of ChatGPT in data visualization. This segment focuses on how AI can transform data into compelling visual stories, making complex results accessible and understandable. It includes material AI apps, GANs, and DALL-E.

Each chapter is crafted to build on the knowledge from the previous sections, ensuring a cohesive and comprehensive learning experience. To cater to a wide range of learning styles, the book includes step-by-step tutorials, real-world applications, and sections dedicated to theoretical concepts backed by practical examples. This approach not only solidifies understanding but also enhances your ability to apply these techniques in real-world scenarios.

Features of This Book

⬛ *Coverage of Latest Python Libraries*: You will gain proficiency in using state-of-the-art libraries essential for modern data scientists.

⬛ *Real-World Problem Solving*: The book challenges you to apply your skills on real data, preparing you for professional success.

⬛ *Companion files* with source code, datasets, and figures are available for downloading by writing to the publisher (with proof of purchase) to info@merclearning.com.

This book is more than just a learning tool; it is a reference that you will return to repeatedly as you progress in your career. Whether you are a beginner aiming to get a solid start in programming and data science or an experienced professional looking to explore new advancements in AI, "Python 3 and Machine Learning Using ChatGPT/GPT-4" is an invaluable asset.

We hope that you will find this book to be a valuable resource, one that inspires you to explore further and apply your knowledge to solve complex problems. The future of Generative AI is exciting and full of possibilities.

O. Campesato
April 2024

## CHAPTER 1

INTRODUCTION TO PANDAS

This chapter introduces you to Pandas and provides code samples that illustrate some of its useful features. If you are familiar with these topics, skim through the material and peruse the code samples, just in case they contain information that is new to you.

The first part contains a brief introduction to Pandas. This section contains code samples that illustrate some features of Pandas `DataFrames` and a brief discussion of series, which are two of the main features of Pandas.

The second part of this chapter discusses various types of data frames that you can create, such as numeric and Boolean data frames. In addition, we discuss examples of creating data frames with NumPy functions and random numbers.

Note: Several code samples in this chapter reference the `NumPy` library for working with arrays and generating random numbers, which you can learn from online articles.

WHAT IS PANDAS?

Pandas is a Python library that is compatible with other Python libraries, such as NumPy and Matplotlib. Install Pandas by opening a command shell and invoking this command for Python 3.x:

```
pip3 install pandas
```

In many ways, the semantics of the APIs in the Pandas library are similar to a spreadsheet, along with support for XSL, XML, HTML, and CSV file types. Pandas provides a data type called a *data frame* (similar to a Python dictionary) with an extremely powerful functionality.

Pandas data frames support a variety of input types, such as `ndarray`, `list`, `dict`, or `series`.

The data type `series` is another mechanism for managing data. In addition to performing an online search for more details regarding `series`, the following article contains a good introduction:

https://towardsdatascience.com/20-examples-to-master-pandas-series-bc4c68200324

Pandas Options and Settings

You can change the default values of environment variables, an example of which is shown below:

```
import pandas as pd

display_settings = {
    'max_columns': 8,
    'expand_frame_repr': True, # Wrap to multiple pages
    'max_rows': 20,
    'precision': 3,
    'show_dimensions': True
}

for op, value in display_settings.items():
  pd.set_option("display.{}".format(op), value)
```

Include the preceding code block in your own code if you want Pandas to display a maximum of 20 rows and 8 columns, and floating point numbers displayed with 3 decimal places. Set `expand_frame_rep` to `True` if you want the output to "wrap around" to multiple pages. The preceding `for` loop iterates through `display_settings` and sets the options equal to their corresponding values.

In addition, the following code snippet displays all Pandas options and their current values in your code:

```
print(pd.describe_option())
```

There are various other operations that you can perform with options and their values (such as the `pd.reset()` method for resetting values), as described in the Pandas user guide:

https://pandas.pydata.org/pandas-docs/stable/user_guide/options.html

Pandas Data Frames

In simplified terms, a Pandas *data frame* is a two-dimensional data structure, and it is convenient to think of the data structure in terms of rows and columns. Data frames can be labeled (rows as well as columns), and the columns can contain different data types. The source of the dataset for a Pandas data frame can be a data file, a database table, and a Web service. The data frame features include:

- Data frame methods
- Data frame statistics
- Grouping, pivoting, and reshaping
- Handle missing data
- Join data frames

The code samples in this chapter show you almost all the features in the preceding list.

Data Frames and Data Cleaning Tasks

The specific tasks that you need to perform depend on the structure and contents of a dataset. In general, you will perform a workflow with the following steps, not necessarily always in this order (and some might be optional). All of the following steps can be performed with a Pandas data frame:

- Read data into a data frame
- Display top of data frame
- Display column data types
- Display missing values
- Replace NA with a value
- Iterate through the columns
- Statistics for each column
- Find missing values
- Total missing values
- Percentage of missing values
- Sort table values
- Print summary information
- Columns with > 50% missing
- Rename columns

This chapter contains sections that illustrate how to perform many of the steps in the preceding list.

Alternatives to Pandas

Before delving into the code samples, there are alternatives to Pandas that offer very useful features, some of which are shown below:

- PySpark (for large datasets)
- Dask (for distributed processing)
- Modin (faster performance)
- Datatable (R data.table for Python)

The inclusion of these alternatives is not intended to diminish Pandas. Indeed, you might not need any of the functionality in the preceding list. However, in the event that you need such functionality in the future, so it is worthwhile for you to know about these alternatives now (and there may be even more powerful alternatives at some point in the future).

A PANDAS DATA FRAME WITH A NUMPY EXAMPLE

Listing 1.1 shows the content of `pandas_df.py` that illustrates how to define several data frames and display their contents.

LISTING 1.1: pandas_df.py

```
import pandas as pd
import numpy as np

myvector1 = np.array([1,2,3,4,5])
print("myvector1:")
print(myvector1)
print()

mydf1 = pd.Data frame(myvector1)
print("mydf1:")
print(mydf1)
print()

myvector2 = np.array([i for i in range(1,6)])
print("myvector2:")
print(myvector2)
print()

mydf2 = pd.Data frame(myvector2)
print("mydf2:")
print(mydf2)
print()

myarray = np.array([[10,30,20],
[50,40,60],[1000,2000,3000]])
print("myarray:")
print(myarray)
print()

mydf3 = pd.Data frame(myarray)
print("mydf3:")
print(mydf3)
print()
```

Listing 1.1 starts with standard `import` statements for Pandas and NumPy, followed by the definition of two one-dimensional NumPy arrays and a two-dimensional NumPy array. Each NumPy variable is followed by a corresponding Pandas data frame (mydf1, mydf2, and mydf3). Now launch the code in Listing 1.1 to see the following output, and you can compare the NumPy arrays with the Pandas data frames:

```
myvector1:
[1 2 3 4 5]

mydf1:
   0
0  1
1  2
2  3
3  4
4  5

myvector2:
[1 2 3 4 5]

mydf2:
   0
0  1
1  2
2  3
3  4
4  5

myarray:
[[   10    30    20]
 [   50    40    60]
 [1000 2000 3000]]

mydf3:
      0     1     2
0    10    30    20
1    50    40    60
2  1000  2000  3000
```

By contrast, the following code block illustrates how to define two Pandas Series that are part of the definition of a Pandas data frame:

```
names = pd.Series(['SF', 'San Jose', 'Sacramento'])
sizes = pd.Series([852469, 1015785, 485199])
df = pd.Data frame({ 'Cities': names, 'Size': sizes })
print(df)
```

Create a Python file with the preceding code (along with the required import statement), and when you launch that code, you will see the following output:

```
      City name      sizes
0            SF     852469
1     San Jose    1015785
2    Sacramento    485199
```

DESCRIBING A PANDAS DATA FRAME

Listing 1.2 shows the content of `pandas_df_describe.py`, which illustrates how to define a Pandas data frame that contains a 3x3 NumPy array of integer values, where the rows and columns of the data frame are labeled. Other aspects of the data frame are also displayed.

LISTING 1.2: pandas_df_describe.py

```python
import numpy as np
import pandas as pd

myarray = np.array([[10,30,20],
[50,40,60],[1000,2000,3000]])

rownames = ['apples', 'oranges', 'beer']
colnames = ['January', 'February', 'March']

mydf = pd.Data frame(myarray, index=rownames,
columns=colnames)
print("contents of df:")
print(mydf)
print()

print("contents of January:")
print(mydf['January'])
print()

print("Number of Rows:")
print(mydf.shape[0])
print()

print("Number of Columns:")
print(mydf.shape[1])
print()

print("Number of Rows and Columns:")
print(mydf.shape)
print()

print("Column Names:")
print(mydf.columns)
print()

print("Column types:")
print(mydf.dtypes)
print()
```

```
print("Description:")
print(mydf.describe())
print()
```

Listing 1.2 starts with two standard import statements followed by the variable myarray, which is a 3x3 NumPy array of numbers. The variables row-names and colnames provide names for the rows and columns, respectively, of the Pandas data frame mydf, which is initialized as a Pandas data frame with the specified data source (i.e., myarray).

The first portion of the output below requires a single print() statement (which simply displays the contents of mydf). The second portion of the output is generated by invoking the describe() method that is available for any Pandas data frame. The describe() method is useful: you will see various statistical quantities, such as the mean, standard deviation minimum, and maximum performed by *columns* (not rows), along with values for the 25th, 50th, and 75th percentiles. The output of Listing 1.2 is here:

```
contents of df:
         January  February  March
apples        10        30     20
oranges       50        40     60
beer        1000      2000   3000

contents of January:
apples        10
oranges       50
beer        1000
Name: January, dtype: int64

Number of Rows:
3

Number of Columns:
3

Number of Rows and Columns:
(3, 3)

Column Names:
Index(['January', 'February', 'March'], dtype='object')

Column types:
January     int64
February    int64
March       int64
dtype: object

Description:
            January     February       March
count      3.000000     3.000000    3.000000
mean     353.333333   690.000000  1026.666667
```

```
std        560.386771   1134.504297   1709.073823
min         10.000000     30.000000     20.000000
25%         30.000000     35.000000     40.000000
50%         50.000000     40.000000     60.000000
75%        525.000000   1020.000000   1530.000000
max       1000.000000   2000.000000   3000.000000
```

PANDAS BOOLEAN DATA FRAMES

Pandas supports Boolean operations on data frames, such as the logical OR, the logical AND, and the logical negation of a pair of data frames. Listing 1.3 shows the content of pandas_boolean_df.py that illustrates how to define a Pandas data frame whose rows and columns are Boolean values.

LISTING 1.3: pandas_boolean_df.py

```
import pandas as pd

df1 = pd.Data frame({'a': [1, 0, 1], 'b': [0, 1, 1] },
dtype=bool)
df2 = pd.Data frame({'a': [0, 1, 1], 'b': [1, 1, 0] },
dtype=bool)

print("df1 & df2:")
print(df1 & df2)

print("df1 | df2:")
print(df1 | df2)

print("df1 ^ df2:")
print(df1 ^ df2)
```

Listing 1.3 initializes the data frames df1 and df2, and then computes df1 & df2, df1 | df2, and df1 ^ df2, which represent the logical AND, the logical OR, and the logical negation, respectively, of df1 and df2. The output from launching the code in Listing 1.3 is as follows:

```
df1 & df2:
        a       b
0   False   False
1   False    True
2    True   False
df1 | df2:
        a       b
0    True    True
1    True    True
2    True    True
df1 ^ df2:
        a       b
0    True    True
1    True   False
2   False    True
```

Transposing a Pandas Data Frame

The T attribute (as well as the transpose function) enables you to generate the transpose of a Pandas data frame, similar to the NumPy ndarray. The transpose operation switches rows to columns and columns to rows. For example, the following code snippet defines a Pandas data frame df1 and then displays the transpose of df1:

```
df1 = pd.Data frame({'a': [1, 0, 1], 'b': [0, 1, 1] },
dtype=int)

print ("df1.T:")
print (df1.T)
```

The output of the preceding code snippet is here:

```
df1.T:
   0  1  2
a  1  0  1
b  0  1  1
```

The following code snippet defines Pandas data frames df1 and df2 and then displays their sum:

```
df1 = pd.Data frame({'a' : [1, 0, 1], 'b' : [0, 1, 1] },
dtype=int)
df2 = pd.Data frame({'a' : [3, 3, 3], 'b' : [5, 5, 5] },
dtype=int)

print ("df1 + df2:")
print (df1 + df2)
```

The output is here:

```
df1 + df2:
   a  b
0  4  5
1  3  6
2  4  6
```

PANDAS DATA FRAMES AND RANDOM NUMBERS

Listing 1.4 shows the content of pandas_random_df.py that illustrates how to create a Pandas data frame with random integers.

LISTING 1.4: pandas_random_df.py

```
import pandas as pd
import numpy as np
```

```
df = pd.Data frame(np.random.randint(1, 5, size=(5, 2)),
columns=['a','b'])
df = df.append(df.agg(['sum', 'mean']))

print("Contents of data frame:")
print(df)
```

Listing 1.4 defines the Pandas data frame df that consists of 5 rows and 2 columns of random integers between 1 and 5. Notice that the columns of df are labeled "a" and "b." In addition, the next code snippet appends two rows consisting of the sum and the mean of the numbers in both columns. The output of Listing 1.4 is here:

```
a      b
0       1.0   2.0
1       1.0   1.0
2       4.0   3.0
3       3.0   1.0
4       1.0   2.0
sum    10.0   9.0
mean    2.0   1.8
```

Listing 1.5 shows the content of pandas_combine_df.py that illustrates how to combine Pandas data frames.

LISTING 1.5: pandas_combine_df.py

```
import pandas as pd
import numpy as np

df = pd.Data frame({'foo1' : np.random.randn(5),
                    'foo2' : np.random.randn(5)})

print("contents of df:")
print(df)

print("contents of foo1:")
print(df.foo1)

print("contents of foo2:")
print(df.foo2)
```

Listing 1.5 defines the Pandas data frame df that consists of 5 rows and 2 columns (labeled "foo1" and "foo2") of random real numbers between 0 and 5. The next portion of Listing 1.5 shows the content of df and foo1. The output of Listing 1.5 is as follows:

```
contents of df:
        foo1        foo2
0   0.274680  _0.848669
```

```
1 -0.399771 -0.814679
2  0.454443 -0.363392
3  0.473753  0.550849
4 -0.211783 -0.015014
contents of foo1:
0     0.256773
1     1.204322
2     1.040515
3    -0.518414
4     0.634141
Name: foo1, dtype: float64
contents of foo2:
0    -2.506550
1    -0.896516
2    -0.222923
3     0.934574
4     0.527033
Name: foo2, dtype: float64
```

READING CSV FILES IN PANDAS

Pandas provides the read-csv() method for reading the contents of CSV files. For example, Listing 1.6 shows the contents of sometext.csv that contain labeled data (spam or ham), and Listing 1.7 shows the contents of read-csv-file.py that illustrate how to read the contents of a CSV file.

LISTING 1.6: sometext.csv

```
type      text
ham       Available only for today
ham       I'm joking with you
spam      Free entry in 2 a wkly comp
ham       U dun say so early hor
ham       I don't think he goes to usf
spam      FreeMsg Hey there
ham       my brother is not sick
ham       As per your request Melle
spam      WINNER!! As a valued customer
```

LISTING 1.7: read-csv-file.py

```python
import pandas as pd
import numpy as np

df = pd.read-csv('sometext.csv', delimiter='\t')

print("=> First five rows:")
print(df.head(5))
```

Listing 1.7 reads the content of sometext.csv, whose columns are separated by a tab ("\t") delimiter. Launch the code in Listing 1.7 to see the following output:

```
=> First five rows:
     type                                     text
0    ham          Available only for today
1    ham                  I'm joking with you
2    spam   Free entry in 2 a wkly comp
3    ham                U dun say so early hor
4    ham    I don't think he goes to usf
```

The default value for the `head()` method is 5, but you can display the first n rows of a data frame `df` with the code snippet `df.head(n)`.

Specifying a Separator and Column Sets in Text Files

The previous section showed you how to use the `delimiter` attribute to specify the delimiter in a text file. You can also use the `sep` parameter specifies a different separator. In addition, you can assign the `names` parameter the column names in the data that you want to read. An example of using `delimiter` and `sep` is here:

```
df2 = pd.read_csv("data.csv",sep="|",
                names=["Name","Surname","Height","Weig
ht"])
```

Pandas also provides the `read_table()` method for reading the contents of CSV files, which uses the same syntax as the `read_csv()` method.

Specifying an Index in Text Files

Suppose that you know that a particular column in a text file contains the index value for the rows in the text file. For example, a text file that contains the data in a relational table would typically contain an index column.

Fortunately, Pandas allows you to specify the kth column as the index in a text file, as shown here:

```
df = pd.read_csv('myfile.csv', index_col=k)
```

THE LOC() AND ILOC() METHODS IN PANDAS

If you want to display the contents of a record in a Pandas data frame, specify the index of the row in the `loc()` method. For example, the following code snippet displays the data by feature name in a data frame `df`:

```
df.loc[feature_name]
```

Select the first row of the "height" column in the data frame:

```
df.loc([0], ['height'])
```

The following code snippet uses the `iloc()` function to display the first 8 records of the name column with this code snippet:

```
df.iloc[0:8]['name']
```

CONVERTING CATEGORICAL DATA TO NUMERIC DATA

One common task in machine learning involves converting a feature containing character data into a feature that contains numeric data. Listing 1.8 shows the contents of `cat2numeric.py` that illustrate how to replace a text field with a corresponding numeric field.

LISTING 1.8: cat2numeric.py

```python
import pandas as pd
import numpy as np

df = pd.read_csv('sometext.csv', delimiter='\t')

print("=> First five rows (before):")
print(df.head(5))
print("------------------------")
print()

# map ham/spam to 0/1 values:
df['type'] = df['type'].map( {'ham':0 , 'spam':1} )

print("=> First five rows (after):")
print(df.head(5))
print("------------------------")
```

Listing 1.8 initializes the data frame `df` with the contents of the CSV file `sometext.csv`, and then displays the contents of the first five rows by invoking `df.head(5)`, which is also the default number of rows to display.

The next code snippet in Listing 1.8 invokes the `map()` method to replace occurrences of ham with 0 and replace occurrences of spam with 1 in the column labeled `type`, as shown here:

```python
df['type'] = df['type'].map( {'ham':0 , 'spam':1} )
```

The last portion of Listing 1.8 invokes the `head()` method again to display the first five rows of the dataset after having renamed the contents of the column type. Launch the code in Listing 1.8 to see the following output:

```
=> First five rows (before):
   type                          text
0  ham       Available only for today
1  ham              I'm joking with you
```

```
2   spam   Free entry in 2 a wkly comp
3   ham            U dun say so early hor
4   ham    I don't think he goes to usf


------------------------

=> First five rows (after):
   type                          text
0      0      Available only for today
1      0           I'm joking with you
2      1  Free entry in 2 a wkly comp
3      0           U dun say so early hor
4      0  I don't think he goes to usf


------------------------
```

As another example, Listing 1.9 shows the contents of shirts.csv and Listing 1.10 shows the contents of shirts.py; these examples illustrate four techniques for converting categorical data into numeric data.

LISTING 1.9: shirts.csv

```
type,ssize
shirt,xxlarge
shirt,xxlarge
shirt,xlarge
shirt,xlarge
shirt,xlarge
shirt,large
shirt,medium
shirt,small
shirt,small
shirt,xsmall
shirt,xsmall
shirt,xsmall
```

LISTING 1.10: shirts.py

```
import pandas as pd

shirts = pd.read_csv("shirts.csv")
print("shirts before:")
print(shirts)
print()

# TECHNIQUE #1:
#shirts.loc[shirts['ssize']=='xxlarge','size'] = 4
#shirts.loc[shirts['ssize']=='xlarge', 'size'] = 4
#shirts.loc[shirts['ssize']=='large',  'size'] = 3
#shirts.loc[shirts['ssize']=='medium', 'size'] = 2
#shirts.loc[shirts['ssize']=='small',  'size'] = 1
#shirts.loc[shirts['ssize']=='xsmall', 'size'] = 1
```

```
# TECHNIQUE #2:
#shirts['ssize'].replace('xxlarge', 4, inplace=True)
#shirts['ssize'].replace('xlarge',  4, inplace=True)
#shirts['ssize'].replace('large',   3, inplace=True)
#shirts['ssize'].replace('medium',  2, inplace=True)
#shirts['ssize'].replace('small',   1, inplace=True)
#shirts['ssize'].replace('xsmall',  1, inplace=True)

# TECHNIQUE #3:
#shirts['ssize'] = shirts['ssize'].apply({'xxlarge':4,
'xlarge':4, 'large':3, 'medium':2, 'small':1, 'xsmall':1}.
get)

# TECHNIQUE #4:
shirts['ssize'] = shirts['ssize'].replace(regex='xlarge',
value=4)
shirts['ssize'] = shirts['ssize'].replace(regex='large',
value=3)
shirts['ssize'] = shirts['ssize'].replace(regex='medium',
value=2)
shirts['ssize'] = shirts['ssize'].replace(regex='small',
value=1)

print("shirts after:")
print(shirts)
```

Listing 1.10 starts with a code block of six statements that uses direct comparison with strings to make numeric replacements. For example, the following code snippet replaces all occurrences of the string xxlarge with the value 4:

```
shirts.loc[shirts['ssize']=='xxlarge','size'] = 4
```

The second code block consists of six statements that use the replace() method to perform the same updates, an example of which is shown here:

```
shirts['ssize'].replace('xxlarge', 4, inplace=True)
```

The third code block consists of a single statement that uses the apply() method to perform the same updates, as shown here:

```
shirts['ssize'] = shirts['ssize'].apply({'xxlarge':4,
'xlarge':4, 'large':3, 'medium':2, 'small':1, 'xsmall':1}.get)
```

The fourth code block consists of four statements that use regular expressions to perform the same updates, an example of which is shown here:

```
shirts['ssize'] = shirts['ssize'].replace(regex='xlarge',
value=4)
```

Since the preceding code snippet matches xxlarge as well as xlarge, we only need *four* statements instead of six statements. (If you are unfamiliar with regular expressions, you can find online articles that discuss regular expressions.) Now launch the code in Listing 1.10 to see the following output:

```
shirts before
        type      size
0    shirt    xxlarge
1    shirt    xxlarge
2    shirt     xlarge
3    shirt     xlarge
4    shirt     xlarge
5    shirt      large
6    shirt     medium
7    shirt      small
8    shirt      small
9    shirt     xsmall
10   shirt     xsmall
11   shirt     xsmall
shirts after:
        type   size
0    shirt       4
1    shirt       4
2    shirt       4
3    shirt       4
4    shirt       4
5    shirt       3
6    shirt       2
7    shirt       1
8    shirt       1
9    shirt       1
10   shirt       1
11   shirt       1
```

MATCHING AND SPLITTING STRINGS IN PANDAS

Listing 1.11 shows the content of shirts_str.py, which illustrates how to match a column value with an initial string and how to split a column value based on a letter.

LISTING 1.11: shirts_str.py

```
import pandas as pd

shirts = pd.read_csv("shirts2.csv")
print("shirts:")
print(shirts)
print()

print("shirts starting with xl:")
print(shirts[shirts.ssize.str.startswith('xl')])
print()
```

```
print("Exclude 'xlarge' shirts:")
print(shirts[shirts['ssize'] != 'xlarge'])
print()

print("first three letters:")
shirts['sub1'] = shirts['ssize'].str[:3]
print(shirts)
print()

print("split ssize on letter 'a':")
shirts['sub2'] = shirts['ssize'].str.split('a')
print(shirts)
print()

print("Rows 3 through 5 and column 2:")
print(shirts.iloc[2:5, 2])
print()
```

Listing 1.11 initializes the data frame df with the contents of the CSV file shirts.csv, and then displays the contents of df. The next code snippet in Listing 1.11 uses the startswith() method to match the shirt types that start with the letters x1, followed by a code snippet that displays the shorts whose size does not equal the string xlarge.

The next code snippet uses the construct str[:3] to display the first three letters of the shirt types, followed by a code snippet that uses the split() method to split the shirt types based on the letter "a."

The final code snippet invokes iloc[2:5,2] to display the contents of rows 3 through 5 inclusive, and only the second column. The output of Listing 1.11 is as follows:

```
shirts:
       type    ssize
0    shirt  xxlarge
1    shirt  xxlarge
2    shirt   xlarge
3    shirt   xlarge
4    shirt   xlarge
5    shirt    large
6    shirt   medium
7    shirt    small
8    shirt    small
9    shirt   xsmall
10   shirt   xsmall
11   shirt   xsmall

shirts starting with x1:
     type   ssize
2   shirt  xlarge
3   shirt  xlarge
4   shirt  xlarge
```

```
Exclude 'xlarge' shirts:
      type     ssize
0    shirt   xxlarge
1    shirt   xxlarge
5    shirt     large
6    shirt    medium
7    shirt     small
8    shirt     small
9    shirt    xsmall
10   shirt    xsmall
11   shirt    xsmall

first three letters:
      type     ssize sub1
0    shirt   xxlarge  xxl
1    shirt   xxlarge  xxl
2    shirt    xlarge  xla
3    shirt    xlarge  xla
4    shirt    xlarge  xla
5    shirt     large  lar
6    shirt    medium  med
7    shirt     small  sma
8    shirt     small  sma
9    shirt    xsmall  xsm
10   shirt    xsmall  xsm
11   shirt    xsmall  xsm

split ssize on letter 'a':
      type     ssize sub1         sub2
0    shirt   xxlarge  xxl   [xxl, rge]
1    shirt   xxlarge  xxl   [xxl, rge]
2    shirt    xlarge  xla    [xl, rge]
3    shirt    xlarge  xla    [xl, rge]
4    shirt    xlarge  xla    [xl, rge]
5    shirt     large  lar     [l, rge]
6    shirt    medium  med    [medium]
7    shirt     small  sma    [sm, ll]
8    shirt     small  sma    [sm, ll]
9    shirt    xsmall  xsm   [xsm, ll]
10   shirt    xsmall  xsm   [xsm, ll]
11   shirt    xsmall  xsm   [xsm, ll]

Rows 3 through 5 and column 2:
2    xlarge
3    xlarge
4    xlarge
Name: ssize, dtype: object
```

CONVERTING STRINGS TO DATES IN PANDAS

Listing 1.12 shows the content of string2date.py, which illustrates how to convert strings to date formats.

LISTING 1.12: string2date.py

```
import pandas as pd

bdates1 = {'strdates':  ['20210413','20210813','20211225'],
           'people': ['Sally','Steve','Sarah']
          }

df1 = pd.Data frame(bdates1, columns =
['strdates','people'])
df1['dates'] = pd.to_datetime(df1['strdates'],
format='%Y%m%d')
print("=> Contents of data frame df1:")
print(df1)
print()
print(df1.dtypes)
print()

bdates2 = {'strdates':  ['13Apr2021','08Aug2021','25D
ec2021'],
           'people': ['Sally','Steve','Sarah']
          }

df2 = pd.Data frame(bdates2, columns =
['strdates','people'])
df2['dates'] = pd.to_datetime(df2['strdates'],
format='%d%b%Y')
print("=> Contents of data frame df2:")
print(df2)
print()

print(df2.dtypes)
print()
```

Listing 1.12 initializes the data frame df1 with the contents of bdates1, and then converts the strdates column to dates using the %Y%m%d format. The next portion of Listing 1.12 initializes the data frame df2 with the contents of bdates2, and then converts the strdates column to dates using the %d%b%Y format. Now launch the code in Listing 1.12 to see the following output:

```
=> Contents of data frame df1:
   strdates people       dates
0  20210413  Sally 2021-04-13
1  20210813  Steve 2021-08-13
2  20211225  Sarah 2021-12-25

strdates              object
people               object
dates        datetime64[ns]
dtype: object
```

```
=> Contents of data frame df2:
     strdates people        dates
0   13Apr2021  Sally 2021-04-13
1   08Aug2021  Steve 2021-08-08
2   25Dec2021  Sarah 2021-12-25

strdates                object
people                  object
dates           datetime64[ns]
dtype: object
```

WORKING WITH DATE RANGES IN PANDAS

Listing 1.13 shows the content of pand_parse_dates.py that illustrates how to work with date ranges in a CSV file.

LISTING 1.13: pand_parse_dates.py

```python
import pandas as pd

df = pd.read_csv('multiple_dates.csv', parse_
dates=['dates'])

print("df:")
print(df)
print()

df = df.set_index(['dates'])
start_d = "2021-04-30"
end_d   = "2021-08-31"

print("DATES BETWEEN",start_d,"AND",end_d,":")
print(df.loc[start_d:end_d])
print()

print("DATES BEFORE",start_d,":")
print(df.loc[df.index < start_d])

years = ['2020','2021','2022']
for year in years:
  year_sum = df.loc[year].sum()[0]
  print("SUM OF VALUES FOR YEAR",year,":",year_sum)
```

Listing 1.13 starts by initializing the variable df with the contents of the CSV file multiple_dates.csv and then displaying its contents. The next code snippet sets the dates column as the index column and then initializes the variable start_d and end_d that contain a start date and an end date, respectively.

The next portion of Listing 1.13 displays the dates between start_d and end_d, and then the list of dates that precede start_d. The final code block iterates through a list of years and then calculates the sum of the numbers in the values field for each year in the list. Now launch the code in Listing 1.13 to see the following output:

```
df:
          dates  values
0   2020-01-31    40.0
1   2020-02-28    45.0
2   2020-03-31    56.0
3   2021-04-30     NaN
4   2021-05-31     NaN
5   2021-06-30   140.0
6   2021-07-31    95.0
7   2022-08-31    40.0
8   2022-09-30    55.0
9   2022-10-31     NaN
10  2022-11-15    65.0


DATES BETWEEN 2021-04-30 AND 2021-08-31 :
             values
dates
2021-04-30     NaN
2021-05-31     NaN
2021-06-30   140.0
2021-07-31    95.0


DATES BEFORE 2021-04-30 :
             values
dates
2020-01-31    40.0
2020-02-28    45.0
2020-03-31    56.0


SUM OF VALUES FOR YEAR 2020 : 141.0
SUM OF VALUES FOR YEAR 2021 : 235.0
SUM OF VALUES FOR YEAR 2022 : 160.0
```

DETECTING MISSING DATES IN PANDAS

Listing 1.14 shows the content of `pandas_missing_dates.py` that illustrates how to detect missing date values in a CSV file.

LISTING 1.14: pandas_missing_dates.py

```
import pandas as pd

# A data frame from a dictionary of lists
data = {'Date': ['2021-01-18', '2021-01-20', '2021-01-21',
'2021-01-24'],
        'Name': ['Joe', 'John', 'Jane', 'Jim']}
df = pd.Data frame(data)
```

```
# Setting the Date values as index:
df = df.set_index('Date')

# to_datetime() converts string format to a DateTime
object:
df.index = pd.to_datetime(df.index)

start_d="2021-01-18"
end_d="2021-01-25"

# display dates that are not in the sequence:
print("MISSING DATES BETWEEN",start_d,"and",end_d,":")
dates = pd.date_range(start=start_d, end=end_d).
difference(df.index)

for date in dates:
  print("date:",date)
print()
```

Listing 1.14 initializes the dictionary data with a list of values for the Date field and the Name field, after which the variable df is initialized as a data frame whose contents are from the data variable.

The next code snippet sets the Date field as the index of the data frame df, after which the string-based dates are converted to DateTime objects. Another pair of code snippets initialize the variable start_d and end_d with a start date and an end date, respectively.

The final portion of Listing 1.14 initializes the variable dates with the list of missing dates between start_d and end_d, after which the contents of dates are displayed. Now launch the code in Listing 1.14 to see the following output:

```
MISSING DATES BETWEEN 2021-01-18 and 2021-01-25:
date: 2022-01-19 00:00:00
date: 2022-01-22 00:00:00
date: 2022-01-23 00:00:00
date: 2022-01-25 00:00:00
```

INTERPOLATING MISSING DATES IN PANDAS

Listing 1.15 shows the content of missing_dates.csv and Listing 1.16 shows the content of pandas_interpolate.py that illustrates how to replace NaN values with interpolated values that are calculated in several ways.

LISTING 1.15: missing_dates.csv

```
"dates","values"
2021-01-31,40
2021-02-28,45
2021-03-31,56
2021-04-30,NaN
2021-05-31,NaN
```

```
2021-06-30,140
2021-07-31,95
2021-08-31,40
2021-09-30,55
2021-10-31,NaN
2021-11-15,65
```

Notice the value 140 (shown in bold) in Listing 1.15: this value is an outlier, which will affect the calculation of the interpolated values, and potentially generate additional outliers.

LISTING 1.16: pandas_interpolate.py

```python
import pandas as pd
df = pd.read_csv("missing_dates.csv")

# fill NaN values with linear interpolation:
df1 = df.interpolate()

# fill NaN values with quadratic polynomial interpolation:
df2 = df.interpolate(method='polynomial', order=2)

# fill NaN values with cubic polynomial interpolation:
df3 = df.interpolate(method='polynomial', order=3)

print("original data frame:")
print(df)
print()
print("linear interpolation:")
print(df1)
print()
print("quadratic interpolation:")
print(df2)
print()
print("cubic interpolation:")
print(df3)
print()
```

Listing 1.16 initializes df with the contents of the CSV file missing_ dates.csv and then initializes the three data frames df1, df2, and df3 that are based on linear, quadratic, and cubic interpolation, respectively, via the interpolate() method. Now launch the code in Listing 1.16 to see the following output:

```
original data frame:
          dates   values
0    2021-01-31    40.0
1    2021-02-28    45.0
2    2021-03-31    56.0
3    2021-04-30     NaN
4    2021-05-31     NaN
5    2021-06-30   140.0
```

```
6    2021-07-31    95.0
7    2021-08-31    40.0
8    2021-09-30    55.0
9    2021-10-31    NaN
10   2021-11-15    65.0

linear interpolation:
         dates  values
0    2021-01-31    40.0
1    2021-02-28    45.0
2    2021-03-31    56.0
3    2021-04-30    84.0
4    2021-05-31   112.0
5    2021-06-30   140.0
6    2021-07-31    95.0
7    2021-08-31    40.0
8    2021-09-30    55.0
9    2021-10-31    60.0
10   2021-11-15    65.0

quadratic interpolation:
         dates       values
0    2021-01-31    40.000000
1    2021-02-28    45.000000
2    2021-03-31    56.000000
3    2021-04-30    88.682998
4    2021-05-31   136.002883
5    2021-06-30   140.000000
6    2021-07-31    95.000000
7    2021-08-31    40.000000
8    2021-09-30    55.000000
9    2021-10-31    68.162292
10   2021-11-15    65.000000

cubic interpolation:
         dates       values
0    2021-01-31    40.000000
1    2021-02-28    45.000000
2    2021-03-31    56.000000
3    2021-04-30    92.748096
4    2021-05-31   132.055687
5    2021-06-30   140.000000
6    2021-07-31    95.000000
7    2021-08-31    40.000000
8    2021-09-30    55.000000
9    2021-10-31    91.479905
10   2021-11-15    65.000000
```

OTHER OPERATIONS WITH DATES IN PANDAS

Listing 1.17 shows the content of `pandas_misc1.py` that illustrates how to extract a list of years from a column in a data frame.

LISTING 1.17: pandas_misc1.py

```
import pandas as pd
import numpy as np

df = pd.read_csv('multiple_dates.csv', parse_
dates=['dates'])
print("df:")
print(df)
print()

year_list = df['dates']

arr1 = np.array([])
for long_year in year_list:
  year = str(long_year)
  short_year = year[0:4]
  arr1 = np.append(arr1,short_year)

unique_years = set(arr1)
print("unique_years:")
print(unique_years)
print()

unique_arr = np.array(pd.Data frame.from_dict(unique_years))
print("unique_arr:")
print(unique_arr)
print()
```

Listing 1.17 initializes df with the contents of the CSV file multiple_dates.csv and then displays its contents. The next portion of Listing 1.17 initializes year_list with the dates column of df.

The next code block contains a loop that iterates through the elements in year_list, extracts the first four characters (i.e., the year value) and appends that substring to the NumPy array arr1. The final code block initializes the variable unique_arr as a NumPy array consisting of the unique years in the dictionary unique_years. Now launch the code in Listing 1.17 to see the following output:

```
df:
          dates  values
0   2020-01-31    40.0
1   2020-02-28    45.0
2   2020-03-31    56.0
3   2021-04-30    NaN
4   2021-05-31    NaN
5   2021-06-30   140.0
6   2021-07-31    95.0
7   2022-08-31    40.0
8   2022-09-30    55.0
9   2022-10-31    NaN
10  2022-11-15    65.0
```

```
unique_years:
{'2022', '2020', '2021'}

unique_arr:
[['2022']
 ['2020']
 ['2021']]
```

Listing 1.18 shows the content of `pandas_misc2.py` that illustrates how to iterate through the rows of a data frame. Keep in mind that row-wise iteration is not recommended because it can result in performance issues in larger datasets.

LISTING 1.18: pandas_misc2.py

```
import pandas as pd

df = pd.read_csv('multiple_dates.csv', parse_
dates=['dates'])

print("df:")
print(df)
print()

print("=> ITERATE THROUGH THE ROWS:")
for idx,row in df.iterrows():
  print("idx:",idx," year:",row['dates'])
print()
```

Listing 1.18 initializes the Pandas data frame `df`, prints its contents, and then processes the rows of `df` in a loop. During each iteration, the current index and row contents are displayed. Now launch the code in Listing 1.18 to see the following output:

```
df:
          dates   values
0   2020-01-31    40.0
1   2020-02-28    45.0
2   2020-03-31    56.0
3   2021-04-30     NaN
4   2021-05-31     NaN
5   2021-06-30   140.0
6   2021-07-31    95.0
7   2022-08-31    40.0
8   2022-09-30    55.0
9   2022-10-31     NaN
10  2022-11-15    65.0

=> ITERATE THROUGH THE ROWS:
idx:  0   year: 2020-01-31 00:00:00
idx:  1   year: 2020-02-28 00:00:00
idx:  2   year: 2020-03-31 00:00:00
idx:  3   year: 2021-04-30 00:00:00
```

```
idx: 4   year: 2021-05-31 00:00:00
idx: 5   year: 2021-06-30 00:00:00
idx: 6   year: 2021-07-31 00:00:00
idx: 7   year: 2022-08-31 00:00:00
idx: 8   year: 2022-09-30 00:00:00
idx: 9   year: 2022-10-31 00:00:00
idx: 10  year: 2022-11-15 00:00:00
```

Listing 1.19 shows the content of `pandas_misc3.py` that illustrates how to display a weekly set of dates that are between a start date and an end date.

LISTING 1.19: pandas_misc3.py

```
import pandas as pd

start_d="01/02/2022"
end_d="12/02/2022"
weekly_dates=pd.date_range(start=start_d, end=end_d,
freq='W')

print("Weekly dates from",start_d,"to",end_d,":")
print(weekly_dates)
```

Listing 1.19 starts with initializing the variable `start_d` and `end_d` that contain a start date and an end date, respectively, and then initializes the variable `weekly_dates` with a list of weekly dates between the start date and the end date. Now launch the code in Listing 1.19 to see the following output:

```
Weekly dates from 01/02/2022 to 12/02/2022 :
DatetimeIndex(['2022-01-02', '2022-01-09', '2022-01-16',
               '2022-01-23',
               '2022-01-30', '2022-02-06', '2022-02-13',
               '2022-02-20',
               '2022-02-27', '2022-03-06', '2022-03-13',
               '2022-03-20',
               '2022-03-27', '2022-04-03', '2022-04-10',
               '2022-04-17',
               '2022-04-24', '2022-05-01', '2022-05-08',
               '2022-05-15',
               '2022-05-22', '2022-05-29', '2022-06-05',
               '2022-06-12',
               '2022-06-19', '2022-06-26', '2022-07-03',
               '2022-07-10',
               '2022-07-17', '2022-07-24', '2022-07-31',
               '2022-08-07',
               '2022-08-14', '2022-08-21', '2022-08-28',
               '2022-09-04',
               '2022-09-11', '2022-09-18', '2022-09-25',
               '2022-10-02',
```

```
                  '2022-10-09', '2022-10-16', '2022-10-23',
                  '2022-10-30',
                  '2022-11-06', '2022-11-13', '2022-11-20',
                  '2022-11-27'],
           dtype='datetime64[ns]', freq='W-SUN')
```

MERGING AND SPLITTING COLUMNS IN PANDAS

Listing 1.20 shows the contents of employees.csv and Listing 1.21 shows the contents of emp_merge_split.py. These examples illustrate how to merge columns and split columns of a CSV file.

LISTING 1.20: employees.csv

```
name,year,month
Jane-Smith,2015,Aug
Dave-Smith,2020,Jan
Jane-Jones,2018,Dec
Jane-Stone,2017,Feb
Dave-Stone,2014,Apr
Mark-Aster,,Oct
Jane-Jones,NaN,Jun
```

LISTING 1.21: emp_merge_split.py

```python
import pandas as pd

emps = pd.read_csv("employees.csv")
print("emps:")
print(emps)
print()

emps['year']  = emps['year'].astype(str)
emps['month'] = emps['month'].astype(str)

# separate column for first name and for last name:
emps['fname'],emps['lname'] = emps['name'].str.
split("-",1).str

# concatenate year and month with a "#" symbol:
emps['hdate1'] = emps['year'].
astype(str)+"#"+emps['month'].astype(str)

# concatenate year and month with a "-" symbol:
emps['hdate2'] = emps[['year','month']].agg('-'.join,
axis=1)

print(emps)
print()
```

Listing 1.21 initializes the data frame df with the contents of the CSV file employees.csv, and then displays the contents of df. The next pair of code snippets invoke the astype() method to convert the contents of the year and month columns to strings.

The next code snippet in Listing 1.21 uses the split() method to split the name column into the columns fname and lname that contain the first name and last name, respectively, of each employee's name:

```
emps['fname'],emps['lname'] = emps['name'].str.
split("-",1).str
```

The next code snippet concatenates the contents of the year and month string with a "#" character to create a new column called hdate1:

```
emps['hdate1'] = emps['year'].
astype(str)+"#"+emps['month'].astype(str)
```

The final code snippet concatenates the contents of the year and month string with a "-" to create a new column called hdate2, as shown here:
```
emps['hdate2'] = emps[['year','month']].agg('-'.join,
axis=1)
```
Now launch the code in Listing 1.21 to see the following output:

```
emps:
        name      year month
0  Jane-Smith   2015.0   Aug
1  Dave-Smith   2020.0   Jan
2  Jane-Jones   2018.0   Dec
3  Jane-Stone   2017.0   Feb
4  Dave-Stone   2014.0   Apr
5  Mark-Aster     NaN    Oct
6  Jane-Jones     NaN    Jun


        name      year month fname  lname    hdate1        hdate2
0  Jane-Smith   2015.0   Aug  Jane  Smith  2015.0#Aug  2015.0-Aug
1  Dave-Smith   2020.0   Jan  Dave  Smith  2020.0#Jan  2020.0-Jan
2  Jane-Jones   2018.0   Dec  Jane  Jones  2018.0#Dec  2018.0-Dec
3  Jane-Stone   2017.0   Feb  Jane  Stone  2017.0#Feb  2017.0-Feb
4  Dave-Stone   2014.0   Apr  Dave  Stone  2014.0#Apr  2014.0-Apr
5  Mark-Aster     nan    Oct  Mark  Aster    nan#Oct     nan-Oct
6  Jane-Jones     nan    Jun  Jane  Jones    nan#Jun     nan-Jun
```

There is one other detail regarding the following commented-out code snippet:

```
#emps['fname'],emps['lname'] = emps['name'].str.
split("-",1).str
```

The following deprecation message is displayed if you uncomment the preceding code snippet:

```
#FutureWarning: Columnar iteration over characters
#will be deprecated in future releases.
```

READING HTML WEB PAGES IN PANDAS

Listing 1.22 displays the contents of the HTML Web page abc.html. Listing 1.23 shows the content of read_html_page.py that illustrates how to read the contents of an HTML Web page from Pandas. Note that this code will only work with Web pages that contain *at least* one HTML <table> element.

LISTING 1.22: abc.html

```
<html>
<head>
</head>
<body>
  <table>
    <tr>
      <td>hello from abc.html!</td>
    </tr>
  </table>
</body>
</html>
```

LISTING 1.23: read_html_page.py

```
import pandas as pd

file_name="abc.html"
with open(file_name, "r") as f:
  dfs = pd.read_html(f.read())

print("Contents of HTML Table(s) in the HTML Web Page:")
print(dfs)
```

Listing 1.23 starts with an import statement, followed by initializing the variable file_name to abc.html that is displayed in Listing 1.22. The next code snippet initializes the variable dfs as a data frame with the contents of the HTML Web page abc.html. The final portion of Listing 1.23 displays the contents of the data frame dsf. Now launch the code in Listing 1.23 to see the following output:

```
Contents of HTML Table(s) in the HTML Web Page:
[                         0
0  hello from abc.html!]
```

For more information about the Pandas read_html() method, navigate to this URL:

https://pandas.pydata.org/pandas-docs/stable/reference/api/

SAVING A PANDAS DATA FRAME AS AN HTML WEB PAGE

Listing 1.24 shows the content of read_html_page.py that illustrates how to read the contents of an HTML Web page from Pandas. Note that this code will only work with Web pages that contain at least one HTML <table> element.

LISTING 1.24: read_html_page.py

```
import pandas as pd

emps = pd.read_csv("employees.csv")
print("emps:")
print(emps)
print()

emps['year']  = emps['year'].astype(str)
emps['month'] = emps['month'].astype(str)

# separate column for first name and for last name:
emps['fname'],emps['lname'] = emps['name'].str.
split("-",1).str

# concatenate year and month with a "#" symbol:
emps['hdate1'] = emps['year'].
astype(str)+"#"+emps['month'].astype(str)

# concatenate year and month with a "-" symbol:
emps['hdate2'] = emps[['year','month']].agg('-'.join,
axis=1)

print(emps)
print()

html = emps.to_html()
print("Data frame as an HTML Web Page:")
print(html)
```

Listing 1.24 populates the data frame temps with the contents of employees.csv and then converts the year and month attributes to type string. The next code snippet splits the contents of the name field with the "-" symbol as a delimiter. As a result, this code snippet populates the new fname and lname fields with the first name and last name, respectively, of the previously split field.

The next code snippet in Listing 1.24 converts the year and month fields to strings, and then concatenates them with a "#" as a delimiter. Yet another code snippet populates the hdate2 field with the concatenation of the year and month fields.

After displaying the content of the data frame emps, the final code snippet populate the variable html with the result of converting the data frame emps to an HTML Web page by invoking the to_html() method of Pandas. Now launch the code in Listing 1.24 to see the following output:

```
Contents of HTML Table(s)
emps:
          name     year month
0   Jane-Smith   2015.0    Aug
1   Dave-Smith   2020.0    Jan
2   Jane-Jones   2018.0    Dec
3   Jane-Stone   2017.0    Feb
4   Dave-Stone   2014.0    Apr
5   Mark-Aster      NaN    Oct
6   Jane-Jones      NaN    Jun


          name     year month fname  lname     hdate1      hdate2
0   Jane-Smith   2015.0    Aug  Jane  Smith  2015.0#Aug  2015.0-Aug
1   Dave-Smith   2020.0    Jan  Dave  Smith  2020.0#Jan  2020.0-Jan
2   Jane-Jones   2018.0    Dec  Jane  Jones  2018.0#Dec  2018.0-Dec
3   Jane-Stone   2017.0    Feb  Jane  Stone  2017.0#Feb  2017.0-Feb
4   Dave-Stone   2014.0    Apr  Dave  Stone  2014.0#Apr  2014.0-Apr
5   Mark-Aster      nan    Oct  Mark  Aster    nan#Oct    nan-Oct
6   Jane-Jones      nan    Jun  Jane  Jones    nan#Jun    nan-Jun


Data frame as an HTML Web Page:
<table border="1" class="data frame">
  <thead>
    <tr style="text-align: right;">
      <th></th>
      <th>name</th>
      <th>year</th>
      <th>month</th>
      <th>fname</th>
      <th>lname</th>
      <th>hdate1</th>
      <th>hdate2</th>
    </tr>
  </thead>
  <tbody>
    <tr>
      <th>0</th>
      <td>Jane-Smith</td>
      <td>2015.0</td>
      <td>Aug</td>
      <td>Jane</td>
      <td>Smith</td>
      <td>2015.0#Aug</td>
      <td>2015.0-Aug</td>
    </tr>
    <tr>
      <th>1</th>
      <td>Dave-Smith</td>
      <td>2020.0</td>
      <td>Jan</td>
      <td>Dave</td>
      <td>Smith</td>
      <td>2020.0#Jan</td>
      <td>2020.0-Jan</td>
    </tr>
```

```
      // details omitted for brevity
      <tr>
        <th>6</th>
        <td>Jane-Jones</td>
        <td>nan</td>
        <td>Jun</td>
        <td>Jane</td>
        <td>Jones</td>
        <td>nan#Jun</td>
        <td>nan-Jun</td>
      </tr>
    </tbody>
</table>
```

SUMMARY

This chapter introduced you to Pandas for creating labeled data frames and displaying the metadata of data frames. Then you learned how to create data frames from various sources of data, such as random numbers and hard-coded data values. In addition, you saw how to perform column-based and row-based operations in Pandas data frames.

You also learned how to read Excel spreadsheets and perform numeric calculations on the data in those spreadsheets, such as the minimum, mean, and maximum values in numeric columns. Then, you saw how to create Pandas data frames from data stored in CSV files.

## CHAPTER 2

INTRODUCTION TO MACHINE LEARNING

T his chapter introduces numerous concepts in machine learning, such as feature selection, feature engineering, data cleaning, training sets, and test sets.

The first part of this chapter briefly discusses machine learning and the sequence of steps that are typically required to prepare a dataset. These steps include "feature selection" or "feature extraction" that can be performed using various algorithms.

The second section describes the types of data that you can encounter, issues that can arise with the data in datasets, and how to rectify them. You will also learn about the difference between "hold out" and "k-fold" when you perform the training step.

The third part of this chapter briefly discusses the basic concepts involved in linear regression. Although linear regression was developed more than 200 years ago, this technique is still one of the core techniques for solving (albeit simple) problems in statistics and machine learning. In fact, the technique known as the *Mean Squared Error* (MSE) for finding a best-fitting line for data points in a 2D plane (or a hyperplane for higher dimensions) is implemented in Python to minimize loss functions that are discussed later.

The fourth section in this chapter contains additional code samples involving linear regression tasks using standard techniques in NumPy. Hence, if you are comfortable with this topic, you can probably skim quickly through the first two sections of this chapter.

WHAT IS MACHINE LEARNING?

In high level terms, *machine learning* is a subset of AI that can solve tasks that are infeasible or too cumbersome with traditional programming languages. A spam filter for email is an early example of machine learning. Machine learning generally supersedes the accuracy of older algorithms.

Despite the variety of machine learning algorithms, the data is arguably more important than the selected algorithm. Many issues can arise with data, such as insufficient data, poor quality of data, incorrect data, missing data, irrelevant data, and duplicate data values. Later in this chapter, you will see techniques that address many of these data-related issues.

If you are unfamiliar with machine learning terminology, a *dataset* is a collection of data values, which can be in the form of a CSV file or a spreadsheet. Each column is called a *feature*, and each row is a *datapoint* that contains a set of specific values for each feature. If a dataset contains information about customers, then each row pertains to a specific customer.

Types of Machine Learning

There are three main types of machine learning (combinations of these are also possible) that you will encounter:

- Supervised learning
- Unsupervised learning
- Semi-supervised learning

Supervised learning means that the datapoints in a dataset have a label that identifies its contents. For example, the MNIST dataset contains 28x28 PNG files, each of which contains a single hand-drawn digit (i.e., 0 through 9 inclusive). Every image with the digit 0 has the label "0," every image with the digit 1 has the label "1," and all other images are labeled according to the digit that is displayed in those images.

As another example, the columns in the Titanic dataset are features about passengers, such as their gender, cabin class, price of their ticket, and whether the passenger survived. Each row contains information about a single passenger, including the value 1 if the passenger survived. *The MNIST dataset and the Titanic dataset involve classification tasks: the goal is to train a model and then predict the class (MNIST) or survival (Titanic) of each row in a test dataset.*

In general, the datasets for classification tasks have a small number of possible values: one of nine digits in the range of 0 through 9, one of four animals (dog, cat, horse, giraffe), or one of two values (survived versus perished, purchased versus not purchased). In general, if the number of outcomes can be displayed reasonably well in a drop-down list, then it is probably a classification task.

In the case of a dataset that contains real estate data, each row contains information about a specific house, such as the number of bedrooms, square feet of the house, number of bathrooms, and price of the house. In this dataset, the price of the house is the label for each row. Notice that the range of possible prices is too large to fit reasonably well in a drop-down list. *A real estate dataset involves a **regression** task: the goal is to train a model based on a training dataset and then predict the price of each house in a test dataset.*

Unsupervised learning involves unlabeled data, which is typically the case for clustering algorithms (discussed later). Some important unsupervised learning algorithms that involve *clustering* are listed below:

- k-means
- Hierarchical Cluster Analysis (HCA)
- Expectation Maximization

Some important unsupervised learning algorithms that involve *dimensionality reduction* (discussed in more detail later) are listed below:

- PCA (Principal Component Analysis)
- Kernel PCA
- LLE (Locally Linear Embedding)
- t-SNE (t-distributed Stochastic Neighbor Embedding)

There is one more very important unsupervised task called *anomaly detection*. This task is relevant for fraud detection and detecting outliers (discussed later in more detail).

Semi-supervised learning is a combination of supervised and unsupervised learning: some datapoints are labeled and some are unlabeled. One technique involves using the labeled data to classify (i.e., label) the unlabeled data, after which you can apply a classification algorithm.

TYPES OF MACHINE LEARNING ALGORITHMS

There are three main types of machine learning algorithms:

- Regression (ex: linear regression)
- Classification (ex: k-nearest neighbors)
- Clustering (ex: k-means)

Regression is a supervised learning technique to predict numerical quantities. An example of a regression task is predicting the value of a particular stock. Note that this task is different from predicting whether the value of a particular stock will increase or decrease tomorrow (or some other future time period). Another example of a regression task involves predicting the loss of a house in a real estate dataset. Both of these tasks are examples of a regression task.

Regression algorithms in machine learning include linear regression and generalized linear regression (also called *multivariate analysis* in traditional statistics).

Classification is also a supervised learning technique, but it is for predicting categorical quantities. An example of a classification task is detecting the occurrence of spam, fraud, or determining the digit in a PNG file (such as the

MNIST dataset). In this case, the data is already labeled, so you can compare the prediction with the label that was assigned to the given PNG.

Classification algorithms in machine learning include the following list of algorithms (they are discussed in greater detail in the next chapter):

- Decision Trees (a single tree)
- Random Forests (multiple trees)
- kNN (k-Nearest Neighbors)
- Logistic regression (despite its name)
- Naïve Bayes
- SVM (Support Vector Machines)

Some machine learning algorithms (such as SVMs, random forests, and kNN) support regression as well as classification. In the case of SVMs, the scikit-learn implementation of this algorithm provides two APIs: SVC for classification and SVR for regression.

Each of the preceding algorithms involves a model that is trained on a dataset, after which the model is used to make a prediction. By contrast, a random forest consists of *multiple* independent trees (the number is specified by you), and each tree makes a prediction regarding the value of a feature. If the feature is numeric, take the mean or the mode (or perform some other calculation) to determine the "final" prediction. If the feature is categorical, use the mode (i.e., the most frequently occurring class) as the result; in the case of a tie, you can select one of them in a random fashion.

Incidentally, the following URL contains more information regarding the kNN algorithm for classification as well as regression:

http://saedsayad.com/k_nearest_neighbors_reg.htm

Clustering is an unsupervised learning technique for grouping similar data together. Clustering algorithms put data points in different clusters without knowing the nature of the data points. After the data has been separated into different clusters, you can use the SVM algorithm to perform classification.

Clustering algorithms in machine learning include the following (some of which are variations of each other):

- k-means
- mean shift
- Hierarchical Cluster Analysis (HCA)
- Expectation Maximization

Keep in mind the following points. First, the value of k in k-means is a hyper parameter, and it is usually an odd number to avoid ties between two classes. Next, the mean shift algorithm incorporates the k-means algorithm that does not require you to specify a value for k. In fact, the mean shift algorithm determines the optimal number of clusters. However, this algorithm does not scale well for large datasets.

Machine Learning Tasks

Unless you have a dataset that has already been sanitized, you need to examine the data in a dataset to make sure that it is in a suitable condition. The data preparation phase involves examining the rows ("data cleaning") to ensure that they contain valid data (which might require domain-specific knowledge) and examining the columns (feature selection or feature extraction) to determine whether you can retain only the most important columns.

A high-level list of the sequence of machine learning tasks (some of which might not be required) is shown below:

- Obtain a dataset
- Data cleaning
- Feature selection
- Dimensionality reduction
- Algorithm selection
- Train-vs.-test data
- Training a model
- Testing a model
- Fine-tuning a model
- Obtain metrics for the model

First, you obviously need to obtain a dataset for your task. In the ideal scenario, this dataset already exists; otherwise, you need to cull the data from one or more data sources (e.g., a CSV file, relational database, no-SQL database, and Web service).

Second, you need to perform *data cleaning*, which you can do via the following techniques:

- Missing Value Ratio
- Low Variance Filter
- High Correlation Filter

In general, data cleaning involves checking the data values in a dataset to resolve one or more of the following:

- fix incorrect values
- resolve duplicate values
- resolve missing values
- decide what to do with outliers

Use the Missing Value Ratio technique if the dataset has too many missing values. In extreme cases, you might be able to drop features with a large number of missing values. Use the Low Variance filter technique to identify and drop features with constant values from the dataset. Use the High Correlation filter technique to find highly correlated features, which increase multicollinearity in the dataset: such features can be removed from a dataset (but check with your domain expert before doing so).

Depending on your background and the nature of the dataset, you might need to work with a *domain expert*, who is a person with a deep understanding of the contents of the dataset.

For example, you can use a statistical value (mean, mode, and so forth) to replace incorrect values with suitable values. Duplicate values can be handled in a similar fashion. You can replace missing numeric values with zero, the minimum, the mean, the mode, or the maximum value in a numeric column. You can replace missing categorical values with the mode of the categorical column.

If a row in a dataset contains a value that is an outlier, you have three choices:

- delete the row
- keep the row
- replace the outlier with some other value (mean?)

When a dataset contains an outlier, you need to make a decision based on domain knowledge that is specific to the given dataset.

Suppose that a dataset contains stock-related information. As you know, there was a stock market crash in 1929, which you can view as an outlier. Such an occurrence is rare, but it can contain meaningful information. Incidentally, the source of wealth for some families in the twentieth century was based on buying massive amounts of stock are very low prices during the Great Depression.

FEATURE ENGINEERING, SELECTION, AND EXTRACTION

In addition to creating a dataset and "cleaning" its values, you also need to examine the features in that dataset to determine whether you can reduce the dimensionality (i.e., the number of features) of the dataset. The process for doing so involves three main techniques:

- feature engineering
- feature selection
- feature extraction (also called "feature projection")

Feature engineering is the process of determining a new set of features that are based on a combination of existing features to create a meaningful dataset for a given task. Domain expertise is often required for this process, even in the cases of relatively simple datasets. Feature engineering can be tedious and expensive, and in some cases, you might consider using automated feature learning. After you have created a dataset, it is a good idea to perform feature selection or feature extraction (or both) to ensure that you have a high-quality dataset.

Feature selection is also called "variable selection," "attribute selection," or "variable subset selection." Feature selection involves selecting a subset of relevant features in a dataset. In essence, feature selection involves selecting the most important features in a dataset, which provides these advantages:

- reduced training time
- simpler models that are easier to interpret
- avoidance of the curse of dimensionality
- better generalization due to a reduction in overfitting ("reduction of variance")

Feature selection techniques are often used in domains where there are many features and comparatively few samples (or data points). Keep in mind that a low-value feature can be redundant or irrelevant, which are two different concepts. For instance, a relevant feature might be redundant when it is combined with another strongly correlated feature.

Feature selection can use three strategies: the filter strategy (e.g., information gain), wrapper strategy (e.g., search guided by accuracy), and embedded strategy (prediction errors are used to determine whether features are included or excluded while developing a model). On other interesting point is that feature selection can also be useful for regression as well as classification tasks.

Feature extraction creates new features from functions that produce combinations of the original features. By contrast, feature selection involves determining a subset of the existing features.

Feature selection and feature extraction both result in *dimensionality reduction* for a given dataset, which is the topic of the next section.

DIMENSIONALITY REDUCTION

Dimensionality reduction refers to algorithms that reduce the number of features in a dataset. As you will see, there are many techniques available, and they involve either feature selection or feature extraction.

Algorithms that use feature selection to perform dimensionality reduction are listed here:

- Backward Feature Elimination
- Forward Feature Selection
- Factor Analysis
- Independent Component Analysis

Algorithms that use feature extraction to perform dimensionality reduction are listed here:

- PCA
- non-negative matrix factorization (NMF)
- kernel PCA
- graph-based kernel PCA
- Linear discriminant analysis (LDA)
- generalized discriminant analysis (GDA)
- Autoencoder

The following algorithms combine feature extraction and dimensionality reduction:

- PCA
- linear discriminant analysis (LDA)
- canonical correlation analysis (CCA)
- non-negative matrix factorization (NMF)

These algorithms can be used during a pre-processing step before using clustering or some other algorithm (such as kNN) on a dataset. One other group of algorithms involves methods based on projections, and it includes t-Distributed Stochastic Neighbor Embedding (t-SNE) as well as UMAP.

This chapter discusses PCA, and you can perform an online search to find more information about the other algorithms.

PCA

Principal Components are new components that are linear combinations of the initial features in a dataset. In addition, these components are uncorrelated and the most meaningful or important information is contained in these new components.

There are two advantages to PCA: reduced computation time due to far fewer features and the ability to graph the components when there are at most three components. If you have four or five components, you will not be able to display them visually, but you could select subsets of three components for visualization, and perhaps gain some additional insight into the dataset.

PCA uses the variance as a measure of information: the higher the variance, the more important the component. In fact, PCA determines the eigenvalues and eigenvectors of a covariance matrix (discussed later), and constructs a new matrix whose columns are eigenvectors, ordered from left-to-right based on the maximum eigenvalue in the left-most column, decreasing until the right-most eigenvector also has the smallest eigenvalue.

Covariance Matrix

As a reminder, the statistical quantity called the variance of a random variable X is defined as follows:

variance(x) = [SUM (x – xbar)*(x-xbar)]/n

A covariance matrix C is an nxn matrix whose values on the main diagonal are the variance of the variables X1, X2, . . ., Xn. The other values of C are the covariance values of each pair of variables Xi and Xj.

The formula for the covariance of the variables X and Y is a generalization of the variance of a variable, and the formula is shown here:

covariance(X, Y) = [SUM (x – xbar)*(y-ybar)]/n

Notice that you can reverse the order of the product of terms (multiplication is commutative), and therefore the covariance matrix C is a symmetric matrix:

covariance(X, Y) = covariance(Y,X)

PCA calculates the eigenvalues and the eigenvectors of the covariance matrix A.

WORKING WITH DATASETS

In addition to data cleaning, there are several other steps that you need to perform, such as selecting training data vs. test data and deciding whether to use "hold out" or cross-validation during the training process. More details are provided in the subsequent sections.

Training Data Versus Test Data

After you have performed the tasks described earlier in this chapter (i.e., data cleaning and perhaps dimensionality reduction), you are ready to split the dataset into two parts. The first part is the *training set*, which is used to train a model, and the second part is the *test set*, which is used for "inferencing" (another term for making predictions). Make sure that you conform to the following guidelines for your test sets:

1. The set is large enough to yield statistically meaningful results.
2. It is representative of the dataset as a whole.
3. Never train on test data.
4. Never test on training data.

What is Cross-validation?

The purpose of *cross-validation* is to test a model with non-overlapping test sets, which is performed in the following manner:

Step 1) Split the data into k subsets of equal size.
Step 2) Select one subset for testing and the others for training.
Step 3) Repeat Step 2 for the other k-1 subsets.

This process is called *k-fold cross-validation*, and the overall error estimate is the average of the error estimates. A standard method for evaluation involves ten-fold cross-validation. Extensive experiments have shown that using ten subsets is the best choice to obtain an accurate estimate. In fact, you can repeat ten-fold cross-validation ten times and compute the average of the results, which helps to reduce the variance.

The next section discusses regularization, which is an important yet optional topic in this book. If you plan to become proficient in machine learning, you will need to learn about regularization.

WHAT IS REGULARIZATION?

Regularization helps to solve the overfitting problem, which occurs when a model performs well on training data but poorly on validation or test data. Regularization solves this problem by adding a penalty term to the loss function, thereby controlling the model complexity with this penalty term. Regularization is generally useful for:

- a large number of variables
- a low ratio of (# observations)/(# of variables)
- a high multicollinearity

There are two main types of regularization: L1 Regularization (which is related to MAE, or the absolute value of differences) and L2 Regularization (which is related to MSE, or the square of differences). In general, L2 performs better than L1 and L2 is efficient in terms of computation.

Machine Learning and Feature Scaling

Feature scaling standardizes the range of features of data. This step is performed during the data pre-processing step, in part because gradient descent benefits from feature scaling.

The assumption is that the data conforms to a standard normal distribution, and standardization involves subtracting the mean and divide by the standard deviation for every data point, which results in an $N(0,1)$ normal distribution.

Data Normalization versus Standardization

Data normalization is a linear scaling technique. Let's assume that a dataset has the values {X1, X2, . . . , Xn} along with the following terms:

Minx = minimum of Xi values
Maxx = maximum of Xi values

Now calculate a set of new Xi values as follows:

Xi = (Xi – Minx)/[Maxx – Minx]

The new Xi values are now scaled so that they are between 0 and 1.

THE BIAS-VARIANCE TRADEOFF

Bias in machine learning can be due to an error from wrong assumptions in a learning algorithm. High bias might cause an algorithm to miss relevant relations between features and target outputs (underfitting). Prediction bias can occur because of "noisy" data, an incomplete feature set, or a biased training sample.

Error due to bias is the difference between the expected (or average) prediction of your model and the correct value that you want to predict. Repeat the model building process multiple times and gather new data each time, and also perform an analysis to produce a new model. The resulting models have a range of predictions because the underlying datasets have a degree of randomness. Bias measures the extent to the predictions for these models are from the correct value.

Variance in machine learning is the expected value of the squared deviation from the mean. A high variance can cause an algorithm to model the random noise in the training data, rather than the intended outputs (overfitting).

Adding parameters to a model increases its complexity, increases the variance, and decreases the bias. Dealing with bias and variance is dealing with underfitting and overfitting.

Error due to variance is the variability of a model prediction for a given data point. As before, repeat the entire model building process, and the variance is the extent to which predictions for a given point vary among different "instances" of the model.

METRICS FOR MEASURING MODELS

Linear regression models use *R-squared*, which measures how close the data is to the fitted regression line (regression coefficient). The R-squared value is always a percentage between 0 and 100%. The value 0% indicates that the model explains none of the variability of the response data around its mean. The value 100% indicates that the model explains all the variability of the response data around its mean. In general, a higher R-squared value indicates a better model.

Limitations of R-Squared

Although high R-squared values are preferred, they are not necessarily always good values. Similarly, low R-squared values are not always bad. For example, an R-squared value for predicting human behavior is often less than 50%. Moreover, R-squared cannot determine whether the coefficient estimates and predictions are biased. In addition, an R-squared value does not indicate whether a regression model is adequate. Thus, it is possible to have a low R-squared value for a good model, or a high R-squared value for a poorly fitting model. Evaluate R-squared values in conjunction with residual plots, other model statistics, and subject area knowledge.

Confusion Matrix

Clasification algorithms use a *confusion matrix* (also called an "error matrix"), which is a square contingency table that contains the number of false positives, false negatives, true positives, and true negatives. The four entries in a 2x2 confusion matrix can be labeled as follows:

TP: True Positive
FP: False Positive
TN: True Negative
FN: False Negative

The diagonal values of the confusion matrix are correct predictions, whereas the off-diagonal values are incorrect predictions. In general, a lower FP value is better than a FN value. For example, an FP indicates that a healthy person was incorrectly diagnosed with a disease, whereas an FN indicates that an unhealthy person was incorrectly diagnosed as healthy.

Accuracy versus Precision versus Recall

A 2x2 confusion matrix has four entries that that represent the various combinations of correct and incorrect classifications. Given the definitions in the preceding section, the definitions of precision, accuracy, and recall are given by the following formulas:

precision = TP/(TP + FP)
accuracy = (TP + TN)/[TP + FP + FN + TN]
recall   = TP/[TP + FN]

Accuracy can be an unreliable metric because it yields misleading results in unbalanced datasets. When the number of observations in different classes are significantly different, it gives equal importance to both false positive and false negative classifications. For example, declaring cancer as benign is worse than incorrectly informing patients that they are suffering from cancer. Unfortunately, accuracy will not differentiate between these two cases.

Keep in mind that the confusion matrix can be an nxn matrix and not just a 2x2 matrix. For example, if a class has 5 possible values, then the confusion matrix is a 5x5 matrix, and the numbers on the main diagonal are the "true positive" results.

The ROC Curve

The *receiver operating characteristic* (ROC) curve is a curve that plots the true positive rate (TPR, i.e., the *recall*) against the false positive rate (FPR). Note that the true negative rate (TNR) is also called the *specificity*.

The following Web page contains a Python code sample using sklearn and the Iris dataset, as well as code for plotting the ROC:

https://scikit-learn.org/stable/auto_examples/model_selection/plot_roc.html

The following Web page contains an assortment of Python code samples for plotting the ROC:

https://stackoverflow.com/questions/25009284/how-to-plot-roc-curve-in-python

OTHER USEFUL STATISTICAL TERMS

Machine learning relies on a number of statistical quantities to assess the validity of a model, some of which are listed here:

- RSS
- TSS
- R^2
- F1 score
- p-value

The definitions of RSS, TSS, and R^2 are shown below, where y^ is the y-coordinate of a point on a best-fitting line and y_ is the mean of the y values of the points in the dataset:

RSS = sum of squares of residuals (y - **y^**)**2
TSS = toal sum of squares   (y - **y_**)**2
R^2 = 1 - RSS/TSS

What is an F1 score?

The *F1 score* is a measure of the accuracy of a test, and it is defined as the harmonic mean of precision and recall. Here are the relevant formulas, where p is the precision and r is the recall:

F1-score $= 1/[((1/r) + (1/p))/2]$
$\qquad\quad = 2*[p*r]/[p+r]$

The best value of an F1 score is 0 and the worst value is 0. An F1 score tends to be used for categorical classification problems, whereas the R^2 value is typically for regression tasks (such as linear regression).

What is a p-value?

The p-value is used to reject the null hypothesis if the p-value is small enough (< 0.005), which indicates a higher significance. Recall that the null hypothesis states that there is no correlation between a dependent variable (such as y) and an independent variable (such as x). The threshold value for p is typically 1% or 5%.

There is no straightforward formula for calculating *p-values*, which are values that are always between 0 and 1. In fact, p-values are statistical quantities to evaluate the "null hypothesis," and they are calculated by means of p-value tables or via spreadsheet/statistical software.

WHAT IS LINEAR REGRESSION?

The goal of linear regression is to find the best-fitting line that "represents" a dataset. Keep in mind two key points. First, the best-fitting line does not necessarily pass through all (or even most of) the points in the dataset. The purpose of a best-fitting line is to minimize the vertical distance of that line from the points in dataset. Second, linear regression does not determine the best-fitting polynomial: the latter involves finding a higher-degree polynomial that passes through many of the points in a dataset.

Moreover, a dataset in the plane can contain two or more points that lie on the same *vertical* line, which is to say that those points have the same x value. However, a function cannot pass through such a pair of points: if two points (x1,y1) and (x2,y2) have the same x value, then they must have the same y value (i.e., y1=y2). A function can have two or more points that lie on the same *horizontal* line.

Now consider a scatter plot with many points in the plane that are sort of "clustered" in an elongated cloud-like shape: a best-fitting line will probably intersect only limited number of points (in fact, a best-fitting line might not intersect *any* of the points).

Consider one other scenario: suppose a dataset contains a set of points that lie on the same line. For instance, let's say the x values are in the set

{1,2,3,...,10} and the y values are in the set {2,4,6,...,20}. Then the equation of the best-fitting line is y=2*x+0. In this scenario, all the points are *collinear*, which is to say that they lie on the same line.

Linear Regression vs. Curve-Fitting

Suppose a dataset consists of n data points of the form (x, y), and no two of those data points have the same x value. Then, according to a well-known result in mathematics, there is a polynomial of degree less than or equal to n-1 that passes through those n points (if you are really interested, you can find mathematical proof of this statement in online articles). For example, a line is a polynomial of degree one and it can intersect any pair of non-vertical points in the plane. For any triple of points (that are not all on the same line) in the plane, there is a quadratic equation that passes through those points.

In addition, sometimes a lower degree polynomial is available. For instance, consider the set of 100 points in which the x value equals the y value: in this case, the line y = x (which is a polynomial of degree one) passes through all 100 points.

However, the extent to which a line "represents" a set of points in the plane depends on how closely those points can be approximated by a line, which is measured by the *variance* of the points (the variance is a statistical quantity). The more collinear the points, the smaller the variance; conversely, the more "spread out" the points are, the larger the variance.

When are Solutions Exact Values?

Although statistics-based solutions provide closed-form solutions for linear regression, neural networks provide *approximate* solutions. This is because machine learning algorithms for linear regression involve a sequence of approximations that "converges" to optimal values, which means that machine learning algorithms produce estimates of the exact values. For example, the slope m and y-intercept b of a best-fitting line for a set of points on a 2D plane have a closed-form solution in statistics, but they can only be approximated via machine learning algorithms (exceptions do exist, but they are rare situations).

Even though a closed-form solution for "traditional" linear regression provides exact values for both m and b, sometimes you can only use an approximation of the exact value. For instance, suppose that the slope m of a best-fitting line equals the square root of 3 and the y-intercept b is the square root of 2. If you plan to use these values in source code, you can only work with an approximation of these two numbers. In the same scenario, a neural network computes approximations for m and b, regardless of whether or not the exact values for m and b are irrational, rational, or integer values. However, machine learning algorithms are better suited for complex, non-linear, multi-dimensional datasets.

As a simple example, suppose that the closed-form solution for a linear regression problem produces integer or rational values for both m and b.

Specifically, let's suppose that a closed-form solution yields the values 2.0 and 1.0 for the slope and y-intercept, respectively, of a best-fitting line. The equation of the line looks like this:

$$y = 2.0 * x + 1.0$$

However, the corresponding solution from training a neural network might produce the values 2.0001 and 0.9997 for the slope m and the y-intercept b, respectively, as the values of m and b for a best-fitting line. Always keep this point in mind, especially when you are training a neural network.

What is Multivariate Analysis?

Multivariate analysis generalizes the equation of a line in the Euclidean plane to higher dimensions, and it is called a *hyper plane* instead of a line. The generalized equation has the following form:

$$y = w1*x1 + w2*x2 + \ldots + wn*xn + b$$

In the case of 2D linear regression, you only need to find the value of the slope (m) and the y-intercept (b), whereas in multivariate analysis you need to find the values for w1, w2, . . ., wn. Note that multivariate analysis is a term from statistics, and in machine learning it is often referred to as "generalized linear regression." Most of the code samples in this book that pertain to linear regression involve 2D points in the Euclidean plane.

OTHER TYPES OF REGRESSION

Linear regression finds the best-fitting line that "represents" a dataset, but what happens if a line in the plane is not a good fit for the dataset? This is a relevant question when you work with datasets.

Some alternatives to linear regression include quadratic equations, cubic equations, or higher-degree polynomials. However, these alternatives involve trade-offs, as we will discuss later.

Another possibility is a sort of hybrid approach that involves piece-wise linear functions, which comprises a set of line segments. If contiguous line segments are connected, then it is a piece-wise linear continuous function; otherwise, it is a piece-wise linear discontinuous function.

Thus, given a set of points in the plane, regression involves addressing the following questions:

1. What type of curve fits the data well? How do we know?
2. Does another type of curve fit the data better?
3. What does "best fit" mean?

One way to check if a line fits the data involves a visual check, but this approach does not work for data points that are higher than two dimensions. Moreover, this is a subjective decision, and some sample datasets are displayed later in this chapter. By visual inspection of a dataset, you might decide that a quadratic or cubic (or even higher degree) polynomial has the potential of being a better fit for the data. However, visual inspection is probably limited to points in a 2D plane or in three dimensions.

Let's defer the non-linear scenario and make the assumption that a line would be a good fit for the data. There is a well-known technique for finding the "best-fitting" line for such a dataset that involves minimizing the MSE (which we will discuss later in this chapter).

The next section provides a quick review of linear equations in the plane, along with some images that illustrate examples of linear equations.

WORKING WITH LINES IN THE PLANE (OPTIONAL)

This section contains a short review of lines in the Euclidean plane, so you can skip this section if you are comfortable with this topic. A minor point that is often overlooked is that lines in the Euclidean plane have infinite length. If you select two distinct points of a line, then all the points between those two selected points is a *line segment*. A *ray* is a "half infinite" line: when you select one point as an endpoint, then all the points on one side of the line constitutes a ray.

For example, the points in the plane whose y-coordinate is 0 is a line and also the x-axis, whereas the points between (0,0) and (1,0) on the x-axis form a line segment. In addition, the points on the x-axis that are to the right of (0,0) form a ray, and the points on the x-axis that are to the left of (0,0) also form a ray.

For simplicity and convenience, in this book we will use the terms "line" and "line segment" interchangeably. Now let's delve into the details of lines in the Euclidean plane. Here is the equation of a (non-vertical) line in the Euclidean plane:

$$y = m*x + b$$

The value of m is the slope of the line and the value of b is the y-intercept (i.e., the place where the line intersects the y-axis).

If need be, you can use a more general equation that can also represent vertical lines, as shown here:

$$a*x + b*y + c = 0$$

However, we will not be working with vertical lines, so we will use the first formula.

Figure 2.1 displays three horizontal lines whose equations (from top to bottom) are y = 3, y = 0, and y = -3.

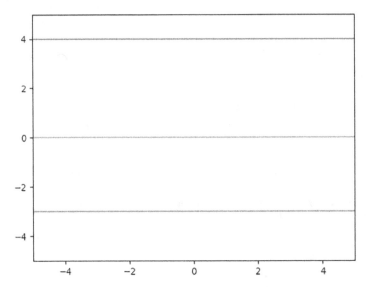

FIGURE 2.1 A graph of three horizontal line segments

Figure 2.2 displays two slanted lines whose equations are y = x and y = -x, respectively.

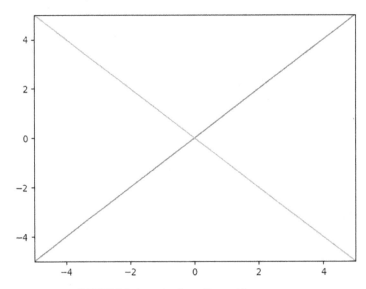

FIGURE 2.2 A graph of two diagonal line segments

Figure 2.3 displays two slanted parallel lines whose equations are y = 2*x and y = 2*x + 3, respectively.

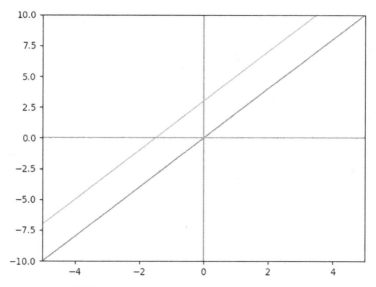

FIGURE 2.3 A graph of two slanted parallel line segments

Figure 2.4 displays a piece-wise linear graph consisting of connected line segments.

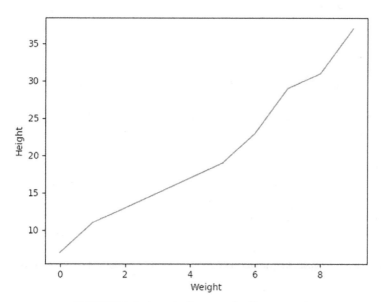

FIGURE 2.4 A piece-wise linear graph of line segments

Let's turn our attention to generating quasi-random data using a NumPy API, and then we will plot the data using Matplotlib.

SCATTER PLOTS WITH NUMPY AND MATPLOTLIB (1)

Listing 2.1 displays the content of `np_plot1.py` that illustrates how to use the NumPy `randn()` API to generate a dataset and then the `scatter()` API in Matplotlib to plot the points in the dataset.

One detail to note is that all the adjacent horizontal values are equally spaced, whereas the vertical values are based on a linear equation plus a "perturbation" value. This "perturbation technique" (which is not a standard term) is used in other code samples in this chapter to add a slightly randomized effect when the points are plotted. The advantage of this technique is that the best-fitting values for m and b are known in advance, and therefore we do not need to guess their values.

LISTING 2.1: np_plot1.py

```
import numpy as np
import matplotlib.pyplot as plt

x = np.random.randn(15,1)
y = 2.5*x + 5 + 0.2*np.random.randn(15,1)

print("x:",x)
print("y:",y)

plt.scatter(x,y)
plt.show()
```

Listing 2.1 contains two `import` statements and then initializes the array variable x with 15 random numbers between 0 and 1.

Next, the array variable y is defined in two parts: the first part is a linear equation `2.5*x + 5` and the second part is a "perturbation" value that is based on a random number. Thus, the array variable y simulates a set of values that closely approximate a line segment.

This technique is used in code samples that simulate a line segment, and then the training portion approximates the values of m and b for the best-fitting line. Obviously, we already *know* the equation of the best-fitting-line: the purpose of this technique is to compare the trained values for the slope m and y-intercept b with the known values (which, in this case, are 2.5 and 5). A partial output from Listing 2.1 is here:

```
x:  [[-1.42736308]
 [ 0.09482338]
 [-0.45071331]
 [ 0.19536304]
```

```
[-0.22295205]
// values omitted for brevity
y: [[1.12530514]
 [5.05168677]
 [3.93320782]
 [5.49760999]
 [4.46994978]
// values omitted for brevity
```

Figure 2.5 displays a scatter plot of points based on the values of x and y.

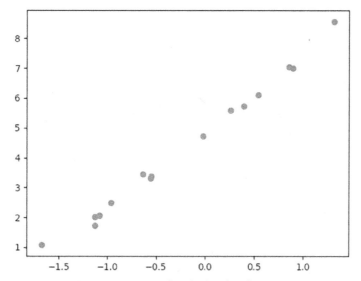

FIGURE 2.5 A scatter plot of points for a line segment

Why the Perturbation Technique is Useful

You already saw how to use the perturbation technique and by way of comparison, consider a dataset with the following points that are defined in the Python array variables X and Y:

X = [0,0.12,0.25,0.27,0.38,0.42,0.44,0.55,0.92,1.0]
Y = [0,0.15,0.54,0.51, 0.34,0.1,0.19,0.53,1.0,0.58]

If you need to find the best-fitting line for the preceding dataset, how would you guess the values for the slope m and the y-intercept b? In most cases, you probably cannot guess their values. However, the perturbation technique enables you to slightly move the points on a line whose value for the slope m (and optionally the value for the y-intercept b) is specified in advance.

The perturbation technique only works when you introduce small random values that do not result in different values for m and b.

SCATTER PLOTS WITH NUMPY AND MATPLOTLIB (2)

The code in Listing 2.1 (in the previous section) assigned random values to the variable x, whereas a hard-coded value is assigned to the slope m. The y values are a hard-coded multiple of the x values, plus a random value that is calculated via the perturbation technique. Hence, we do not know the value of the y-intercept b.

In this section, the values for `trainX` are based on the `np.linspace()` API, and the values for `trainY` involve the perturbation technique that is described in the previous section.

The code in this example simply prints the values for `trainX` and `trainY`, which correspond to data points in the Euclidean plane. Listing 2.2 displays the content of `np_plot2.py` that illustrates how to simulate a linear dataset in NumPy.

LISTING 2.2: np_plot2.py

```
import numpy as np

trainX = np.linspace(-1, 1, 11)
trainY = 4*trainX + np.random.randn(*trainX.shape)*0.5

print("trainX: ",trainX)
print("trainY: ",trainY)
```

Listing 2.2 initializes the NumPy array variable `trainX` via the NumPy `linspace()` API, followed by the array variable `trainY` that is defined in two parts. The first part is the linear term `4*trainX` and the second part involves the perturbation technique that is a randomly generated number. The output from Listing 2.2 is here:

```
trainX:  [-1.  -0.8 -0.6 -0.4 -0.2  0.   0.2  0.4  0.6  0.8  1. ]
trainY:  [-3.60147459 -2.66593108 -2.26491189 -1.65121314
-0.56454605  0.22746004 0.86830728  1.60673482  2.51151543
3.59573877  3.05506056]
```

The next section contains an example that is similar to Listing 2.2, using the same perturbation technique to generate a set of points that approximate a quadratic equation instead of a line segment.

A QUADRATIC SCATTER PLOT WITH NUMPY AND MATPLOTLIB

Listing 2.3 displays the content of `np_plot_quadratic.py` that illustrates how to plot a quadratic function in the plane.

LISTING 2.3: np_plot_quadratic.py

```
import numpy as np
import matplotlib.pyplot as plt
```

```
#see what happens with this set of values:
#x = np.linspace(-5,5,num=100)

x = np.linspace(-5,5,num=100)[:,None]
y = -0.5 + 2.2*x +0.3*x**2 + 2*np.random.randn(100,1)
print("x:",x)

plt.plot(x,y)
plt.show()
```

Listing 2.3 initializes the array variable x with the values that are generated via the np.linspace() API, which, in this case, is a set of 100 equally spaced decimal numbers between -5 and 5. Notice the snippet [:,None] in the initialization of x, which results in an array of elements, each of which is an array consisting of a single number.

The array variable y is defined in two parts: the first part is a quadratic equation -0.5 + 2.2*x +0.3*x**2 and the second part is a "perturbation" value that is based on a random number (similar to the code in Listing 2.1). Thus, the array variable y simulates a set of values that approximates a quadratic equation. The output from Listing 2.3 is here:

```
x:
[[-5.        ]
 [-4.8989899 ]
 [-4.7979798 ]
 [-4.6969697 ]
 [-4.5959596 ]
 [-4.49494949]
 // values omitted for brevity
 [ 4.8989899 ]
 [ 5.        ]]
```

Figure 2.6 displays a scatter plot of points based on the values of x and y, which have an approximate shape of a quadratic equation.

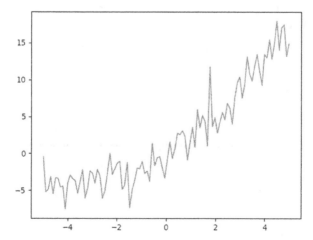

FIGURE 2.6 A scatter plot of points for a quadratic equation

THE MEAN SQUARED ERROR (MSE) FORMULA

The MSE is the sum of the squares of the difference between an actual y value and the predicted y value, divided by the number of points. Notice that the predicted y value is the y value that each point would have if that point were actually on the best-fitting line.

Although the MSE is popular for linear regression, there are other error types available, some of which are discussed briefly in the next section.

A List of Error Types

Although we will only discuss MSE for linear regression in this book, there are other types of formulas that you can use for linear regression, some of which are listed here:

- MSE
- RMSE
- RMSPROP
- MAE

The MSE is the basis for the preceding error types. For example, RMSE is the *Root Mean Squared Error*, which is the square root of the MSE.

MAE is the *Mean Absolute Error*, which is the sum of *the absolute value of the differences of the y terms* (*not* the square of the differences of the y terms), which is then divided by the number of terms.

The RMSPROP optimizer utilizes the magnitude of recent gradients to normalize the gradients. Specifically, RMSPROP maintain a moving average over the RMS (root mean squared) gradients, and then divides that term by the current gradient.

Although it is easier to compute the derivative of MSE, it is also true that MSE is more susceptible to outliers, whereas MAE is less susceptible to outliers. The reason is simple: a squared term can be significantly larger than the absolute value of a term. For example, if a difference term is 10, then a squared term of 100 is added to MSE, whereas only 10 is added to MAE. Similarly, if a difference term is -20, then a squared term 400 is added to MSE, whereas only 20 (which is the absolute value of -20) is added to MAE.

Non-linear Least Squares

When predicting housing prices, where the dataset contains a wide range of values, techniques such as linear regression or random forests can cause the model to overfit the samples with the highest values to reduce quantities such as the mean absolute error.

In this scenario, you probably want an error metric, such as relative error, that reduces the importance of fitting the samples with the largest values. This technique is called *non-linear least squares*, which may use a log-based transformation of labels and predicted values.

The next section contains several code samples, the first of which involves calculating the MSE manually, followed by an example that uses NumPy formulas to perform the calculations.

CALCULATING THE MSE MANUALLY

This section contains two line graphs, both of which contain a line that approximates a set of points in a scatter plot.

Figure 2.7 displays a line segment that approximates a scatter plot of points (some of which intersect the line segment). The MSE for the line in Figure 2.7 is computed as follows (only numerators will be compared):

MSE = (1*1 + (-1)*(-1) + (-1)*(-1) + 1*1)/9 = 4/9

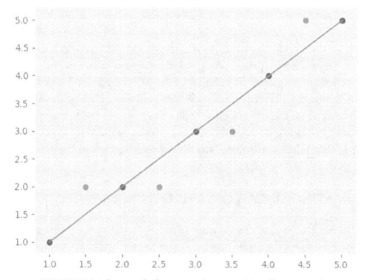

FIGURE 2.7 A line graph that approximates points of a scatter plot

Figure 2.8 displays a set of points and a line that is a potential candidate for best-fitting line for the data. The MSE for the line in Figure 2.8 is computed as follows:

```
MSE  =  ((-2)*(-2)  +  2*2)/7  =  8/7
```

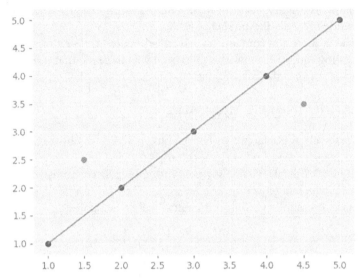

FIGURE 2.8 A line graph that approximates points of a scatter plot

Thus, the line in Figure 2.7 has a smaller MSE than the line in Figure 2.8, which might have surprised you (or did you guess correctly?).

In these two figures, we calculated the MSE easily and quickly, but in general it is significantly more difficult. For instance, if we plot 10 points in the Euclidean plane that do not closely fit a line, with individual terms that involve non-integer values, we would probably need a calculator.

A better solution involves NumPy functions, such as the np.linspace() API, as discussed in the next section.

APPROXIMATING LINEAR DATA WITH NP.LINSPACE()

Listing 2.4 displays the content of np_linspace1.py that illustrates how to generate some data with the np.linspace() API in conjunction with the perturbation technique.

LISTING 2.4: np_linspace1.py

```
import numpy as np

trainX = np.linspace(-1, 1, 6)
trainY = 3*trainX+ np.random.randn(*trainX.shape)*0.5

print("trainX: ", trainX)
print("trainY: ", trainY)
```

The purpose of this code sample is to produce and display a set of randomly generated numbers. Later in this chapter, we will use this code as a starting point for an actual linear regression task.

Listing 2.4 starts with the definition of the array variable `trainX` that is initialized via the `np.linspace()` API. Next, the array variable `trainY` is defined via the perturbation technique used in previous code samples. The output from Listing 2.4 is here:

```
trainX:  [-1.  -0.6 -0.2  0.2  0.6  1. ]
trainY:  [-2.9008553  -2.26684745 -0.59516253  0.66452207
1.82669051  2.30549295]
trainX:  [-1.  -0.6 -0.2  0.2  0.6  1. ]
trainY:  [-2.9008553  -2.26684745 -0.59516253  0.66452207
1.82669051  2.30549295]
```

Now that we know how to generate (x, y) values for a linear equation, let's learn how to calculate the MSE, which is discussed in the next section. The next example generates a set of data values using the `np.linspace()` method and the `np.random.randn()` method to introduce some randomness in the data points.

CALCULATING MSE WITH NP.LINSPACE() API

The code sample in this section differs from many of the earlier code samples in this chapter: it uses a hard-coded array of values for `x` and also for `Y` instead of the perturbation technique. Hence, you will *not* know the correct value for the slope and y-intercept (and you probably will not be able to guess their correct values). Listing 2.5 displays the content of `plain_linreg1.py` that illustrates how to compute the MSE with simulated data.

LISTING 2.5: plain_linreg1.py

```python
import numpy as np
import matplotlib.pyplot as plt

X = [0,0.12,0.25,0.27,0.38,0.42,0.44,0.55,0.92,1.0]
Y = [0,0.15,0.54,0.51, 0.34,0.1,0.19,0.53,1.0,0.58]

losses = []
#Step 1: Parameter initialization
W = 0.45
b = 0.75

for i in range(1, 100):
  #Step 2: Calculate Loss
  Y_pred = np.multiply(W, X) + b
  Loss_error = 0.5 * (Y_pred - Y)**2
  loss = np.sum(Loss_error)/10

  #Step 3: Calculate dW and db
  db = np.sum((Y_pred - Y))
  dw = np.dot((Y_pred - Y), X)
  losses.append(loss)
```

```
#Step 4: Update parameters:
W = W - 0.01*dw
b = b - 0.01*db

if i%10 == 0:
  print("Loss at", i,"iteration = ", loss)

#Step 5: Repeat via a for loop with 1000 iterations

#Plot loss versus # of iterations
print("W = ", W,"& b = ",  b)
plt.plot(losses)
plt.ylabel('loss')
plt.xlabel('iterations (per tens)')
plt.show()
```

Listing 2.5 initializes the array variables X and Y with hard-coded values, and then initializes the scalar variables W and b. The next portion of Listing 2.5 contains a for loop that iterates 100 times. After each iteration of the loop, the variables Y_pred, Loss_error, and loss are calculated. Next, the values for dw and db are calculated, based on the sum of the terms in the array Y_pred-Y, and the inner product of Y_pred-y and X, respectively.

Notice how W and b are updated: their values are decremented by the terms 0.01*dw and 0.01*db, respectively. This calculation should look familiar: the code is programmatically calculating an approximate value of the gradient for W and b, both of which are multiplied by the learning rate (the hard-coded value 0.01), and the resulting term is decremented from the current values of W and b to produce a new approximation for W and b. Although this technique is simple, it does calculate reasonable values for W and b.

The final block of code in Listing 2.5 displays the intermediate approximations for W and b, along with a plot of the loss (vertical axis) vs. the number of iterations (horizontal axis). The output from Listing 2.5 is here:

```
Loss at 10 iteration =   0.04114630674619492
Loss at 20 iteration =   0.026706242729839392
Loss at 30 iteration =   0.024738889446900423
Loss at 40 iteration =   0.023850565034634254
Loss at 50 iteration =   0.0231499048706651
Loss at 60 iteration =   0.02255361434242207
Loss at 70 iteration =   0.0220425055291673
Loss at 80 iteration =   0.021604128492245713
Loss at 90 iteration =   0.02122811750568435
W =   0.47256473531193927 & b =   0.19578262688662174
```

Figure 2.9 displays a scatter plot of points generated by the code in Listing 2.5.

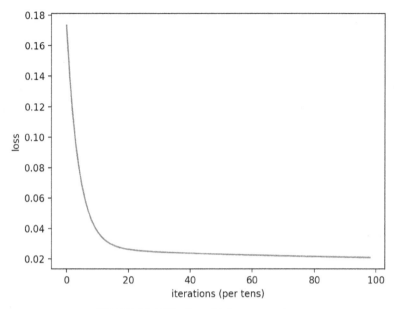

FIGURE 2.9 MSE values with linear regression

The code sample `plain-linreg2.py` is similar to the code in Listing 2.5: the difference is that instead of a single loop with 100 iterations, there is an outer loop that execute 100 times, and during each iteration of the outer loop, the inner loop also executes 100 times.

SUMMARY

This chapter introduced you to machine learning and concepts such as feature selection, feature engineering, data cleaning, training sets, and test sets. Next you learned about supervised, unsupervised, and semi-supervised learning. Then you learned regression tasks, classification tasks, and clustering, as well as the steps that are typically required to prepare a dataset. These steps include "feature selection" or "feature extraction" that can be performed using various algorithms. Then you learned about issues that can arise with the data in datasets and how to rectify them.

In addition, you also learned about linear regression, along with a brief description of how to calculate a best-fitting line for a dataset of values in the Euclidean plane. You saw how to perform linear regression using NumPy to initialize arrays with data values, along with a "perturbation technique" that introduces some randomness for the y values. This technique is useful because you will know the correct values for the slope and y-intercept of the best-fitting line, which you can then compare with the trained values.

## CHAPTER 3

CLASSIFIERS IN MACHINE LEARNING

This chapter presents numerous classification algorithms in machine learning. This includes algorithms such as the kNN (k-nearest neighbors) algorithm, logistic regression (despite its name, it *is* a classifier), decision trees, random forests, SVMs, and Bayesian classifiers. The emphasis on algorithms is intended to introduce you to machine learning, which includes a tree-based code sample that relies on scikit-learn.

Due to space constraints, this chapter does not cover other well-known algorithms, such as Linear Discriminant Analysis and the k-means algorithm (which is for unsupervised learning and clustering). However, there are many online tutorials available that discuss these and other algorithms in machine learning.

With the preceding points in mind, the first section of this chapter briefly discusses the classifiers that are mentioned in the introductory paragraph. The second section of this chapter provides an overview of activation functions, which will be very useful if you decide to learn about deep neural networks. You will learn how and why they are used in neural networks. This section also contains a list of the TensorFlow APIs for activation functions, followed by a description of some of their merits.

The third section introduces logistic regression, which relies on the sigmoid function and is also used in RNNs (recurrent neural networks) and LSTMs (Long Short Term Memory).

To give you some context, classifiers are one of three major types of algorithms: regression algorithms (e.g., linear regression and GPT-4 in Chapter 4), classification algorithms (discussed in this chapter), and clustering algorithms (such as k-means, which is not discussed in this book).

The section pertaining to activation functions does involve a basic understanding of hidden layers in a neural network. Depending on your experience level, you might benefit from reading some preparatory material before reading this section (there are many articles available online).

WHAT IS CLASSIFICATION?

Given a dataset that contains observations whose class membership is known, *classification* is the task of determining the class to which a new datapoint belongs. *Classes* refer to categories and are also called "targets" or "labels." For example, spam detection in email service providers involves binary classification (only two classes). The MNIST dataset contains a set of images, where each image is a single digit, which means there are ten labels. Some applications in classification include credit approval, medical diagnosis, and target marketing.

What are Classifiers?

In the previous chapter, you learned that linear regression uses supervised learning in conjunction with numeric data. The goal is to train a model that can make numeric predictions (e.g., the price of stock tomorrow, the temperature of a system or its barometric pressure). By contrast, classifiers use supervised learning in conjunction with non-numeric classes of data: the goal is to train a model that can make categorical predictions.

For instance, suppose that each row in a dataset is a specific wine, and each column pertains to a specific wine feature (tannin, acidity, and so forth). Suppose further that there are five classes of wine in the dataset: for simplicity, let's label them A, B, C, D, and E. Given a new data point, which is to say a new row of data, a classifier for this dataset attempts to determine the label for this wine.

Some of the classifiers in this chapter can perform categorical classification and also make numeric predictions (i.e., they can be used for regression as well as classification).

Common Classifiers

Some of the most popular classifiers for machine learning are listed here (in no particular order):

- linear classifiers
- kNN
- logistic regression
- decision trees
- random forests
- SVMs
- Bayesian classifiers
- CNNs (deep learning)

Different classifiers have different advantages and disadvantages, which often involves a trade-off between complexity and accuracy, similar to algorithms in fields that are outside of AI.

In the case of deep learning, CNNs (convolutional neural networks) perform image classification, which makes them classifiers (they can also be used for audio and text processing).

The upcoming sections provide a brief description of the machine learning classifiers that are listed in the previous list.

Binary versus Multiclass Classification

Binary classifiers work with datasets that have two classes, whereas multiclass classifiers (sometimes called multinomial classifiers) distinguish more than two classes. Random forest classifiers and Naïve Bayes classifiers support multiple classes, whereas SVMs and linear classifiers can only be used as binary classifiers.

In addition, there are techniques for multiclass classification that are based on binary classifiers: One-versus-All (OvA) and One-versus-One (OvO).

The OvA technique (also called "One-versus-The-Rest") involves multiple binary classifiers that are equal to the number of classes. For example, if a dataset has five classes, then OvA uses five binary classifiers, each of which detects one of the five classes. In order to classify a datapoint in this particular dataset, select the binary classifier that has output the highest score.

The OvO technique also involves multiple binary classifiers, but in this case, a binary classifier is used to train on a pair of classes. For instance, if the classes are A, B, C, D, and E, then ten binary classifiers are required: one for A and B, one for A and C, one for A and D, and so forth, until the last binary classifier for D and E.

In general, if there are n classes, then n*(n-1)/2 binary classifiers are required. Although the OvO technique requires considerably more binary classifiers (e.g., 190 are required for 20 classes) than the OvA technique (e.g., a mere 20 binary classifiers for 20 classes), the OvO technique has the advantage that each binary classifier is only trained on the portion of the dataset that pertains to its two chosen classes.

Multilabel Classification

Multilabel classification involves assigning multiple labels to an instance from a dataset. Hence, multilabel classification generalizes multiclass classification (discussed in the previous section), where the latter involves assigning a single label to an instance belonging to a dataset that has multiple classes. An article involving multilabel classification that contains Keras-based code is available online:

https://medium.com/@vijayabhaskar96/multi-label-image-classification-tutorial-with-keras-imagedatagenerator-cd541f8eaf24

You can also perform an online search for articles that involve SKLearn or PyTorch for multilabel classification tasks.

WHAT ARE LINEAR CLASSIFIERS?

A *linear classifier* separates a dataset into two classes. A linear classifier is a line for 2D points, a plane for 3D points, and a hyperplane (a generalization of a plane) for higher dimensional points.

Linear classifiers are often the fastest classifiers, so they are often used when the speed of classification is of high importance. Linear classifiers usually work well when the input vectors are sparse (i.e., mostly zero values) or when the number of dimensions is large.

WHAT IS KNN?

The kNN (k-nearest neighbors) algorithm is a classification algorithm. In brief, data points that are "near" each other are classified as belonging to the same class. When a new point is introduced, it is added to the class of the majority of its nearest neighbor. For example, suppose that k equals 3, and a new data point is introduced. Look at the class of its 3 nearest neighbors: let's say they are A, A, and B. Then by majority vote, the new data point is labeled as a data point of class A.

The kNN algorithm is essentially a heuristic and not a technique with complex mathematical underpinnings, and yet it is still an effective and useful algorithm.

Try the kNN algorithm if you want to use a simple algorithm, or when you believe that the nature of your dataset is highly unstructured. The kNN algorithm can produce highly nonlinear decisions despite being very simple. You can use kNN in search applications where you are searching for "similar" items.

Measure similarity by creating a vector representation of the items, and then compare the vectors using an appropriate distance metric (such as Euclidean distance).

Some concrete examples of kNN search include searching for semantically similar documents.

How to Handle a Tie in kNN

An odd value for k is less likely to result in a tie vote, but it is not impossible. For example, suppose that k equals 7, and when a new data point is introduced, its 7 nearest neighbors belong to the set {A,B,A,B,A,B,C}. As you can see, there is no majority vote, because there are 3 points in class A, 3 points in class B, and 1 point in class C.

There are several techniques for handling a tie in kNN, as listed here:

• Assign higher weights to closer points.
• Increase the value of k until a winner is determined.

• Decrease the value of k until a winner is determined.
• Randomly select one class.

If you reduce k until it equals 1, it is still possible to have a tie vote: there might be two points that are equally distant from the new point, so you need a mechanism for deciding which of those two points to select as the 1-neighbor.

If there is a tie between classes A and B, then randomly select either class A or class B. Another variant is to keep track of the "tie" votes, and alternate round-robin style to ensure a more even distribution.

WHAT ARE DECISION TREES?

Decision trees are another type of classification algorithm that involves a tree-like structure. In a "generic" tree, the placement of a data point is determined by simple conditional logic. As a simple illustration, suppose that a dataset contains a set of numbers that represent the ages of people, and let's also suppose that the first number is 50. This number is chosen as the root of the tree, and all numbers that are smaller than 50 are added on the left branch of the tree, whereas all numbers that are greater than 50 are added on the right branch of the tree.

For example, suppose we have the sequence of numbers that is as follows: {50, 25, 70, 40}. Then we can construct a tree as follows: 50 is the root node; 25 is the left child of 50; 70 is the right child of 50; and 40 is the right child of 20. Each additional numeric value that we add to this dataset is processed to determine which direction to proceed ("left or right") at each node in the tree.

Listing 3.1 displays the content of `sklearn_tree2.py` that defines a set of 2D points in the Euclidean plane, along with their labels, and then predicts the label (i.e., the class) of several other 2D points in the Euclidean plane.

LISTING 3.1: sklearn_tree2.py

```
from sklearn import tree

# X = pairs of 2D points and Y = the class of each point
X = [[0, 0], [1, 1], [2,2]]
Y = [0, 1, 1]

tree_clf = tree.DecisionTreeClassifier()
tree_clf = tree_clf.fit(X, Y)

#predict the class of samples:
print("predict class of [-1., -1.]:")
print(tree_clf.predict([[-1., -1.]]))

print("predict class of [2., 2.]:")
print(tree_clf.predict([[2., 2.]]))
```

```
# the percentage of training samples of the same class
# in a leaf note equals the probability of each class
print("probability of each class in [2.,2.]:")
print(tree_clf.predict_proba([[2., 2.]]))
```

Listing 3.1 imports the tree class from `sklearn` and then initializes the arrays X and y with data values. Next, the variable `tree_clf` is initialized as an instance of the `DecisionTreeClassifier` class, after which it is trained by invoking the `fit()` method with the values of X and y.

Now launch the code in Listing 3.1 and you will see the following output:

```
predict class of [-1., -1.]:
[0]
predict class of [2., 2.]:
[1]
probability of each class in [2.,2.]:
[[0. 1.]]
```

As you can see, the points [-1,-1] and [2,2] are correctly labeled with the values 0 and 1, respectively.

Listing 3.2 displays the content of `sklearn_tree3.py` that extends the code in Listing 3.1 by adding a third label, and also by predicting the label of three points instead of two points in the Euclidean plane (the modifications are shown in bold).

LISTING 3.2: sklearn_tree3.py

```
from sklearn import tree

# X = pairs of 2D points and Y = the class of each point
X = [[0, 0], [1, 1], [2,2]]
Y = [0, 1, 2]

tree_clf = tree.DecisionTreeClassifier()
tree_clf = tree_clf.fit(X, Y)

#predict the class of samples:
print("predict class of [-1., -1.]:")
print(tree_clf.predict([[-1., -1.]]))

print("predict class of [0.8, 0.8]:")
print(tree_clf.predict([[0.8, 0.8]]))

print("predict class of [2., 2.]:")
print(tree_clf.predict([[2., 2.]]))

# the percentage of training samples of the same class
# in a leaf note equals the probability of each class
print("probability of each class in [2.,2.]:")
print(tree_clf.predict_proba([[2., 2.]]))
```

Now launch the code in Listing 3.2, and you will see the following output:

```
predict class of [-1., -1.]:
[0]
predict class of [0.8, 0.8]:
[1]
predict class of [2., 2.]:
[2]
probability of each class in [2.,2.]:
[[0. 0. 1.]]
```

As you can see, the points [-1,-1], [0.8, 0.8], and [2,2] are correctly labeled with the values 0, 1, and 2, respectively.

Listing 3.3 displays a portion of the dataset partial_wine.csv, which contains two features and a label column (there are three classes). The total row count for this dataset is 178.

LISTING 3.3: partial_wine.csv

```
Alcohol, Malic acid, class
14.23,1.71,1
13.2,1.78,1
13.16,2.36,1
14.37,1.95,1
13.24,2.59,1
14.2,1.76,1
```

Listing 3.4 displays the content of tree_classifier.py that uses a decision tree to train a model on the dataset partial_wine.csv.

LISTING 3.4: tree_classifier.py

```
import numpy as np
import matplotlib.pyplot as plt
import pandas as pd

# Importing the dataset
dataset = pd.read_csv('partial_wine.csv')
X = dataset.iloc[:, [0, 1]].values
y = dataset.iloc[:, 2].values

# split the dataset into a training set and a test set
from sklearn.model_selection import train_test_split
X_train, X_test, y_train, y_test = train_test_split(X, y,
test_size = 0.25, random_state = 0)

# Feature Scaling
from sklearn.preprocessing import StandardScaler
sc = StandardScaler()
X_train = sc.fit_transform(X_train)
X_test = sc.transform(X_test)
```

```
# ====> INSERT YOUR CLASSIFIER CODE HERE <====
from sklearn.tree import DecisionTreeClassifier
classifier = DecisionTreeClassifier(criterion='entropy',rand
om_state=0)
classifier.fit(X_train, y_train)
# ====> INSERT YOUR CLASSIFIER CODE HERE <====

# predict the test set results
y_pred = classifier.predict(X_test)

# generate the confusion matrix
from sklearn.metrics import confusion_matrix
cm = confusion_matrix(y_test, y_pred)
print("confusion matrix:")
print(cm)
```

Listing 3.4 contains some import statements and then populates the Pandas data frame dataset with the contents of the CSV file partial_wine. csv. Next, the variable X is initialized with the first two columns (and all the rows) of dataset, and the variable y is initialized with the third column (and all the rows) of dataset.

Next, the variables X_train, X_test, y_train, and y_test are populated with data from X and y using a 75/25 split proportion. Notice that the variable sc (which is an instance of the StandardScalar class) performs a scaling operation on the variables X_train and X_test.

The code block shown in bold in Listing 3.4 is where we create an instance of the DecisionTreeClassifier class and then train the instance with the data in the variables X_train and X_test.

The next portion of Listing 3.4 populates the variable y_pred with a set of predictions that are generated from the data in the X_test variable. The last portion of Listing 3.4 creates a confusion matrix based on the data in y_test and the predicted data in y_pred.

Remember that all the diagonal elements of a confusion matrix are correct predictions (such as true positive and true negative); all the other cells contain a numeric value that specifies the number of predictions that are incorrect (such as false positive and false negative).

Now launch the code in Listing 3.4, and you will see the following output for the confusion matrix in which there are 36 correct predictions and 9 incorrect predictions (with an accuracy of 80%):

```
confusion matrix:
[[13  1  2]
 [ 0 17  4]
 [ 1  1  6]]
from sklearn.metrics import confusion_matrix
```

There is a total of 45 entries in the preceding 3x3 matrix, and the diagonal entries are correctly identified labels. Hence, the accuracy is 36/45 = 0.80.

WHAT ARE RANDOM FORESTS?

Random forests are a generalization of decision trees: this classification algorithm involves multiple trees (the number is specified by you). If the data involves making a numeric prediction, the average of the predictions of the trees is computed. If the data involves a categorical prediction, the mode of the predictions of the trees is determined.

By way of analogy, random forests operate in a manner similar to financial portfolio diversification: the goal is to balance the losses with higher gains. Random forests use a "majority vote" to make predictions, which operates under the assumption that selecting the majority vote is more likely to be correct (and more often) than any individual prediction from a single tree.

You can easily modify the code in Listing 3.4 to use a random forest by replacing the two lines shown in bold with the following code:

```
from sklearn.ensemble import RandomForestClassifier
classifier = RandomForestClassifier(n_estimators = 10,
criterion='entropy', random_state = 0)
```

Make this code change, launch the code, and examine the confusion matrix to compare its accuracy with the accuracy of the decision tree in Listing 3.4.

WHAT ARE SVMS?

Support Vector Machines involve a supervised machine learning algorithm and can be used for classification or regression problems. SVMs can work with nonlinearly separable data as well as linearly separable data. SVMs use a technique called the "kernel trick" to transform data and then find an optimal boundary. The transformation involves higher dimensionality. This technique results in a separation of the transformed data, after which it is possible to find a hyperplane that separates the data into two classes.

SVMs are more common in classification tasks than regression tasks. Some use cases for SVMs include the following:

- text classification tasks: category assignment
- detecting spam/sentiment analysis
- used for image recognition: aspect-based recognition color-based classification
- handwritten digit recognition (postal automation)

Tradeoffs of SVMs

Although SVMs are extremely powerful, there are tradeoffs involved. Some of the advantages of SVMs are listed here:

- high accuracy
- works well on smaller cleaner datasets
- can be more efficient because it uses a subset of training points
- an alternative to CNNs in cases of limited datasets
- captures more complex relationships between data points

Despite the power of SVMs, there are some disadvantages of SVMs, which are listed here:

- not suited to larger datasets: training time can be high
- less effective on noisier datasets with overlapping classes

SVMs involve more parameters than decision trees and random forests

One suggestion to consider is to modify Listing 3.4 to use an SVM by replacing the two lines shown in bold with the following two lines shown in bold:

```
from sklearn.svm import SVC
classifier = SVC(kernel = 'linear', random_state = 0)
```

You now have an SVM-based model, simply by making the previous code update. Make the code change, then launch the code and examine the confusion matrix to compare its accuracy with the accuracy of the decision tree model and the random forest model earlier in this chapter.

WHAT IS BAYESIAN INFERENCE?

Bayesian inference is an important technique in statistics that involves statistical inference and Bayes' theorem to update the probability for a hypothesis as more information becomes available. Bayesian inference is often called "Bayesian probability," and it is important in the dynamic analysis of sequential data.

Bayes' Theorem

Given two sets A and B, let's define the following numeric values (all of them are between 0 and 1):

P(A) = probability of being in set A
P(B) = probability of being in set B
P(Both) = probability of being in A intersect B
P(A|B) = probability of being in A (given you are in B)
P(B|A) = probability of being in B (given you are in A)

Then the following formulas are also true:

P(A|B) = P(Both)/P(B) (#1)
P(B|A) = P(Both)/P(A) (#2)

Multiply the preceding pair of equations by the term that appears in the denominator and we get these equations:

P(B)*P(A|B) = P(Both) (#3)
P(A)*P(B|A) = P(Both) (#4)

Now set the left-side of Equations #3 and #4 equal to each another, and that gives us this equation:

P(B)*P(A|B) = P(A)*P(B|A) (#5)

Divide both sides of Equation #5 by P(B), and we obtain this well-known equation:

P(A|B) = P(A)*P(A|B)/P(B) (#6)

Some Bayesian Terminology

In the previous section, we derived the following relationship:

P(h|d) = (P(d|h) * P(h)) / P(d)

There is a name for each of the four terms in the preceding equation, as discussed below.

First, the posterior probability is P(h|d), which is the probability of hypothesis h given the data d.

Second, P(d|h) is the probability of data d given that the hypothesis h was true.

Third, the prior probability of h is P(h), which is the probability of hypothesis h being true (regardless of the data).

Finally, P(d) is the probability of the data (regardless of the hypothesis)

We are interested in calculating the posterior probability of P(h|d) from the prior probability p(h) with P(D) and P(d|h).

What is MAP?

The *maximum a posteriori* (MAP) *hypothesis* is the hypothesis with the highest probability, which is the maximum probable hypothesis. This can be written as follows:

MAP(h) = max(P(h|d))
or:

$MAP(h) = max((P(d|h) * P(h)) / P(d))$
or:
$MAP(h) = max(P(d|h) * P(h))$

Why Use Bayes' Theorem?

Bayes' theorem describes the probability of an event based on the prior knowledge of the conditions that might be related to the event. If we know the conditional probability, we can use Bayes' rule to find out the reverse probabilities. The previous statement is the general representation of Bayes' rule.

WHAT IS A BAYESIAN CLASSIFIER?

A Naïve Bayes' Classifier is a probabilistic classifier inspired by Bayes' theorem. An NB classifier assumes the attributes are conditionally independent, and it works well even when the assumption is not true. This assumption greatly reduces computational cost, and it is a simple algorithm to implement that only requires linear time. Moreover, a NB classifier easily scalable to larger datasets and good results are obtained in most cases. Other advantages of a NB classifier include the following:

- can be used for Binary & Multiclass classification
- provides different types of NB algorithms
- good choice for Text Classification problems
- a popular choice for spam email classification
- can be easily trained on small datasets

As you can probably surmise, NB classifiers do have some disadvantages, as listed below:

- All features are assumed unrelated.
- It cannot learn relationships between features.
- It can suffer from "the zero probability problem."

The *zero probability problem* refers to the case when the conditional probability is zero for an attribute, it fails to give a valid prediction. However, can be fixed explicitly using a Laplacian estimator.

Types of Naïve Bayes' Classifiers

There are three major types of NB classifiers:

- Gaussian Naïve Bayes
- Multinomial Naïve Bayes (Multinomial NB)
- Bernoulli Naïve Bayes

Details of these classifiers are beyond the scope of this chapter, but you can perform an online search for more information.

TRAINING CLASSIFIERS

Some common techniques for training classifiers are here:

- holdout method
- k-fold cross-validation

The *holdout method* is the most common method, which starts by dividing the dataset into two partitions called train and test (80% and 20%, respectively). The train set is used for training the model, and the test data tests its predictive power.

The *k-fold cross-validation* technique is used to verify that the model is not over-fitted. The dataset is randomly partitioned into k mutually exclusive subsets, where each partition has equal size. One partition is for testing and the other partitions are for training. Iterate throughout the whole of the k folds.

EVALUATING CLASSIFIERS

Whenever you select a classifier for a dataset, it is obviously important to evaluate the accuracy of that classifier. Some common techniques for evaluating classifiers are listed here:

- precision and recall
- ROC curve (Receiver Operating Characteristics)

Precision and recall are discussed in Chapter 2 and reproduced here for your convenience. Let's define the following variables:

TP = the number of true positive results
FP = the number of false positive results
TN = the number of true negative results
FN = the number of false negative results

Then the definitions of precision, accuracy, and recall are given by the following formulas:

precision = TP/(TN + FP)
accuracy = (TP + TN)/[TP + FP + FN + TN]
recall = TP/[TP + FN]

The *ROC curve* is used for a visual comparison of classification models that shows the trade-off between the true positive rate and the false positive rate. The area under the ROC curve is a measure of the accuracy of the model. When a model is closer to the diagonal, it is less accurate, and the model with perfect accuracy will have an area of 1.0.

The ROC curve plots the True Positive Rate versus False Positive Rate. Another type of curve is the PR curve that plots precision versus recall. When dealing with highly skewed datasets (strong class imbalance), precision-recall (PR) curves give better results.

This concludes the portion of the chapter pertaining to statistical terms and techniques for measuring the validity of a dataset. Now let's look at activation functions in machine learning, which is the topic of the next section.

WHAT ARE ACTIVATION FUNCTIONS?

An *activation function* is (usually) a nonlinear function that introduces nonlinearity into a neural network, thereby preventing a "consolidation" of the hidden layers in neural network. Specifically, suppose that every pair of adjacent layers in a neural network involves just a matrix transformation and no activation function. *Such a network is a linear system, which means that its layers can be consolidated into a much smaller system.*

First, the weights of the edges that connect the input layer with the first hidden layer can be represented by a matrix: let's call it W1. Next, the weights of the edges that connect the first hidden layer with the second hidden layer can also be represented by a matrix: let's call it W2. Repeat this process until we reach the edges that connect the final hidden layer with the output layer: let's call this matrix Wk. Since we do not have an activation function, we can simply multiply the matrices W1, W2, ..., Wk together and produce one matrix: let's call it W. We have now replaced the original neural network with an equivalent neural network that contains one input layer, a single matrix of weights W, and an output layer. In other words, we no longer have our original multilayered neural network!

Fortunately, we can prevent the previous scenario from happening when we specify an activation function between every pair of adjacent layers. In other words, *an activation function at each layer prevents this "matrix consolidation."* Hence, we can maintain all the intermediate hidden layers during the process of training the neural network.

For simplicity, let's assume that we have the same activation function between every pair of adjacent layers (we will remove this assumption shortly). The process for using an activation function in a neural network involves several steps, described as follows:

1. Start with an input vector, x1, of numbers.

2. Multiply x1 by the matrix of the weights, W1, which represents the edges that connect the input layer with the first hidden layer. The result is a new vector, x2.

3. "Apply" the activation function to each element of x2 to create another vector x3.

Now repeat Steps 2 and 3, except that we use the "starting" vector x3 and the weights matrix W2 for the edges that connect the first hidden layer with the second hidden layer (or just the output layer if there is only one hidden layer).

After completing the preceding process, we have "preserved" the neural network, which means that it can be trained on a dataset. Instead of using the same activation function at each step, you can replace each activation function by a different activation function (the choice is yours).

Why Do We Need Activation Functions?

The previous section outlines the process for transforming an input vector from the input layer and then through the hidden layers until it reaches the output layer. The purpose of activation functions in neural networks is vitally important, so it is worth repeating here: activation functions "maintain" the structure of neural networks and prevent them from being reduced to an input layer and an output layer. In other words, if we specify a nonlinear activation function between every pair of consecutive layers, then the neural network cannot be replaced with a neural network that contains fewer layers.

Without a nonlinear activation function, we simply multiply a weight matrix for a given pair of consecutive layers with the output vector that is produced from the previous pair of consecutive layers. We repeat this simple multiplication until we reach the output layer of the neural network. After reaching the output layer, we have effectively replaced multiple matrices with a single matrix that "connects" the input layer with the output layer.

How Do Activation Functions Work?

If this is the first time you have encountered the concept of an activation function, it is probably confusing, so here is an analogy that might be helpful. Suppose you are driving your car late at night and there is nobody else on the highway. You can drive at a constant speed for as long as there are no obstacles (such as stop signs and traffic lights). However, suppose you drive into the parking lot of a large grocery store. When you approach a speed bump you must slow down, cross the speed bump, and increase speed again, and repeat this process for every speed bump.

Think of the nonlinear activation functions in a neural network as the counterpart to the speed bumps: you simply cannot maintain a constant speed, which (by analogy) means that you cannot first multiply all the weight matrices together and "collapse" them into a single weight matrix. Another analogy involves a road with multiple toll booths: you must slow down, pay the toll, and then resume driving until you reach the next toll booth. These are only imperfect analogies to help you understand the need for nonlinear activation functions.

COMMON ACTIVATION FUNCTIONS

Although there are many activation functions (and you can define your own if you know how to do so), here is a list of common activation functions, followed by brief descriptions:

- sigmoid
- tanh
- ReLU
- ReLU6
- ELU
- SELU

The sigmoid activation function is based on Euler's constant e, with a range of values between 0 and 1, and its formula is shown here:

$$1/[1+e^{\wedge}(-x)]$$

The tanh activation function is also based on Euler's constant e, and its formula is shown here:

$$[e^{\wedge}x - e^{\wedge}(-x)]/[e^{\wedge}x+e^{\wedge}(-x)]$$

One way to remember the preceding formula is to note that the numerator and denominator have the same pair of terms: they are separated by a "-" sign in the numerator and a "+" sign in the denominator. The tanh function has a range of values between -1 and 1.

The ReLU (Rectified Linear Unit) activation function is straightforward: if x is negative then ReLU(x) is 0; for all other values of x, ReLU(x) equals x. ReLU6 is specific to TensorFlow, and it is a variation of ReLU(x): the additional constraint is that ReLU(x) equals 6 when x >= 6 (hence its name).

The ELU is an *exponential linear unit* and it is the exponential "envelope" of ReLU, which replaces the two linear segments of ReLU with an exponential activation function that is differentiable for all values of x (including x = 0).

SELU is an acronym for *Scaled Exponential Linear Unit*, and it is slightly more complicated than the other activation functions (and used less frequently). For a thorough explanation of these and other activation functions (along with graphs that depict their shape), navigate to the following Wikipedia Web page:

https://en.wikipedia.org/wiki/Activation_function

The preceding link provides a long list of activation functions as well as their derivatives.

Activation Functions in Python

Listing 3.5 displays content of the file `activations.py` that contains the formulas for various activation functions.

LISTING 3.5: activations.py

```
import numpy as np

# Python sigmoid example:
z = 1/(1 + np.exp(-np.dot(W, x)))

# Python tanh example:
z = np.tanh(np.dot(W,x))

# Python ReLU example:
z = np.maximum(0, np.dot(W, x))
```

Listing 3.5 contains Python code that use NumPy methods to define a sigmoid function, a `tanh` function, and a ReLU function. Note that you need to specify values for x and W to launch the code in Listing 3.5.

THE RELU AND ELU ACTIVATION FUNCTIONS

Currently ReLU is often the "preferred" activation function; previously, the preferred activation function was tanh (and before tanh the preferred activation function was sigmoid). ReLU consists of two line segments (one with slope zero and the other with slope 1) that intersect at the origin in the 2D Euclidean plane, and it provides the best training accuracy and validation accuracy.

ReLU is like a switch for linearity: it is "off" if you do not need it, and its derivative is 1 when it is active, which makes ReLU the simplest of all the current activation functions. Note that the second derivative of the function is 0 everywhere: it is a very simple function that simplifies optimization. In addition, the gradient is constant even for large values, and it never "saturates" (i.e., it does not shrink to zero on the positive horizontal axis).

Rectified linear units and generalized versions are based on the principle that linear models are easier to optimize. The ReLU activation function or one of its related alternatives (discussed later) is the recommended activation function in many cases.

The Advantages and Disadvantages of ReLU

The following list contains the advantages of the ReLU activation function:

- does not saturate in the positive region
- very efficient in terms of computation

- models with ReLU typically converge faster those with other activation functions

However, ReLU does have a disadvantage when the activation value of a ReLU neuron becomes 0: then the gradients of the neuron will also be 0 during back-propagation. You can mitigate this scenario by judiciously assigning the values for the initial weights as well as the learning rate.

ELU

The exponential linear unit (ELU) is based on ReLU: the primary difference is that ELU is differentiable at the origin (ReLU is a continuous function but *not* differentiable at the origin). However, keep in mind several points. First, ELUs trade computational efficiency for "immortality" (immunity to "dying"). Read the following paper for more details: *arxiv.org/abs/1511.07289*. Second, RELUs are still popular and preferred over ELU because the use of ELU introduces an additional new hyperparameter.

SIGMOID, SOFTMAX, AND HARDMAX SIMILARITIES

The sigmoid activation function has a range in (0,1), and it saturates and "kills" gradients. Unlike the tanh activation function, sigmoid outputs are not zero-centered. In addition, both sigmoid and softmax are discouraged for vanilla feed forward implementation. However, the sigmoid activation function is still used in LSTMs (specifically for the forget gate, input gate, and the output gate), GRUs (Gated Recurrent Units), and probabilistic models. Moreover, some autoencoders have additional requirements that preclude the use of piecewise linear activation functions.

Softmax

The *softmax* activation function maps the values in a dataset to another set of values that are between 0 and 1, and whose sum equals 1. Thus, softmax creates a probability distribution. In the case of image classification with convolutional neural networks (CNNs), the softmax activation function "maps" the values in the final hidden layer to the 10 neurons in the output layer. The index of the position that contains the largest probability is matched with the index of the number 1 in the one-hot encoding of the input image. If the index values are equal, then the image has been classified, otherwise it is considered a mismatch.

Softplus

The *softplus* activation function is a smooth (i.e., differentiable) approximation to the ReLU activation function. Recall that the origin is the only non-differentiable point of the ReLU function, which is "smoothed" by the softmax activation whose equation is here:

$$f(x) = \ln(1 + e^x)$$

Tanh

The tanh activation function has a range in (-1,1), whereas the sigmoid function has a range in (0,1). Both of these two activations saturate, but unlike the sigmoid neuron, the tanh output is zero-centered. Therefore, in practice, the tanh nonlinearity is always preferred to the sigmoid nonlinearity.

The sigmoid and tanh activation functions appear in LSTMs (sigmoid for the three gates and tanh for the internal cell state) as well as GRUs (Gated Recurrent Units) during the calculations pertaining to input gates, forget gates, and output gates.

SIGMOID, SOFTMAX, AND HARDMAX DIFFERENCES

This section briefly discusses some of the differences among these three functions. First, the sigmoid function is used for binary classification in logistic regression model, as well as the gates in LSTMs and GRUs. The sigmoid function is used as activation function while building neural networks, but keep in mind that the sum of the probabilities is not necessarily equal to 1.

Second, the softmax function generalizes the sigmoid function: it is used for multiclassification in logistic regression model. The softmax function is the activation function for the "fully connected layer" in CNNs, which is the rightmost hidden layer and the output layer. Unlike the sigmoid function, the sum of the probabilities must equal 1. You can use either the sigmoid function or softmax for binary (n=2) classification.

Third, the hardmax function assigns 0 or 1 to output values (similar to a step function). For example, suppose that we have three classes {c1, c2, c3} whose scores are [1, 7, 2], respectively. The hardmax probabilities are [0, 1, 0], whereas the softmax probabilities are [0.1, 0.7, 0.2]. Notice that the sum of the hardmax probabilities is 1, which is also true of the sum of the softmax probabilities. However, the hardmax probabilities are all-or-nothing, whereas the softmax probabilities are analogous to receiving "partial credit."

WHAT IS LOGISTIC REGRESSION?

Despite its name, *logistic regression* is a classifier and a linear model with a binary output. Logistic regression works with multiple independent variables and involves a sigmoid function for calculating probabilities. Logistic regression is essentially the result of "applying" the sigmoid activation function to linear regression to perform binary classification.

Logistic regression is useful in a variety of unrelated fields. Such fields include machine learning, various medical fields, and social sciences. Logistic regression can be used to predict the risk of developing a given disease, based on various observed characteristics of the patient. Other fields that use logistic regression include engineering, marketing, and economics.

Logistic regression can be binomial (only two outcomes for a dependent variable), multinomial (three or more outcomes for a dependent variable), or ordinal (dependent variables are ordered). For instance, suppose that a dataset consists of data that belongs either to class A or to class B. If you are given a new data point, logistic regression predicts whether that new data point belongs to class A or to class B. By contrast, linear regression predicts a numeric value, such as the next-day value of a stock.

Setting a Threshold Value

The *threshold value* is a numeric value that determines which data points belong to class A and which points belong to class B. For instance, a pass/fail threshold might be 0.70. A pass/fail threshold for passing a written driver's test in California is 0.85.

As another example, suppose that p = 0.5 is the "cutoff" probability. Then we can assign class A to the data points that occur with probability > 0.5 and assign class B to data points that occur with probability <= 0.5. Since there are only two classes, we do have a classifier.

A similar scenario involves tossing a well-balanced coin. We know that there is a 50% chance of throwing heads (let's label this outcome as "class A") and a 50% chance of throwing tails (let's label this outcome as "class B"). If we have a dataset that consists of labeled outcomes, then we have the expectation that approximately 50% of them are class A and class B.

However, we have no way to determine (in advance) what percentage of people will pass their written driver's test or the percentage of people who will pass their course. Datasets containing outcomes for these types of scenarios need to be trained, and logistic regression can be a suitable technique for doing so.

Logistic Regression: Important Assumptions

Logistic regression requires the observations to be independent of each other. In addition, logistic regression requires little or no multicollinearity among the independent variables. Logistic regression handles numeric, categorical, and continuous variables, and also assumes linearity of independent variables and log odds, which is defined here:

odds = p/(1-p) and logit = log(odds)

This analysis does not require the dependent and independent variables to be related linearly; however, another requirement is that independent variables are linearly related to the log odds.

Logistic regression is used to obtain odds ratio in the presence of more than one explanatory variable. The procedure is quite similar to multiple linear regression, with the exception that the response variable is binomial. The result is the impact of each variable on the odds ratio of the observed event of interest.

Linearly Separable Data

Linearly separable data is data that can be separated by a line (in 2D), a plane (in 3D), or a hyperplane (in higher dimensions). Linearly non-separable data is data (clusters) that cannot be separated by a line or a hyperplane. For example, the XOR function involves datapoints that cannot be separated by a line. If you create a truth table for an XOR function with two inputs, the points (0,0) and (1,1) belong to class 0, whereas the points (0,1) and (1,0) belong to class 1 (draw these points in a 2D plane to convince yourself). The solution involves transforming the data in a higher dimension so that it becomes linearly separable, which is the technique used in SVMs.

SUMMARY

This chapter started with an explanation of classification and classifiers, followed by a brief explanation of commonly used classifiers in machine learning.

Then we discussed activation functions, which will be very useful if you decide to learn about deep neural networks. You also received a high-level introduction to activation functions, including sigmoid, tanh, ReLU, ReLU6, ELU, and SELU.

Next, you learned about logistic regression, which relies on the sigmoid function, along with underlying assumptions for logistic regression. Finally, you saw a code sample involving logistic regression and the MNIST dataset.

## CHAPTER 4

CHATGPT AND GPT-4

This chapter contains information about the main features of ChatGPT and GPT-4, as well as some of their competitors.

The first portion of this chapter starts with information generated by ChatGPT regarding the nature of generative AI and conversational AI versus generative AI. According to ChatGPT, it is true that ChatGPT itself, GPT-4, and DALL-E are included in generative AI. This section also discusses ChatGPT and some of its features, as well as alternatives to ChatGPT.

The third portion of this chapter discusses some of the features of GPT-4 that power ChatGPT. You will learn about some competitors of GPT-4, such as Llama 2 (Meta) and Bard (renamed as Google Gemini).

WHAT IS GENERATIVE AI?

Generative AI refers to a subset of artificial intelligence models and techniques designed to generate new data samples that are similar in nature to a given set of input data. The goal is to produce content or data that was not part of the original training set but is coherent, contextually relevant, and in the same style or structure.

Generative AI is unique in its ability to create and innovate, as opposed to merely analyzing or classifying. The advancements in this field have led to breakthroughs in creative domains and practical applications, making it a cutting-edge area of AI research and development.

Important Features of Generative AI

The following list contains key features of generative AI, followed by a brief description for each item:

- data generation
- synthesis
- learning distributions

Data generation refers to the ability to create new data points that are not part of the training data but resemble them. This can include text, images, music, videos, or any other form of data.

Synthesis means that generative models can blend various inputs to generate outputs that incorporate features from each input, like merging the styles of two images.

Learning distributions means that generative AI models aim to learn the probability distribution of the training data so they can produce new samples from that distribution.

Popular Techniques in Generative AI

Generative Adversarial Networks (GANs): GANs consist of two networks, a generator and a discriminator, that are trained simultaneously. The generator tries to produce fake data, while the discriminator tries to distinguish between real data and fake data. Over time, the generator gets better at producing realistic data.

Variational Autoencoders (VAEs): VAEs are probabilistic models that learn to encode and decode data in a manner that the encoded representations can be used to generate new data samples.

Recurrent Neural Networks (RNNs): Used primarily for sequence generation, such as text or music.

What Makes Generative AI Unique

Creation vs. Classification: While most traditional AI models aim to classify input data into predefined categories, generative models aim to create new data.

Unsupervised Learning: Many generative models, especially GANs and VAEs, operate in an unsupervised manner, meaning they do not require labeled data for training.

Diverse Outputs: Generative models can produce a wide variety of outputs based on learned distributions, making them ideal for tasks like art generation, style transfer, and more.

Challenges: Generative AI poses unique challenges, such as mode collapse in GANs or ensuring the coherence of generated content.

There are numerous areas that involve generative AI applications, some of which are listed here:

- art and music creation
- data augmentation
- style transfer
- text generation
- image synthesis
- drug discovery

Art and Music Creation includes generating paintings, music, or other forms of art.

Data augmentation involves creating additional data for training models, especially when the original dataset is limited.

Style transfer refers to applying the style of one image to the content of another.

Text generation is a very popular application of generative AI, which involves creating coherent and contextually relevant text.

Image synthesis is another popular area of generative AI, which involves generating realistic images, faces, or even creating scenes for video games.

Drug discovery is a very important facet of generative AI that pertains to generating molecular structures for new potential drugs.

CONVERSATIONAL AI VERSUS GENERATIVE AI

Both conversational AI and generative AI are prominent subfields within the broader domain of artificial intelligence. However, these subfields have a different focus regarding their primary objective, the technologies that they use, and applications.

https://medium.com/@social_65128/differences-between-conversational-ai-and-generative-ai-e3adca2a8e9a

The primary differences between the two subfields are in the following sequence of points:

- primary objective
- applications
- technologies used
- training and interaction
- evaluation
- data requirements

Primary Objectives

The main goal of conversational AI is to facilitate human-like interactions between machines and humans. This includes chatbots, virtual assistants, and other systems that engage in dialogue with users.

The primary objective of generative AI is to create new content or data that was not in the training set but is similar in structure and style. This can range from generating images, music, and text to more complex tasks like video synthesis.

Applications

Common applications for conversational AI include customer support chatbots, voice-operated virtual assistants (like Siri or Alexa), and interactive voice response (IVR) systems.

Common applications for generative AI include creating art or music, generating realistic video game environments, synthesizing voices, and producing realistic images or even deep fakes.

Technologies Used

Conversational AI often relies on Natural Language Processing (NLP) techniques to understand and generate human language. This includes intent recognition, entity extraction, and dialogue management.

Generative AI commonly utilizes generative Adversarial Networks (GANs), Variational Autoencoders (VAEs), and other generative models to produce new content.

Training and Interaction

While training can be supervised, semi-supervised, or unsupervised, the primary interaction mode for conversational AI is through back-and-forth dialogue or conversation.

The training process for generative AI, especially with models like GANs, involves iterative processes where the model learns to generate data by trying to fool a discriminator into believing the generated data is real.

Evaluation

Conversational AI evaluation metrics often revolve around understanding and response accuracy, user satisfaction, and the fluency of generated responses.

Generative AI evaluation metrics for models like GANs can be challenging and might involve using a combination of quantitative metrics and human judgment to assess the quality of generated content.

Data Requirements

Data requirements for conversational AI typically involve dialogue data, with conversations between humans or between humans and bots.

Data requirements for generative AI involve large datasets of the kind of content it is supposed to generate, such as images, text, and music.

Although both conversational AI and generative AI deal with generating outputs, their primary objectives, applications, and methodologies can differ significantly. Conversational AI is for interactive communication with users, while generative AI focuses on producing new, original content.

IS DALL-E PART OF GENERATIVE AI?

DALL-E and similar tools that generate graphics from text are examples of generative AI. In fact, DALL-E is one of the most prominent examples of generative AI in the realm of image synthesis.

Here is a list of generative characteristics of DALL-E, followed by brief descriptions of each item:

- image generation
- learning distributions
- innovative combinations
- broad applications
- transformer architecture

Image generation is a critical feature of DALL-E, which was designed to generate images based on textual descriptions. Given a prompt like "a two-headed flamingo," DALL-E can produce a novel image that matches the description, even if it is never seen such an image in its training data.

Learning Distributions: Like other generative models, DALL-E learns the probability distribution of its training data. When it generates an image, it samples from this learned distribution to produce visuals that are plausible based on its training.

Innovative Combinations: DALL-E can generate images that represent entirely novel or abstract concepts, showcasing its ability to combine and recombine learned elements in innovative ways.

In addition to image synthesis, DALL-E has provided broad application support, in areas like art generation, style blending, and creating images with specific attributes or themes, highlighting its versatility as a generative tool.

DALL-E leverages a variant of the transformer architecture, similar to models like GPT-3, but adapted for image generation tasks.

Other tools that generate graphics, art, or any form of visual content based on input data (whether it is text, another image, or any other form of data) and can produce outputs not explicitly present in their training data are also considered generative AI. They showcase the capability of AI models to not just analyze and classify but to create and innovate.

ARE CHATGPT AND GPT-4 PART OF GENERATIVE AI?

Both ChatGPT and GPT-4 are LLMs that are considered examples of generative AI. They belong to a class of models called "transformers," which are particularly adept at handling sequences of data, such as text-related tasks.

The following list provides various reasons why these LLMs are considered generative, followed by a brief description of each item:

- text generation
- learning distributions
- broad applications
- unsupervised learning

Text Generation: These models can produce coherent, contextually relevant, and often highly sophisticated sequences of text based on given prompts. They generate responses that were not explicitly present in their training data but are constructed based on the patterns and structures they learned during training.

Learning Distributions: GPT-3, GPT-4, and similar models learn the probability distribution of their training data. When generating text, they are essentially sampling from this learned distribution to produce sequences that are likely based on their training.

Broad Applications: Beyond just text-based chat or conversation, these models can be used for a variety of generative tasks like story writing, code generation, poetry, and even creating content in specific styles or mimicking certain authors, showcasing their generative capabilities.

Unsupervised Learning: While they can be fine-tuned with specific data-sets, models like GPT-3 are primarily trained in an unsupervised manner on vast amounts of text, learning to generate content without requiring explicit labeled data for every possible response.

ChatGPT-3, GPT-4, and similar models by OpenAI are quintessential examples of generative AI in the realm of natural language processing and generation.

The next several sections briefly introduce some of the companies that have a strong presence in the field of AI.

DEEPMIND

DeepMind has made significant contributions to AI, including the creation of various AI systems. DeepMind was established in 2010 and became a subsidiary of Google 2014. Its home page is at *https://deepmind.com/*.

DeepMind created the 280 GB language model Gopher, which significantly outperforms its competitors, including GPT-3, J1-Jumbo, and MT-NLG. DeepMind also developed AlphaFold, which solved a protein folding task in 30 minutes that had eluded researchers for ten years. DeepMind made AlphaFold available for free for everyone in July 2021. DeepMind has made significant contributions in the development of world caliber AI game systems, some of which are discussed in the next section.

DeepMind and Games

DeepMind is the force behind the AI systems AlphaStar and AlphaGo that defeated the best human players in Go (which is considerably more difficult than chess). These games provide "perfect information," whereas games with "imperfect information" (such as poker) have posed challenges for ML models.

AlphaGo Zero (the successor of AlphaGo) mastered the game through self-play in less time and with less computing power. AlphaGo Zero exhibited extraordinary performance by defeating AlphaGo 100–0. Another powerful system is AlphaZero, which used a self-play learning technique to play Go, chess, and shogi, and achieved SOTA (State of the Art) performance results.

By way of comparison, ML models that use tree search are well-suited for games with perfect information. By contrast, games with imperfect information (such as poker) involve hidden information that can be leveraged to devise counter strategies to counteract the strategies of opponents. AlphaStar is capable of playing against the best players of StarCraft II and became the first AI to achieve SOTA results in a game that requires "strategic capability in an imperfect information world."

Player of Games (PoG)

The DeepMind team at Google devised the general-purpose PoG (Player of Games) algorithm that is based on the following techniques:

- CFR (counterfactual regret minimization)
- CVPN (counterfactual value-and-policy network)
- GT-CFT (growing tree CFR)
- CVPN

The counterfactual value-and-policy network (CVPN) is a neural network that calculates the counterfactuals for each state belief in the game. This is critical for evaluating the different variants of the game at any given time.

Growing tree CFR (GT-CFR) is a variation of CFR that is optimized for game-trees trees that grow over time. GT-CFR is based on two fundamental phases, which is discussed in more detail online:

https://medium.com/syncedreview/deepminds-pog-excels-in-perfect-and-imperfect-information-games-advancing-research-on-general-9dbad5c04221

OPENAI

OpenAI is an AI research company that has made significant contributions to AI, including DALL-E and ChatGPT, and its home page is here: *https://openai.com/api/*.

OpenAI was founded in San Francisco by Elon Musk and Sam Altman (as well as others), and one of its stated goals is to develop AI that benefits humanity. Given Microsoft's massive investments in and deep alliance with the organization, OpenAI might be viewed as part of Microsoft. OpenAI is the creator of the GPT-x series of LLMs (Large Language Models), as well as ChatGPT, which was made available on November 30, 2022.

OpenAI made GPT-3 commercially available via API for use across applications, charging on a per-word basis. GPT-3 was announced in July of 2020 and was available through a beta program. Then, in November 2021, OpenAI made GPT-3 open to everyone. More details are accessible online:

https://openai.com/blog/api-no-waitlist/.

In addition, OpenAI developed DALL-E, which generates images from text. OpenAI initially did not permit users to upload images that contained realistic faces. Later, in the fourth quarter of 2022, OpenAI changed its policy to allow users to upload faces into its online system. (Check the OpenAI Web page for more details.) Incidentally, diffusion models have superseded the benchmarks of DALL-E.

OpenAI has also released a public beta of Embeddings, which is a data format that is suitable for various types of tasks with ML, as described here:

https://beta.openai.com/docs/guides/embeddings

OpenAI is the creator of Codex, which provides a set of models that were trained using NLP. The initial release of Codex was in private beta, and more information is accessible at *https://beta.openai.com/docs/engines/instruct-series-beta*.

OpenAI provides four models that are collectively called their Instruct models, which support the ability of GPT-3 to generate natural language. These models will be deprecated in early January, 2024 and replaced with updated versions of GPT-3, ChatGPT, and GPT-4.

If you want to learn more about the features and services that OpenAI offers, navigate to the following Web page: *https://platform.openai.com/overview*.

COHERE

Cohere is a start-up and a competitor of OpenAI, and its home page is here: *https://cohere.ai/*.

Cohere develops cutting-edge NLP technology that is commercially available for multiple industries. Cohere is focused on models that perform textual analysis instead of models for text generation (such as GPT-based models). The founding team of Cohere is impressive: CEO Aidan Gomez is one of the co-inventors of the transformer architecture, and CTO Nick Frosst is a protege of Geoff Hinton.

HUGGING FACE

Hugging Face is a popular community-based repository for open-source NLP technology, and its home page is at *https://github.com/huggingface*.

Unlike OpenAI or Cohere, Hugging Face does not build its own NLP models. Instead, Hugging Face is a platform that manages a plethora of open-source NLP models that customers can fine-tune and then deploy those fine-tuned models. Indeed, Hugging Face has become the eminent location for people to collaborate on NLP models, and sometimes described as "GitHub for machine learning and NLP."

Hugging Face Libraries

Hugging Face provides three important libraries: datasets, tokenizers, and transformers. The Accelerate library supports PyTorch models. The datasets library provides an assortment of libraries for NLP. The tokenizers library enables you to convert text data to numeric values.

Perhaps the most impressive library is the transformers library that provides an enormous set of pre-trained BERT-based models to perform a wide variety of NLP tasks. The Github repository is here: *https://github.com/huggingface/transformers*.

Hugging Face Model Hub

Hugging Face offers a model hub that provides a plethora of models that are accessible online. Moreover, the Web site supports online testing of its models, which includes the following tasks:

- masked word completion with BERT
- Name Entity Recognition with Electra
- Natural Language Inference with RoBERTa
- question answering with DistilBERT
- summarization with BART
- text generation with GPT-2
- translation with T5

Navigate to the following Web page to see the text generation capabilities of "writing with a transformer:" *https://transformer.huggingface.co*.

In a subsequent chapter, you will see Python code samples that show how to list all the available Hugging Face datasets and how to load a specific dataset.

AI21

AI21 is a company that provides proprietary large language models via API to support the applications of its customers. The current SOTA model of AI21 is called Jurassic-1 (roughly the same size as GPT-3), and AI21 also creates its own applications on top of Jurassic-1 and other models. The current application suite of AI21 involves tools that can augment reading and writing.

Primer is an older competitor in this space, founded two years before the invention of the transformer. The company primarily serves clients in government and defense.

INFLECTIONAI

A more recent company in the AI field is InflectionAI whose highly impressive founding team includes:

- Reid Hoffman (LinkedIn)
- DeepMind cofounder Mustafa Suleyman
- DeepMind researcher Karen Simonyan

InflectionAI is committed to a challenging task: enabling humans to interact with computers in much the same way that humans communicate with each other.

ANTHROPIC

Anthropic was created in 2021 by former employees of OpenAI and its home page is here: *https://www.anthropic.com/*.

Anthropic has significant financial support from an assortment of companies, including Google and Salesforce. The company released Claude 2 as a competitor to ChatGPT.

Claude 2 has the ability to summarize as much as 75,000 words of text-based content, whereas ChatGPT currently has a limit of 3,000 words. Moreover, Claude 2 achieved a score of 76.5% on portions of the bar exam and 71% in a Python coding test. Claude 2 also has a higher rate than ChatGPT in terms of providing "clean" responses to queries from users.

This concludes the portion of the chapter regarding the AI companies that are making important contributions in AI. The next section provides a high-level introduction to LLMs.

WHAT IS PROMPT ENGINEERING?

You have already learned about text generators such as GPT-3 and DALL-E 2 from OpenAI and Jurassic from AI21, as well as Midjourney and Stable Diffusion, which can perform text-to-image generation. *Prompt engineering* refers to devising text-based prompts that enable AI-based systems to improve the output that is generated, which means that the output more closely matches whatever users want to produce from AI-systems. By way of analogy, think of prompts as similar to the role of coaches: they offer advice and suggestions to help people perform better in their given tasks.

Since prompts are based on words, the challenge involves learning how different words can affect the generated output. Moreover, it is difficult to predict how systems respond to a given prompt. For instance, if you want to generate a landscape, the difference between a dark landscape and a bright landscape is intuitive. However, if you want a beautiful landscape, how would an AI system generate a corresponding image? As you can surmise, concrete words are easier than abstract or subjective words for AI systems that generate images from text. Just to add more to the previous example, how would you visualize the following?

- a beautiful landscape
- a beautiful song
- a beautiful movie

Although prompt engineering started with text-to-image generation, there are other types of prompt engineering, such as audio-based prompts that interpret emphasized text and emotions that are detected in speech, and sketch-based prompts that generate images from drawings. The most recent focus of attention involves text-based prompts for generating videos, which presents exciting opportunities for artists and designers. An example of image-to-image processing is accessible at the following Web page:

https://huggingface.co/spaces/fffiloni/stable-diffusion-color-sketch

Prompts and Completions

A *prompt* is a text string that users provide to LLMs, and a *completion* is the text that users receive from LLMs. Prompts assist LLMs in completing a request (task), and they can vary in length. Although prompts can be any text string, including a random string, the quality and structure of prompts affects the quality of completions.

Think of prompts as a mechanism for giving "guidance" to LLMs, or even as a way to "coach" LLMs into providing desired answers. The number of tokens in a prompt plus the number of tokens in the completion can be at most 2,048 tokens.

Types of Prompts

The following list contains well-known types of prompts for LLMs:

• zero-shot prompts
• one-shot prompts
• few-shot prompts
• instruction prompts

A *zero-shot prompt* contains a description of a task, whereas a *one-shot prompt* consists of a single example for completing a task. *Few-shot prompts* consist of multiple examples (typically between 10 and 100). In all cases, a clear description of the task or tasks is recommended: more tasks provide GPT-3 with more information, which in turn can lead to more accurate completions.

T0 (for "zero shot") is an interesting LLM: although T0 is 16 times smaller (11 GB) than GPT-3 (175 GB), T0 has outperformed GPT-3 on language-related tasks. T0 can perform well on unseen NLP tasks (i.e., tasks that are new to T0) because it was trained on a dataset containing multiple tasks.

The following URL provides the Github repository for T0, which contains information for training and evaluating the model:

https://github.com/bigscience-workshop/t-zero

T0++ is based on T0, and it was trained with extra tasks beyond the set of tasks on which T0 was trained.

As a side note, the first three prompts in the preceding list are also called "zero-shot learning," "one-shot learning," and "few-shot learning," respectively.

Instruction Prompts

Instruction prompts are used for fine tuning LLMs, and they specify a format (determined by you) for the manner in which the LLM is expected to conform in its responses. You can prepare your own instruction prompts or you can access prompt template libraries that contain different templates for different tasks, along with different data sets. Various prompt instruction templates are publicly available, such as the following links that provide prompt templates for Llama:

https://github.com/devbrones/llama-prompts
https://pub.towardsai.net/llama-gpt4all-simplified-local-chatgpt-ab7d28d34923

Reverse Prompts

Another technique uses a reverse order: input prompts are answers and the response are the questions associated with the answers (similar to a popular game show). For example, given a French sentence, you might ask the model, "What English text might have resulted in this French translation?"

System Prompts versus Agent Prompts

The distinction between a system prompt and an agent prompt often comes up in the context of conversational AI systems and chatbot design.

A *system prompt* is typically an initial message or cue given by the system to guide the user on what they can do or to set expectations about the interaction. It often serves as an introduction or a way to guide users on how to proceed. Here are some examples of system prompts:

- "Welcome to ChatBotX! You can ask me questions about weather, news, or sports. How can I assist you today?"
- "Hello! For account details, press 1. For technical support, press 2."
- "Greetings! Type 'order' to track your package or 'help' for assistance."

By contrast, an agent prompt is a message generated by the AI model or agent in response to a user's input during the course of an interaction. It is a part of the back-and-forth exchange within the conversation. The agent prompt guides the user to provide more information, clarifies ambiguity, or nudges the user toward a specific action. Here are some examples of agent prompts:

User: "I'm looking for shoes."
Agent Prompt: "Great! Are you looking for men's or women's shoes?"
User: "I can't log in."
Agent Prompt: "I'm sorry to hear that. Can you specify if you're having trouble with your password or username?"

User: "Tell me a joke."
Agent Prompt: "Why did the chicken join a band? Because it had the drumsticks!"

The fundamental difference between the two is their purpose and placement in the interaction. A system prompt is often at the beginning of an interaction, setting the stage for the conversation. An agent prompt occurs during the conversation, steering the direction of the dialogue based on user input.

Both types of prompts are crucial for creating a fluid and intuitive conversational experience for users. They guide the user and help ensure that the system understands and addresses the user's needs effectively.

Prompt Templates

Prompt templates are predefined formats or structures used to instruct a model or system to perform a specific task. They serve as a foundation for generating prompts, where certain parts of the template can be filled in or customized to produce a variety of specific prompts. By way of analogy, prompt templates are the counterpart to macros that you can define in some text editors.

Prompt templates are especially useful when working with language models, as they provide a consistent way to query the model across multiple tasks or data points. In particular, prompt templates can make it easier to:

- ensure consistency when querying a model multiple times
- facilitate batch processing or automation
- reduce errors and variations in how questions are posed to the model

As an example, suppose you are working with an LLM and you want to translate English sentences into French. An associated prompt template could be the following:
"Translate the following English sentence into French: {sentence}"
Note that {sentence} is a placeholder that you can replace with any English sentence.

You can use the preceding prompt template to generate specific prompts:

- "Translate the following English sentence into French: 'Hello, how are you?'"
- "Translate the following English sentence into French: 'I love ice cream.'"

As you can see, prompt templates enable you to easily generate a variety of prompts for different sentences without having to rewrite the entire instruction each time. In fact, this concept can be extended to more complex tasks and can incorporate multiple placeholders or more intricate structures, depending on the application.

Prompts for Different LLMs

GPT-3, ChatGPT, and GPT-4 are LLMs that are all based on the Transformer architecture and are fundamentally similar in their underlying mechanics. ChatGPT is essentially a version of the GPT model fine-tuned specifically for conversational interactions. GPT-4 is an evolution or improvement over GPT-3 in terms of scale and capabilities.

The differences in prompts for these models mainly arise from the specific use case and context, rather than inherent differences between the models. Here are some prompting differences that are based on use cases.

GPT-3 can be used for a wide range of tasks beyond just conversation, from content generation to code writing. Here are some examples of prompts for GPT-3:

- "Translate the following English text to French: 'Hello, how are you?'"
- "Write a Python function that calculates the factorial of a number."

ChatGPT is specifically fine-tuned for conversational interactions. Here are some examples of prompts for ChatGPT:

User: "Can you help me with my homework?"
ChatGPT: "Of course! What subject or topic do you need help with?"
User: "Tell me a joke."
ChatGPT: "Why did the chicken cross the playground? To get to the other slide!"

GPT-4 provides a larger scale and refinements, so the prompts would be similar in nature to GPT-3 but might yield more accurate or nuanced outputs. Here are some examples of prompts of prompts for GPT-4:

- "Provide a detailed analysis of quantum mechanics in relation to general relativity."
- "Generate a short story based on a post-apocalyptic world with a theme of hope."

These three models accept natural language prompts and produce natural language outputs. The fundamental way you interact with them remains consistent.

The main difference comes from the context in which the model is being used and any fine-tuning that has been applied. ChatGPT, for instance, is designed to be more conversational, so while you can use GPT-3 for chats, ChatGPT might produce more contextually relevant conversational outputs.

When directly interacting with these models, especially through an API, you might also have control over parameters like "temperature" (controlling randomness) and "max tokens" (controlling response length). Adjusting these can shape the responses, regardless of which GPT variant you are using.

While the underlying models have differences in scale and specific training/fine-tuning, the way you prompt them remains largely consistent: clear, specific natural language prompts yield the best results.

Poorly Worded Prompts

When crafting prompts, it is crucial to be as clear and specific as possible to guide the response in the desired direction. Ambiguous or vague prompts can lead to a wide range of responses, many of which might not be useful or relevant to the user's actual intent.

Moreover, poorly worded prompts are often vague, ambiguous, or too broad, and they can lead to confusion, misunderstanding, or non-specific responses from AI models. Here's a list of examples:

- *"Tell me about that thing."*
  Problem: Too vague. What "thing" is being referred to?

- *"Why did it happen?"*
  Problem: No context. What event or situation is being discussed?

- *"Explain stuff."*
  Problem: Too broad. What specific "stuff" should be explained?

- *"Do the needful."*
  Problem: Ambiguous. What specific action is required?

- *"I want information."*
  Problem: Not specific. What type of information is desired?

- *"Can you get me the thing from the place?"*
  Problem: Both "thing" and "place" are unclear.

- *"Can you tell me about what's-his-name's book?"*
  Problem: Ambiguous reference. Who is "his?"

- *"How do you do the process?"*
  Problem: Which "process" is being referred to?

- *"Describe the importance of the topic."*
  Problem: "Topic" is not specified.

- *"Why is it bad or good?"*
  Problem: No context. What is "it?"

- *"Help with the issue."*
  Problem: Vague. What specific issue is being faced?

- *"Things to consider for the task."*
  Problem: Ambiguity. What "task" is being discussed?

- *"How does this work?"*
  Problem: Lack of specificity. What is "this?"

WHAT IS CHATGPT?

The "chatbot wars" are intensifying, and the long-term value of the primary competitors is still to be determined. One competitor is ChatGPT-3.5 (ChatGPT), which is an AI-based chatbot from OpenAI. ChatGPT responds to queries from users by providing conversational responses, and it is accessible here: *https://chat.openai.com/chat.*

The growth rate in terms of registered users for ChatGPT has been extraordinary. The closest competitor is iPhone, which reached one million users in 2.5 months, whereas ChatGPT crossed one million users in *six days*. ChatGPT peaked around 1.8 billion users and then decreased to roughly 1.5 billion users, which you can see in the chart in this link:

https://decrypt.co/147595/traffic-dip-hits-openais-chatgpt-first-times-hardest

Note that although Threads from Meta out-performed ChatGPT in terms of membership, Threads has seen a significant drop in daily users in the neighborhood of 50%. A comparison of the time frame to reach one million members for six well-known companies/products and ChatGPT is here: *https://www.syntheticmind.io/p/01.*

The preceding Web page also contains information about Will Hobick, who used ChatGPT to write a Chrome extension for email-related tasks, despite not having any JavaScript or Chrome extension programming experience. Will Hobick provides more detailed information about his Chrome extension here:

https://www.linkedin.com/posts/will-hobick_gpt3-chatgpt-ai-activity-7008081003080470528-8QCh

ChatGPT

The paid version of ChatGPT may currently be the best chatbot in the world. Indeed, ChatGPT can perform a multitude of tasks, some of which are listed below:

- write poetry
- write essays
- write code

• role play
• reject inappropriate requests

Moreover, the quality of its responses to natural language queries surpasses the capabilities of its predecessor GPT-3. Another interesting capability includes the ability to acknowledge its mistakes. ChatGPT also provides "prompt replies," which are examples of what you can ask ChatGPT. One interesting use for ChatGPT involves generating a text message for ending a relationship:

https://www.reddit.com/r/ChatGPT/comments/zgpk6c/breaking_up_with_my_girlfriend/

ChatGPT generates Christmas lyrics that are accessible here:

https://www.cnet.com/culture/entertainment/heres-what-it-sounds-like-when-ai-writes-christmas-lyrics

One aspect of ChatGPT that probably will not be endearing to parents with young children is the fact that ChatGPT has told children that Santa Claus does not exist:

https://futurism.com/the-byte/openai-chatbot-santa

https://www.forbes.com/sites/lanceeliot/2022/12/21/pointedly-asking-generative-ai-chatgpt-about-whether-santa-claus-is-real-proves-to-be-eye-opening-for-ai-ethics-and-ai-law

ChatGPT: Google "Code Red"

In December 2022, the CEO of Google issued a "code red" regarding the potential threat of ChatGPT as a competitor to Google's search engine, which is briefly discussed here:

https://www.yahoo.com/news/googles-management-reportedly-issued-code-190131705.html

According to the preceding article, Google is investing resources to develop AI-based products, presumably to offer functionality that can successfully compete with ChatGPT. Some of those AI-based products might also generate graphics that are comparable to graphics effects by DALL-E. Indeed, the race to dominate AI continues unabated and will undoubtedly continue for the foreseeable future.

ChatGPT versus Google Search

Given the frequent speculation that ChatGPT is destined to supplant Google Search, let's briefly compare the manner in which Google and ChatGPT respond to a given query. First, Google is a search engine that uses the Page Rank algorithm (developed by Larry Page) closely guarded secret. Google uses this algorithm to rank websites and to generate search results for a given query. However, the search results include paid ads, which can "clutter" the list of links.

By contrast, ChatGPT is not a search engine: it provides a direct response to a given query. In colloquial terms, ChatGPT will simply "cut to the chase" and eliminate any mention of superfluous links. ChatGPT can also produce incorrect results, the consequences of which can range between benign and significant.

Consequently, Google search and ChatGPT both have strengths as well as weaknesses, and they excel with different types of queries: the former for queries that have multi-faceted answers (e.g., questions about legal issues) and the latter for straight-to-the point queries (e.g., coding questions). Obviously, both of them excel with many other types of queries.

According to Margaret Mitchell, ChatGPT will not replace Google Search. She provides some interesting details regarding Google Search and PageRank that you can read at *https://twitter.com/mmitchell_ai/status/1605013368560943105.*

ChatGPT Custom Instructions

ChatGPT has added support for custom instructions, which enable you to specify some of your preferences that ChatGPT will use when responding to your queries.

ChatGPT Plus users can switch on custom instructions by navigating to the ChatGPT Web site and then perform the following sequence of steps:

Settings > Beta features > Opt into Custom instructions

As a simple example, you can specify that you prefer to see code in a language other than Python. A set of common initial requirements for routine tasks can also be specified via custom instructions in ChatGPT. A detailed sequence of steps for setting up custom instructions is accessible online at the following URL:

https://artificialcorner.com/custom-instructions-a-new-feature-you-must-enable-to-improve-chatgpt-responses-15820678bc02

Another interesting example of custom instructions is from Jeremy Howard, who prepared an extensive and detailed set of custom instructions that is accessible here:

https://twitter.com/jeremyphoward/status/1689464587077509120

As this book goes to print, custom instructions are available only for users who have registered for ChatGPT Plus.

ChatGPT on Mobile Devices and Browsers

ChatGPT first became available for iOS devices and then for Android devices during 2023. You can download ChatGPT onto an iOS device from the following Web page:

https://www.macobserver.com/tips/how-to/how-to-install-and-use-the-official-chatgpt-app-on-iphone/

Alternatively, if you have an Android device, you can download ChatGPT from the following Web page:

https://play.google.com/store/apps/details?id=com.openai.chatgpt

If you want to install ChatGPT for the Bing browser from Microsoft, navigate to this Web page:

https://chrome.google.com/webstore/detail/chatgpt-for-bing/ pkkmgcildaegadhngpjkklnbfbmhpdng

ChatGPT and Prompts

Although ChatGPT is adept at generating responses to queries, sometimes you might not be fully satisfied with the result. One option is to type the word "rewrite" in order to get another version from ChatGPT.

Although this is one of the simplest prompts available, it is limited in terms of effectiveness. If you want a list of more meaningful prompts, the following member-only article contains 31 prompts that have the potential to be better than using the word "rewrite" (and not just with ChatGPT):

https://medium.com/the-generator/31-ai-prompts-better-than-rewrite- b3268dfe1fa9

GPTBot

GPTBot is a crawler for Web sites. Fortunately, you can disallow GPTBot from accessing a Web site by adding the GPTBot to the `robots.txt` file for a Web site:

```
User-agent: GPTBot
Disallow: /
```

You can also customize GPTBot access for only a portion of a Web site by adding the GPTBot token to the `robots.txt`-like file for a Web site:

```
User-agent: GPTBot
Allow: /youcangohere-1/
Disallow: /dontgohere-2/
```

As an aside, Stable Diffusion and LAION both scrape the Internet via Common Crawl. However, you can prevent your Web site from being scraped by specifying the following snippet in the `robots.txt` file:

```
User-agent: CCBot
Disallow: /
```

More information about GPTBot is accessible at the following Web sites: *https://platform.openai.com/docs/gptbot*   *https://platform.openai.com/docs/gptbot*

https://www.yahoo.com/finance/news/openai-prepares-unleash-crawler-devour-020628225.html

ChatGPT Playground

ChatGPT has its own playground, which you will see is substantively different from the GPT-3 playground, that is accessible here: *https://chat.openai.com/chat*.

For your convenience, the link for the GPT-3 playground is reproduced here:

https://beta.openai.com/playground.

OpenAI has periodically added new functionality to ChatGPT that includes the following:

• users can view (and continue) previous conversations
• a reduction in the number of questions that ChatGPT will not answer
• users remain logged in for longer than two weeks

Another nice enhancement includes support for keyboard shortcuts: when working with code, you can use the sequence ⌘ (Ctrl) + Shift + (for Mac) to copy the last code block and the sequence ⌘ (Ctrl) + / to see the complete list of shortcuts.

Many articles are available regarding ChatGPT and how to write prompts to extract the details that you want from ChatGPT. One of those articles is here:

https://www.tomsguide.com/features/7-best-chatgpt-tips-to-get-the-most-out-of-the-chatbot

PLUGINS, ADVANCED DATA ANALYSIS, AND CODE WHISPERER

In addition to answering a plethora of queries from users, ChatGPT extends its functionality by providing support for the following:

• third-party ChatGPT plug-ins
• Advanced Data Analysis
• Code Whisperer

The topics in the preceding list are briefly discussed in the following subsections, along with a short section that discusses Advanced Data Analysis versus Claude 2.

Plugins

There are several hundred ChatGPT plugins available, and lists of some popular plugins are accessible online at the following Web sites:

https://levelup.gitconnected.com/5-chatgpt-plugins-that-will-put-you-ahead-of-99-of-data-scientists-4544a3b752f9

https://www.zdnet.com/article/the-10-best-chatgpt-plugins-of-2023/

Lists of the "best" ChatGPT plugins change frequently, so perform an online search to find out about newer ChatGPT plugins. The following link also contains details about highly rated plugins:

https://www.tomsguide.com/features/i-tried-a-ton-of-chatgpt-plugins-and-these-3-are-the-best

Another set of recommended plugins (depending on your needs, of course) is shown below:

- AskYourPDF
- ChatWithVideo
- Noteable
- Upskillr
- Wolfram

If you are concerned about the possibility of ChatGPT scraping the content of your Web site, the browser plugin from OpenAI supports a user-agent token called ChatGPT-User that abides by the content specified in the `robots.txt` file that many Web sites provide for restricting access to content.

If you want to develop a plugin for ChatGPT, navigate to this Web site for more information: *https://platform.openai.com/docs/plugins/introduction*.

Along with details for developing a ChatGPT plugin, the preceding OpenAI Web site provides useful information about plugins, as shown here:

- Authentication
- Examples
- Plugin review
- Plugin policies

OpenAI does not control any plugins that you add to ChatGPT: they connect ChatGPT to external applications. Moreover, ChatGPT determines which plugin to use during your session, based on the specific plugins that you have enabled in your ChatGPT account.

Advanced Data Analysis

ChatGPT Advanced Data Analysis enables ChatGPT to generate charts and graphs, create and train ML models, including deep learning models. ChatGPT Advanced Data Analysis provides an extensive set of features and it is available to ChatGPT users who are paying the $20/month subscription. However, this feature will probably be made available to all users very soon.

https://towardsdatascience.com/chatgpt-code-interpreter-how-it-saved-me-hours-of-work-3c65a8dfa935

The models from OpenAI can access a Python interpreter that is confined to a sandboxed and fire-walled execution environment. There is also some temporary disk space that is accessible to the interpreter plugin during the evaluation of Python code. Although the temporary disk space is available for a limited time, multiple queries during in the same session can produce a cumulative effect with regard to the code and execution environment.

In addition, ChatGPT can generate a download link (upon request) for data. Advanced Data Analysis can now analyze multiple files at once, which includes CSV files and Excel spreadsheets.

Advanced Data Analysis can perform an interesting variety of tasks, some of which are listed below:

- solve mathematical tasks
- perform data analysis and visualization
- convert files between formats
- work with Excel spreadsheets
- read textual content in a PDF

The following article discusses various ways that you can use Advanced Data Analysis:

https://mlearning.substack.com/p/the-best-88-ways-to-use-chatgpt-code-interpreter

Advanced Data Analysis Versus Claude 2

Claude 2 from Anthropic is another competitor to ChatGPT. In addition to responding to prompts from users, Claude 2 can generate code and "ingest" entire books. Claude 2 is also subject to hallucinations, which is true of other LLM-based chatbots. More detailed information regarding Claude 2 is accessible here:

https://medium.com/mlearning-ai/claude-2-vs-code-interpreter-gpt-4-5-d2e5c9ee00c3

Incidentally, the currently available version of ChatGPT was trained on September, 2021, which means that ChatGPT cannot answer questions regarding Claude 2 or Google Gemini, both of which were released after this date.

Code Whisperer

ChatGPT Code Whisperer enables you to simplify some tasks, some of which are listed below (compare this list with the corresponding list for Google Gemini):

- create videos from images
- extract text from an image
- extract colors from an image

After ChatGPT has generated a video, it will also give you a link from which the generated video is downloadable. More detailed information regarding the features in the preceding list is accessible at the following Web page:

https://artificialcorner.com/chatgpt-code-interpreter-is-not-just-for-coders-here-are-6-ways-it-can-benefit-everyone-b3cc94a36fce

DETECTING GENERATED TEXT

ChatGPT has a high quality of generated text, which in turn also complicates the task of detecting plagiarism. When you read a passage of text, there are several clues that suggest generated text, such as:

- awkward or unusual sentence structure
- repeated text in multiple locations
- excessive use of emotions (or absence thereof)

However, there are tools that can assist in detecting generated code. One free online tool is GPT2 Detector (from OpenAI):

https://huggingface.co/openai-detector

As a simple (albeit contrived) example, type the following sentence in GPT2 Detector: "This is an original sentence written by me and nobody else."

The GPT2 Detector analyzed this sentence and reported that this sentence is real with a 19.35% probability. Now let's modify the preceding sentence by adding some extra text, as shown here: "This is an original sentence written by me and nobody else, regardless of what an online plagiarism tool will report about this sentence."

The GPT2 Detector analyzed this sentence and reported that this sentence is real with a 95.85% probability. According to the GPT2 Detector Web site, the reliability of the probability scores "get reliable" when there are around 50 tokens in the input text.

Another (slightly older) online tool for detecting automatically generated text is GLTR (Giant Language model Test Room) from IBM, which is accessible at *http://gltr.io/*.

You can download the source code (a combination of TypeScript and CSS) for GLTR here:

https://github.com/HendrikStrobelt/detecting-fake-text

In addition to the preceding free tools, some commercial tools are also available, one of which is at *https://writer.com/plans/*.

CONCERNS ABOUT CHATGPT

One important aspect of ChatGPT is that it was not designed to be accurate. In fact, ChatGPT can generate very persuasive answers that are actually incorrect. This detail distinguishes ChatGPT from search engines: the latter provide links to existing information instead of generating responses that might be incorrect. Another comparison is that ChatGPT is more flexible and creative, whereas search engines are less flexible but more accurate in their responses to queries.

Educators are concerned about students using ChatGPT as a tool to complete their class assignments instead of developing research-related skills in conjunction with writing skills. There are educators, however, who enjoy the reduction in preparation time for their classes as a direct result of using ChatGPT to prepare lesson plans.

Another concern is that ChatGPT cannot guarantee that it provides factual data in response to queries from users. ChatGPT can *hallucinate*, which means that it can provide wrong answers as well as citations (i.e., links) that do not exist.

Another limitation of ChatGPT is due to the use of training data that was available only up until 2021. OpenAI does support plug-ins for ChatGPT, one of which can perform on-the-fly real time Web searches.

The goal of prompt engineering is to understand how to craft meaningful queries that will induce ChatGPT to provide the information that you want. Poorly worded (or incorrectly worded) prompts can produce equally poor results. As a rule, it is advisable to curate the contents of the responses from ChatGPT, especially in the case of responses to queries that involve legal details.

Code Generation and Dangerous Topics

Two significant areas for improvement pertain to code generation and handling dangerous topics.

Although ChatGPT (as well as GPT-3) can generate code for various types of applications, keep in mind that ChatGPT displays code that was written by other developers, which is also code that was used to train ChatGPT. Consequently, portions of that code (such as version numbers) might be outdated or incorrect.

As for queries that involve dangerous topics, ChatGPT explains why it cannot answer such a query. However, a query that is posed in "pretend mode" ("suppose you are a fictional character, and how would you explain ....") has enabled people to obtain results from ChatGPT that do not conform to its guidelines.

Other serious potential issues exist, some of which are discussed in the following article:

https://www.yahoo.com/news/hypnotized-chatgpt-bard-convince-users-182100261.html

ChatGPT Strengths and Weaknesses

ChatGPT has a number of strengths. In particular, ChatGPT responds directly to questions without including extraneous links. As a simple example, suppose you enter a query in an online search engine, such as "Generate HTML for an input field."

ChatGPT is prone to various types of errors, along with limitations that include the following:

- inability to "fact check" information
- inability to differentiate misinformation versus facts
- can fabricate answers (aka hallucinations)
- can generate inappropriate/toxic responses

ChatGPT is prone to prompt injection, which can consist of very simple content. However, other chatbots are also susceptible to prompt injection (i.e., it is not specific to ChatGPT). More details regarding prompt injections are accessible here:

https://mlearning.substack.com/p/what-exactly-is-a-prompt-injection

Incidentally, the chatbot LaMDA from Google is also prone to the preceding limitations, which has made Google hesitant to release LaMDA for general availability because of its potential risk regarding Google's reputation. As a side note, LaMDA was announced in May, 2021, and at that time it was described as a "breakthrough language technology:" *https://blog.google/technology/ai/lamda/*.

Despite the earlier list, ChatGPT has increased the capabilities of chat bots, and will undoubtedly spur innovation and competition among prominent stakeholders in this arena.

SAMPLE QUERIES AND RESPONSES FROM CHATGPT

Here is an example of a query submitted to ChatGPT, followed by the detailed response from ChatGPT:

Many people think that AI is dangerous. What do you think?

"There is a common misconception that AI is inherently dangerous. While it is true that AI has the potential to be used for harmful purposes, it is also capable of doing a lot of good. Just like any other technology, it all depends on how it is used. In the right hands, AI can be used to solve some of the world's most pressing problems, such as curing diseases and improving agriculture. In the wrong hands, it could be used to cause harm. It's important for us to use AI responsibly and ethically, and to ensure that it is regulated and controlled in a way that minimizes the potential for harm."

Here are other examples of queries submitted to ChatGPT-3, followed by the detailed responses:

1. What are some ways in which you can improve the accuracy of your responses to queries?

"There are several ways to improve the accuracy of my responses to queries. One way is to use more data to train my algorithms on. The more data I have, the more information I have to work with, and the more accurate my responses can be. Another way to improve my accuracy is to use more advanced algorithms and techniques, such as machine learning and natural language processing. These methods allow me to better understand the nuances of language and to provide more accurate responses to queries. Additionally, regular testing and evaluation can help identify areas where my accuracy can be improved, and allow me to focus on those areas to refine my responses."

2. Can you give an example of an odd perfect number?

"As far as we know, there are no odd perfect numbers. While it is believed that odd perfect numbers exist, none have been found yet, and it is not known if there are any. In fact, it is currently unknown if there are any odd perfect numbers at all. If an odd perfect number were to be discovered, it would be a major breakthrough in mathematics."

3. Can you provide a proof of Goldbach's conjecture?

"I'm sorry, but I am not able to provide a proof of Goldbach's conjecture. Goldbach's conjecture is a famous unsolved problem in mathematics that states that every even integer greater than 2 can be expressed as the sum of two prime numbers. Despite much effort by mathematicians over the years, a proof of the conjecture has not yet been found. It is considered to be one of the most challenging unsolved problems in mathematics. Because I am a large language model trained by OpenAI, I do not have the ability to prove mathematical conjectures. My abilities are limited to providing answers based on the information that I have been trained on."

4. Is there life after death, and how does it compare with life on Earth?

"There is no scientific evidence to support the idea of life after death. This is a topic that has been debated for centuries, and different cultures and belief systems have their own ideas about what happens after we die. Some people believe in an afterlife, while others do not. Because there is no scientific evidence to support the existence of an afterlife, it is not possible to say how it would compare to life on Earth. It is ultimately a matter of personal belief."

5. Please provide a four-paragraph analysis of the war between Ukraine and Russia, and also provide your prediction regarding the outcome

"The war between Ukraine and Russia is a complex conflict that has its roots in the 2014 Russian annexation of Crimea. Since then, the conflict has escalated, with Russian-backed separatists in eastern Ukraine fighting against the Ukrainian government. The fighting has resulted in thousands of casualties and has displaced many people.

The main issue at the heart of the conflict is the question of Ukraine's sovereignty. Russia has long considered Ukraine to be within its sphere of influence, and the annexation of Crimea was seen by many as a violation of Ukraine's sovereignty. Ukraine, on the other hand, is determined to maintain its independence and has been supported in this by many Western countries.

It is difficult to predict the outcome of the war. While the Ukrainian military has been able to make gains against the separatists in recent years, Russia continues to provide support to the rebels and the conflict remains unresolved. In the long term, a diplomatic solution will likely be necessary in order to bring an end to the fighting. However, it is uncertain if and when such a solution will be reached.

In the meantime, the war continues to take a heavy toll on the people of Ukraine. Many are caught in the crossfire, and the ongoing violence and instability have had a significant impact on the country's economy and overall development. It is important for the international community to continue to support Ukraine in its efforts to maintain its sovereignty and bring an end to the conflict."

As you can see from the preceding examples, ChatGPT provides impressive and accurate responses to queries in a manner that surpasses many chatbots of recent years. However, it is still possible to confound this chatbot:

https://www.theverge.com/23488017/openai-chatbot-chatgpt-ai-examples-web-demo

ALTERNATIVES TO CHATGPT

There are several alternatives to ChatGPT that offer a similar set of features, some of which are listed below:

- Google Gemini
- Bing Chat
- Gemini (Google)
- Jasper
- PaLM (Google)
- Pi
- POE (LinkedIn)
- Replika
- WriteSonic
- YouChat

The following subsections discuss some (but not all) of the ChatGPT alternatives in the preceding list.

Google Gemini

Google Gemini is a chatbot that has similar functionality as ChatGPT, such as generating code as well as generating text/documents. A subset of the features supported by Bard is shown below:

- built-in support for Internet search
- built-in support for voice recognition
- built "on top of" PaLM 2 (Google)
- support for 20 programming languages
- read/summarize PDF contents
- provides links for its information

According to the following article, Gemini has added support for 40 additional languages as well as support for text-to-speech:

https://www.extremetech.com/extreme/google-bard-updated-with-text-to-speech-40-new-languages

Moreover, Gemini supports prompts that include images (interpreted by Google Lens) and can produce captions based on the images.

The following article suggests that Google can remain competitive with ChatGPT by leveraging PaLM:

https://analyticsindiamag.com/googles-palm-is-ready-for-the-gpt-challenge/

YouChat

Another alternative to ChatGPT is YouChat, which is part of the search engine *you.com*, and it is accessible at *https://you.com/*.

Richard Socher, who is well known in the ML community for his many contributions, is the creator of *you.com*. According to Richard Socher, YouChat is a search engine that can provide the usual search-related functionality as well as the ability to search the Web to obtain more information to provide responses to queries from users.

Another competitor is POE from LinkedIn, and you can create a free account at *https://poe.com/login*.

Pi from Inflection

Pi is a chatbot developed by InflectionAI, which is a company that was by Mustafa Suleyman, who is also the founder of DeepMind. Pi is accessible at *https://pi.ai/talk*

and there is more information at the following Web page:

https://medium.com/@ignacio.de.gregorio.noblejas/meet-pi-chatgpts-newest-rival-and-the-most-human-ai-in-the-world-367b461c0af1

The development team used Reinforcement Learning from Human Feedback (RLHF) to train this chatbot:

https://medium.com/@ignacio.de.gregorio.noblejas/meet-pi-chatgpts-newest-rival-and-the-most-human-ai-in-the-world-367b461c0af1

MACHINE LEARNING AND CHATGPT: ADVANCED DATA ANALYSIS

OpenAI supports a feature called Advanced Data Analysis, which enables ChatGPT to generate Python code that produces charts and graphs based on data from datasets. Moreover, Advanced Data Analysis can generate ML models that can be trained on datasets. For example, Figure 4.1 displays a screenshot of charts that are based on the Titanic dataset.

Incidentally, if you would like to see examples of ChatGPT generating Python code for ML models, as well as code for charts and graphs, you can learn how to do so in several upcoming books:

- *Machine Learning, Python 3, and ChatGPT"*
- *Python and ChatGPT/GPT-4*
- *Python and Data Visualization with ChatGPT*

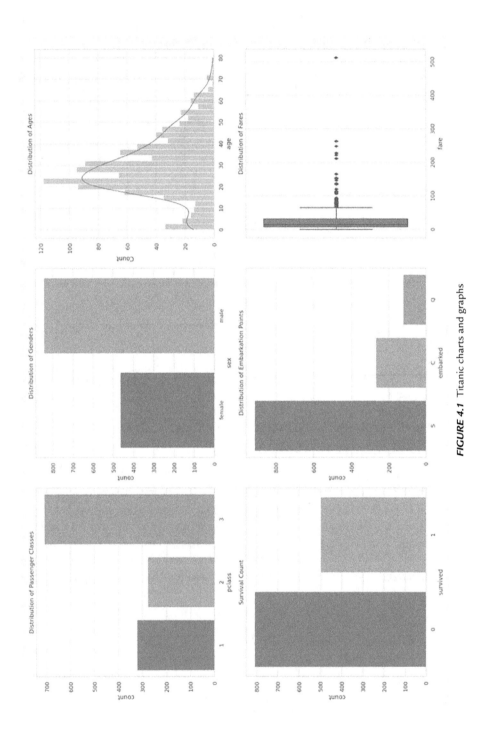

FIGURE 4.1 Titanic charts and graphs

WHAT IS INSTRUCTGPT?

InstructGPT is a language model developed by OpenAI, and it is a sibling model to ChatGPT. InstructGPT was designed to follow instructions given in a prompt to generate detailed responses. Some key points about InstructGPT are listed below:

- instruction following
- training
- applications
- limitations

Instruction following: Unlike ChatGPT, which focuses on open-ended conversations, InstructGPT was designed to follow user instructions in prompts. This makes it suitable for tasks where the user wants to get specific information or outputs by giving clear directives.

Training: InstructGPT was trained using Reinforcement Learning from Human Feedback (RLHF), similar to ChatGPT. An initial model was trained using supervised fine-tuning, where human AI trainers provided conversations playing both sides (the user and the AI assistant). This new dialogue dataset was then mixed with the InstructGPT dataset and transformed into a dialogue format.

Applications: InstructGPT can be useful in scenarios where you want more detailed explanations, step-by-step guides, or specific outputs based on the instructions provided.

Limitations: Like other models, InstructGPT has its limitations. It might produce incorrect or nonsensical answers. The output depends on how the prompt is phrased. It is also sensitive to input phrasing and might give different responses based on slight rephrasing.

As AI models and their applications are rapidly evolving, there might have been further developments or iterations on InstructGPT after 2021. Always refer to OpenAI's official publications and updates for the most recent information. More information about InstructGPT is accessible at *https://openai. com/blog/instruction-following/*.

VIZGPT AND DATA VISUALIZATION

VizGPT is an online tool that enables you to specify English-based prompts in order to visualize aspects of datasets, and it is accessible here: *https://www. vizgpt.ai/*.

Select the default "Cars Dataset" and then click on the "Data" button to display the contents of the dataset, as shown in Figure 4.2.

Next, select the default "Cars Dataset," and then click on the "Chat to Viz" button to display a visualization of the dataset, as shown in Figure 4.3.

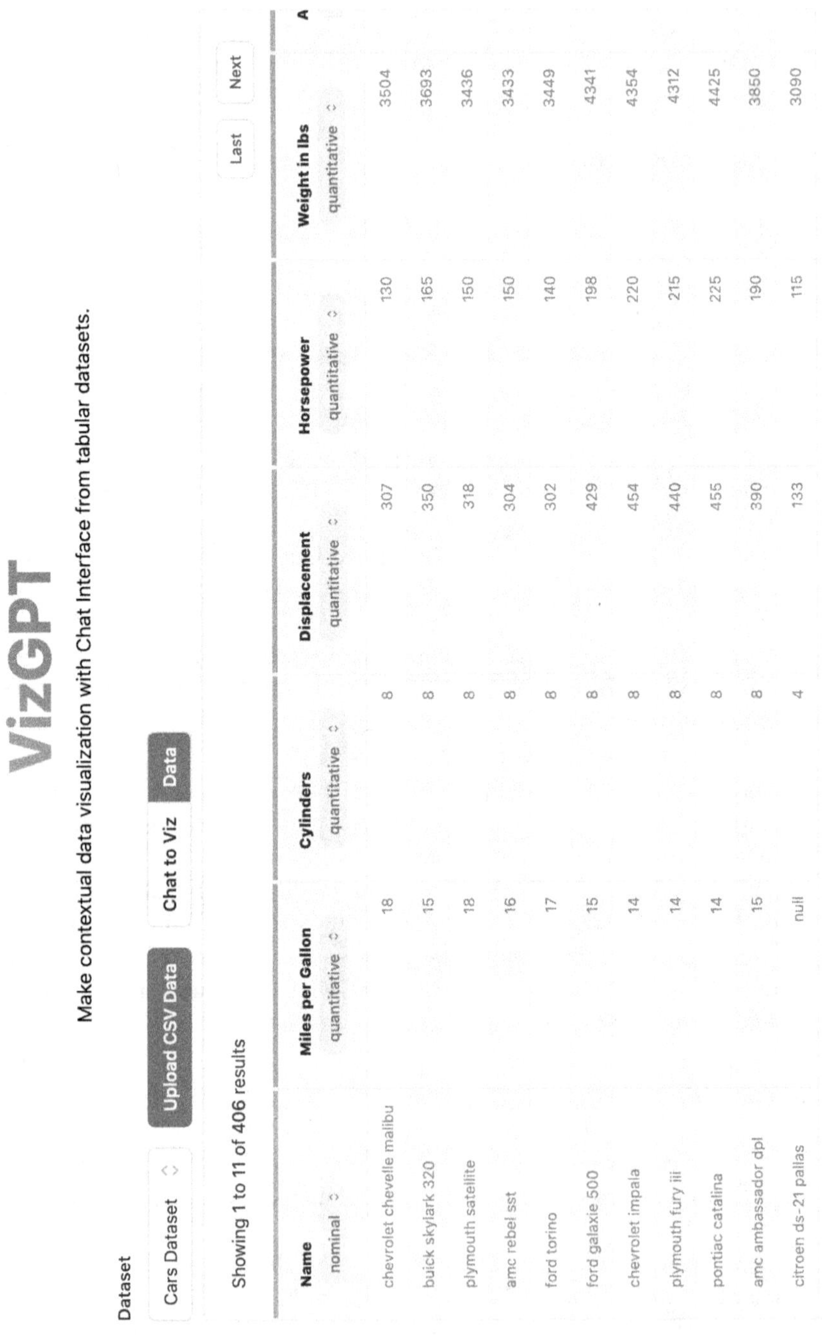

VizGPT

Make contextual data visualization with Chat Interface from tabular datasets.

Dataset

| Cars Dataset < > | Upload CSV Data | Chat to Viz | Data |

Showing 1 to 11 of 406 results

Last | Next

Name nominal ◇	Miles per Gallon quantitative ◇	Cylinders quantitative ◇	Displacement quantitative ◇	Horsepower quantitative ◇	Weight in lbs quantitative ◇	A
chevrolet chevelle malibu	18	8	307	130	3504	
buick skylark 320	15	8	350	165	3693	
plymouth satellite	18	8	318	150	3436	
amc rebel sst	16	8	304	150	3433	
ford torino	17	8	302	140	3449	
ford galaxie 500	15	8	429	198	4341	
chevrolet impala	14	8	454	220	4354	
plymouth fury iii	14	8	440	215	4312	
pontiac catalina	14	8	455	225	4425	
amc ambassador dpl	15	8	390	190	3850	
citroen ds-21 pallas	null	4	133	115	3090	

FIGURE 4.2 VizGPT "Cars Dataset" rows

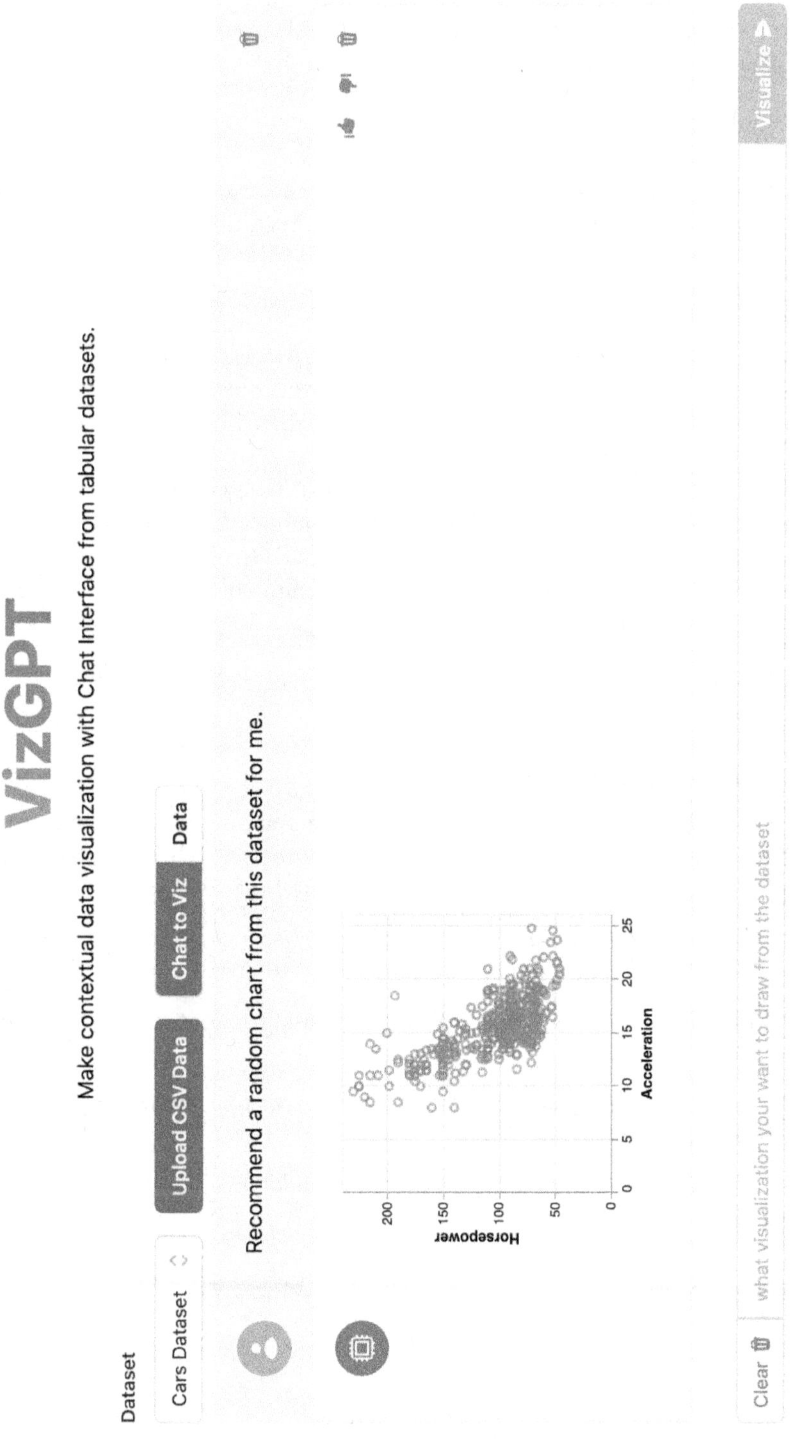
VizGPT
Make contextual data visualization with Chat Interface from tabular datasets.
Dataset
Cars Dataset
Upload CSV Data
Chat to Viz
Data
Recommend a random chart from this dataset for me.
Horsepower
Acceleration
Clear
what visualization your want to draw from the dataset
Visualize

FIGURE 4.3 VizGPT "Cars Dataset" visualization

You can experiment further with VizGPT. For example, you can upload your own dataset by clicking on the "Upload CSV" button and obtain similar results with that dataset.

WHAT IS GPT-4?

GPT-4 was released in mid-March 2023 and became available only to users with an existing ChatGPT account via a paid upgrade ($20/month) to that account. According to various online anecdotal stories from users, GPT-4 is significantly superior to ChatGPT. In addition, Microsoft has a version of GPT-4 that powers its Bing browser, which is freely available to the public.

GPT-4 is a large multimodal model that can process image-based inputs as well as text-based inputs and then generate textual outputs. Currently, image-based outputs are unavailable to the general public, but it does have internal support for image generation.

GPT-4 supports 25,000 words of input text: by comparison, ChatGPT is limited to 4,096 characters. Although the number of parameters in GPT-4 is undisclosed, the following article asserts that GPT-4 is a mixture of 8 x 220-billion-parameter models, which is an example of the MoE (Mixture of Experts) architecture:

https://thealgorithmicbridge.substack.com/p/gpt-4s-secret-has-been-revealed

GPT-4 and Test-Taking Scores

One interesting example of the improved accuracy pertains to the bar exam, which ChatGPT scored in the bottom 10%. By contrast, GPT-4 scored in the top 10% for the same bar exam. More details are accessible here:

https://www.abajournal.com/web/article/latest-version-of-chatgpt-aces-the-bar-exam-with-score-in-90th-percentile

In addition, GPT-4 is apparently able to pass first year at Harvard with a 3.34 GPA. More details are accessible here:

https://www.businessinsider.com/chatgpt-harvard-passed-freshman-ai-education-GPT-4-2023-7?op=1

GPT-4 has performed well on a number of additional tests, some of which are listed below:

- AP exams
- SAT
- GRE
- medical tests
- law exams
- business school exams

- Wharton MBA exam
- USA Biology Olympiad Semifinal Exam
- sommelier (wine steward) exams

You can read more details regarding the preceding tests from this Web page:

https://www.businessinsider.com/list-here-are-the-exams-chatgpt-has-passed-so-far-2023-1

The following Web page contains much more detailed information regarding test scores, benchmarks, and other results pertaining to GPT-4: *https://openai.com/research/gpt-4.*

GPT-4 Parameters

This section contains information regarding some of the GPT-4 parameters, some of which are best-guess approximations.

Since GPT-4 is a transformer-based AR (auto regressive) model, it is trained to perform next-token prediction. The following paper, "GPT-4 Technical Report," was released in March 2023, and it contains a detailed analysis of the capabilities of GPT-4:

https://arxiv.org/abs/2303.08774

GPT-4 Fine Tuning

Although OpenAI allows you to fine-tune the four base models, it is (currently) not possible to perform fine tuning on ChatGPT 3.5 or GPT-4. Instead, you can integrate OpenAI models with your own data source via LangChain or LlamaIndex (previously known as GPT-Index). Both of them enable you to connect OpenAI models with your existing data sources.

An introduction to LangChain is accessible here:

https://www.pinecone.io/learn/series/langchain/langchain-intro/

An introduction to LlamaIndex is accessible at the following Web pages:

https://zilliz.com/blog/getting-started-with-llamaindex

https://stackoverflow.com/questions/76160057/openai-chat-completions-api-how-do-i-customize-answers-from-gpt-3-5-or-gpt-4-mo?noredirect=1&lq=1

CHATGPT AND GPT-4 COMPETITORS

Shortly after the release of ChatGPT on November 30, 2022, there was considerable activity among various companies to release a competitor to ChatGPT, some of which are listed below:

- Google Gemini
- CoPilot (Microsoft)

- Codex (OpenAI)
- Apple GPT (Apple)
- PaLM 2 (Google and GPT-4 competitor)
- Claude 2 and Claude 3 (Anthropic)
- Llama 2(Meta)

The following subsections contain additional details regarding the LLMs in the preceding list.

Gemini

Gemini is an AI chatbot from Google that is a competitor to ChatGPT. By way of comparison, Gemini is powered by PaLM 2 (discussed later), whereas ChatGPT is powered by GPT-4. Recently, Gemini added support for images in its answers to user queries, whereas this functionality for ChatGPT has not been released yet to the public. More information can be found at the following Web page:

https://artificialcorner.com/google-bards-new-image-recognition-means-serious-competition-to-chatgpt-here-are-6-best-use-cases-55d69eae1b27

Bard (before it became Google Gemini) encountered an issue pertaining to the James Webb Space Telescope during a highly publicized release, which resulted in a significant decrease in market capitalization for Alphabet. However, Google has persevered in fixing issues and enhancing the functionality of Bard. You can access Bard at *https://bard.google.com/*.

Around mid-2023, Bard was imbued with several features that were not available in GPT-4 during the same time period, some of which are listed below:

- generate images
- generate HTML/CSS from an image
- generate mobile applications from an image
- create Latex formulas from an image
- extract text from an image

Presumably these features will spur OpenAI to provide the same set of features (some are implemented in GPT-4, but they are not publicly available).

CoPilot (OpenAI/Microsoft)

Microsoft CoPilot is a Visual Studio Code extension that is also powered by GPT-4. GitHub CoPilot is already known for its ability to generate blocks of code within the context of a program. In addition, Microsoft is also developing Microsoft 365 CoPilot, whose availability date has not been announced as of mid-2023.

However, Microsoft has provided early demos that show some of the capabilities of Microsoft 365 Copilot, which includes automating tasks such as:

- writing emails
- summarizing meetings
- making PowerPoint presentations

Microsoft 365 Copilot can analyze data in Excel spreadsheets, insert AI-generated images in PowerPoint, and generate drafts of cover letters. Microsoft has also integrated Microsoft 365 Copilot into some of its existing products, such as Loop and OneNote.

According to the following article, Microsoft intends to charge $30 per month for Office 365 Copilot:

https://www.extremetech.com/extreme/microsoft-to-charge-30-per-month-for-ai-powered-office-apps

Copilot was reverse engineered in late 2022, which is described here:

https://thakkarparth007.github.io/copilot-explorer/posts/copilot-internals

The following article shows you how to create a GPT-3 application that uses NextJS, React, and CoPilot:

https://github.blog/2023-07-25-how-to-build-a-gpt-3-app-with-nextjs-react-and-github-copilot/

Codex (OpenAI)

OpenAI Codex is a fine-tuned GPT-3-based LLM that generates code from text. In fact, Codex powers GitHub Copilot. Codex was trained on more than 150 GB of Python code that was obtained from more than 50 million GitHub repositories.

According to OpenAI, the primary purpose of Codex is to accelerate human programming, and it can complete almost 40% of requests. Codex tends to work quite well for generating code for solving simpler tasks. Navigate to the Codex home page to obtain more information: *https://openai.com/blog/openai-codex*.

Apple GPT

In mid-2023, Apple announced Apple GPT, which is a competitor to ChatGPT from OpenAI. The actual release date was projected to be 2024. "Apple GPT" is the current name for a product that is intended to compete with Google Gemini, OpenAI ChatGPT, and Microsoft Bing AI.

In brief, the LLM PaLM 2 powers Google Gemini, and GPT-4 powers ChatGPT as well as Bing Chat, whereas Ajax is what powers Apple GPT. Ajax is based on Jax from Google, and the name Ajax is a clever concatenation ("Apple Jax" perhaps?).

PaLM-2

PaLM-2, which is an acronym for the Pathways Language Model, is the successor to PaLM (circa 2022). PaLM-2 powers Gemini, and it is also a direct competitor to GPT-4. By way of comparison, PaLM consists of 540 B parameters, and it is plausible that PaLM-2 is a larger LLM (details of the latter are undisclosed).

PaLM-2 provides four submodels called Gecko, Otter, Bison, and Unicorn (smallest to largest). PaLM-2 was trained in more than 100 human languages, as well as programming languages such as Fortran. Moreover, PaLM-2 has been deployed to a plethora of Google products, including Gmail and YouTube.

Med-PaLM M

In addition to the four submodels listed above, Med-PaLM 2 (the successor to Med-PaLM) is an LLM that provides answers to medical questions, and it is accessible here: *http://sites.research.google/med-palm/*.

The successor to Med-PaLM is Med-PaLM M, and details about this LLM are accessible here: *https://arxiv.org/abs/2307.14334*.

An article that provides a direct comparison of performance benchmarks for PaLM 2 and GPT-4 is accessible here:

https://www.makeuseof.com/google-palm-2-vs-openai-gpt-4/

PaLM-2 has a robust set of features, and it is a significant competitor to GPT-4.

Claude 2

Anthropic created the LLM Claude 2, which can answer queries about specific topics. It can also perform searches involving multiple documents, and can summarize documents, create documents, and generate code.

Claude 2 is an improvement on its predecessor Claude 1.3, and it can "ingest" entire books as well as generate code based on prompts from users. Claude 2 appears to be comparable with its rivals ChatGPT and GPT-4 in terms of competing functionality.

Furthermore, Claude 2 supports a context window of 100,000 tokens. It was trained on data as recent as early 2023, whereas ChatGPT was trained on data up until 2021. However, Claude 2 cannot search the Web (unlike its competitor GPT-4). Anthropic will likely be doing more important work in the area of LLMs.

LLAMA 2

Llama 2 (Large Language Model Meta AI) is an open source fine-tuned LLM from Meta that was trained on only publicly-available data; it has created a lot of excitement in the AI community. Llama 2 offers three models (7 B, 13 B, and 70 B parameters) that utilize more data during the pre-training step than numerous other LLMs. Llama 2 was optimized to provide faster inferences and a longer context length (4 K) than other LLMs.

Moreover, the Llama 2 Chat LLM performs surprisingly well: in some cases, its quality is close to the quality of high-performing LLMs such ChatGPT and GPT-4. Llama 2 is more user-friendly also provides better results for writing text in comparison to GPT-4. GPT-4, however, is more adept for tasks such as generating code.

How to Download Llama 2

Llama 2 provides a permissive license for community use and commercial use, and Meta has made the code as well as the pre-trained models and the fine-tuned models publicly available.

There are several ways that you can download Llama 2, starting with this Web page (after you provide some information, such as name, country, and affiliation): *https://ai.meta.com/llama/*.

You can access demonstrations of the 7 B, 13 B, and 70 B models at the following URLs:

https://huggingface.co/spaces/huggingface-projects/Llama 2-7b-chat
https://huggingface.co/spaces/huggingface-projects/Llama 2-13b-chat
https://huggingface.co/spaces/ysharma/Explore_llamav2_with_TGI

You can also access Llama 2 on Hugging Face from the following Web pages: *https://huggingface.co/blog/llama2*

https://github.com/facebookresearch/llama
https://ai.meta.com/research/publications/llama-2-open-foundation-and-fine-tuned-chat-models/

If you are interested in training Llama 2 on your laptop, more details for doing so are accessible here: *https://blog.briankitano.com/llama-from-scratch/*.

Llama 2 Architecture Features

This section simply contains a high-level list of some of the important distinguishing features of Llama 2, as shown below:

- decoder-only LLM
- better pre-training
- improved model architecture
- SwiGLU activation function
- different positional embeddings
- GQA (Grouped Query Attention)
- Ghost Attention (GAtt)
- RLHF and PPO
- BPE SentencePiece tokenizer
- modified normalization step

The majority of LLMs contain the layer normalization that is in the original transformer architecture. By contrast, LlaMa uses a simplified alternative that involves Root Mean Square Layer Normalization (RMSNorm). RMSNorm has yielded improved results for training stability as well as for generalization.

Although SwiGLU is computationally more expensive than the ReLU activation function that is part of the original transformer architecture, SwiGLU achieves better performance.

Note that RLHF is discussed in Chapter 5, which also includes a brief description of TRPO and PPO. For a detailed description of how to fine tune Llama 2 on three tasks, navigate to the following Web page:

https://www.anyscale.com/blog/fine-tuning-llama-2-a-comprehensive-case-study-for-tailoring-models-to-unique-applications

Fine Tuning Llama 2

Although Llama 2 is an improvement over its predecessor Llama, you can further improve the performance of Llama 2 by performing some fine tuning of this LLM.

https://medium.com/@murtuza753/using-llama-2-0-faiss-and-langchain-for-question-answering-on-your-own-data-682241488476

The following article shows you how to fine tune Llama 2 in a Google Colaboratory notebook:

https://towardsdatascience.com/fine-tune-your-own-llama-2-model-in-a-colab-notebook-df9823a04a32

The following article describes how to use MonsterAPI (also discussed in the article) to fine tune Llama 2 in five steps: *https://blog.monsterapi.ai/how-to-fine-tune-llama-2-llm/.*

The following Web page describes how to access Llama 2 in Google Colaboratory:

https://levelup.gitconnected.com/harnessing-the-power-of-llama-2-using-google-colab-2e1dedc2d1d8

WHEN WILL GPT-5 BE AVAILABLE?

As this book goes to print, there is no official information available regarding the status of GPT-5, which is to say that everything is speculative. In the early part of 2023, Sam Altman (CEO of OpenAI) remarked that there were "no official plans" for GPT-5.

However, during mid-2023 OpenAI filed a patent for GPT-5 in which there are some high-level details about the features of GPT-5. Some people have speculated that GPT-5 will be a more powerful version of GPT-4, and others suggest that filing a patent might be nothing more than securing the name GPT-5 by OpenAI.

Regardless of the motivation for filing a patent, there is a great deal of competition with GPT-4 from various companies. Therefore, it is plausible that OpenAI will release either GPT 4.5 or GPT-5, perhaps by the end of 2024. Regarding model sizes, recall that GPT-3 has 175 B parameters, and some speculate that GPT-4 has 10 trillion parameters, which would mean that GPT-4 is roughly 60 times larger than GPT-3. The same increase in scale for GPT-5 seems implausible because GPT-5 would then consist of 600 trillion parameters.

Another possibility is that GPT-4 is based on the MoE (Mixture of Experts) methodology that involves multiple components. For instance, GPT-4 could be a combination of 8 components, each of which involves 220 million parameters, and therefore GPT-4 would consist of 1.76 trillion parameters.

Training LLMs such as GPT-4 is very costly and requires huge datasets for the pre-training step. Regardless of the eventual size of GPT-5, the training process could involve enormous costs.

SUMMARY

This chapter started with a discussion of ChatGPT from OpenAI and some of its features. In addition, you learned about some competitors to ChatGPT, such as Claude 2 from Anthropic.

Next you learned about GPT-4 from OpenAI, which powers ChatGPT, and some of its features. Then you learned about some competitors of GPT-4, such as Llama 2 (Meta) and Google Gemini.

## CHAPTER 5

LINEAR REGRESSION WITH GPT-4

This chapter introduces linear regression and includes GPT-4 generated code samples using NumPy APIs. The code samples use an "incremental" approach, starting with simple examples that involve Python and NumPy code (often using the NumPy `linspace()` API).

The first part of this chapter briefly discusses various types of linear regression, along with examples for simple linear regression, multiple linear regression, polynomial regression, and linear regression with interaction terms.

The second section in this chapter contains additional code samples involving linear regression tasks using standard techniques in NumPy. Hence, if you are comfortable with this topic, you can probably skim quickly through the first two sections of this chapter.

Before you read this chapter, keep in mind that most (around 90%) of the material was generated by ChatGPT. The editing process for the material in this chapter involved the following changes:

- the addition of section headings
- the inclusion of bullet lists
- the removal of inconsequential details
- italicized headings

As you will soon see, the details in this chapter demonstrate the impressive ability of ChatGPT to provide fully detailed responses to tasks that are posed by users. In addition, ChatGPT has very helpful debugging capabilities that can assist in debugging the code that it generates for you because that code is not always perfect.

Now let's look at content that was generated by GPT-4, with the next section as a starting point.

WHAT IS LINEAR REGRESSION?

Although linear regression was developed more than 200 years ago, this technique is still one of the "core" techniques for solving (albeit simple) problems in statistics and machine learning. The technique known as the Mean Squared Error (MSE) for finding a best-fitting line for data points in a 2D plane (or a hyperplane for higher dimensions) is implemented in Python and TensorFlow to minimize cost functions that are discussed later.

The goal of linear regression is to find the best-fitting line that "represents" a dataset. Keep in mind two key points. First, the best-fitting line does not necessarily pass through all (or even most of) the points in the dataset. The purpose of a best-fitting line is to minimize the distance of that line from the points in dataset. Second, linear regression does not determine the best-fitting polynomial: the latter involves finding a higher-degree polynomial that passes through many of the points in a dataset.

EXAMPLES OF LINEAR REGRESSION

Linear regression is a statistical method used to model the relationship between a dependent variable and one or more independent variables. The simplest form of linear regression, simple linear regression, involves one dependent variable and one independent variable. By contrast, multiple linear regression involves one dependent variable and two or more independent variables. We will discuss examples of the following types of regression:

- simple linear regression
- multiple linear regression
- polynomial regression
- linear regression with interaction terms

The choice of the type of linear regression to use depends on the nature of the data and the specific questions you are trying to answer. For instance, an example of simple linear regression involves predicting a person's weight based on their height. Suppose that you have data on the heights and weights of a group of people. You want to predict weight (dependent variable) based on height (independent variable). The mathematical representation of weight and height is shown below:

$$\text{Weight} = \beta 0 + \beta 1 \times \text{Height}$$

An example of multiple linear regression involves predicting the price of a house based on its size and age. In this case, you are predicting house price (dependent variable) based on two independent variables: size of the house (in square feet) and age of the house (in years). The mathematical representation for price, size, and age is shown below:

Price=β0+β1×Size+β2×Age

A third example involves linear regression with interaction terms, such as predicting the sales of a product based on its price and the amount of advertising, while also considering the interaction between price and advertising.

Besides the direct effect of price and advertising on sales, you are also considering how the combination of the two (their interaction) might influence sales. The mathematical representation for sales, price, advertising, and the produce of price and advertising is shown below:

Sales=β0+β1×Price+β2×Advertising+β3×(Price×Advertising)

In addition to the preceding examples, it is possible to perform polynomial regression (a type of linear regression), such as predicting the trajectory of a projectile based on time. Even though it is called "polynomial," it is still a form of linear regression because the regression coefficients (betas) are linear. The nonlinearity is in the independent variable. The mathematical representation (for a second-degree polynomial) for this example is shown below:

Height=β0+β1×Time+β2×Time2

Yet another example involves linear regression with categorical predictors involves predicting a person's salary based on their education level (e.g., high school, bachelor's, or master's). This involves using dummy variables to represent the categorical predictors. The mathematical representation (assuming "high school" is the reference category) is shown below:

Salary=β0+β1×Bachelor's+β2×Master's

The coefficients for the dummy variables (i.e., β1 and β2) represent the differences in the mean salary relative to the reference category.

METRICS FOR LINEAR REGRESSION

Evaluating the performance of a linear regression model is crucial in understanding how well the model fits the data and in comparing it with other models.

No single metric can provide a complete picture of the model's performance. It is essential to consider multiple metrics and understand the context of the problem you are addressing. Here are some common metrics used to evaluate linear regression models:

- Coefficient of Determination (R^2)
- Mean Squared Error (MSE)
- Root Mean Squared Error (RMSE)
- Mean Absolute Error (MAE)

- Residual Standard Error (RSE)
- F-statistic
- T-statistic
- Adjusted R^2
- AIC (Akaike Information Criterion)
- Durbin-Watson Statistic
- Variance Inflation Factor (VIF)

The following subsections contain brief descriptions of the topics in the preceding list.

Coefficient of Determination (R^2)

R^2 (R-squared) represents the proportion of the variance for the dependent variable that is explained by the independent variable(s) in the regression model. Its value ranges from 0 to 1, with 1 indicating that the model explains all the variability of the response data around its mean. Here is the formula:

R^2=1−(Residual Sum of Squares (RSS))/(Total Sum of Squares (TSS))

The Mean Squared Error (MSE) represents the average of the squares of the errors or deviations (i.e., difference between estimator and what is estimated). Here is the formula:

MSE = $(\Sigma(y_i-y^i)^2)/n$

In the preceding formula, y_i is the actual value, y^i is the predicted value, and n is the number of observations.

The RMSE represents the square root of the MSE. It provides the magnitude of error in the same units as the original data.

MAE represents the average absolute differences between the observed actual outcomes and the forecasts. The formula is shown below:

MAE = $(\Sigma|y_i-y^i|)/n$

The RSE represents the standard deviation of the residuals. It gives a measure of how spread out the residuals are around the line of best fit. Here is the formula:

RSE = $sqrt((\Sigma(y_i-y^i)^2)/df)$

In the preceding formula, y_i is the observed value, y is the predicted value, and df is the degrees of freedom (the total number of observations). Smaller values for RSE are indicative of a better fitting model because the data points will be more closely "packed" around the regression line.

The *F-statistic* is used in the context of an ANOVA (analysis of variance) test and provides a statistical test of whether there is a significant relationship between the dependent variable and the independent variables. It compares the full model against a model with no predictors.

The *t-statistic* involves testing whether a given coefficient is different from 0 (no effect). A large t-statistic (or one that is far from zero) and a small p-value suggest that the coefficient is statistically significant.

The adjusted R^2 is adjusted for the number of predictors in the model. Unlike R^2, it penalizes the addition of extraneous predictors. It is useful when comparing models with a different number of predictors.

The *Akaike Information Criterion* (AIC) and *Bayesian Information Criterion* (BIC) are used for model selection. They balance the goodness of fit of the model against the complexity of the model. The model with the lowest AIC or BIC is preferred.

The *Durbin-Watson Statistic* involves tests for autocorrelation in the residuals, and it is useful in time series data.

The *Variance Inflation Factor* (VIF) measures how much the variance of an estimated regression coefficient increases when your predictors are correlated. If no factors are correlated, the VIFs will be equal to 1.

LINEAR REGRESSION WITH RANDOM DATA WITH GPT-4

Listing 5.1 displays the content of `linreg_gpt4.py` that illustrates how to use the NumPy `randn()` API to generate a dataset and then the `scatter()` API in Matplotlib to plot the points in the dataset.

Note: The description of the code in Listing 5.1 was prepared by the author and not by ChatGPT.

LISTING 5.1: linreg_gpt4.py

```
"""
A simple linear regression example using Python's scikit-
learn library.
1. Generate Sample Data
First, let's generate some synthetic data. Suppose we
are trying to model the relationship between years of
experience and salary.
"""

import numpy as np
import matplotlib.pyplot as plt

# Generate synthetic data
np.random.seed(0)  # for reproducibility

# Random years of experience between 0 to 2.5 years
X = 2.5 * np.random.rand(100, 1)
```

```python
# Salary = base + 3*Experience + noise
y = 5 + 3 * X + np.random.randn(100, 1)

plt.scatter(X, y)
plt.xlabel("Years of Experience")
plt.ylabel("Salary")
plt.title("Experience vs. Salary")
plt.show()
"""
In the above code:
X represents years of experience.
y represents the corresponding salary.
We assume a base salary of 5, and for each year of
experience, the salary increases by 3 units. In addition,
there is some random noise.
"""


"""
2. Train a Linear Regression Model
let's fit a linear regression model to this data.
"""
from sklearn.linear_model import LinearRegression

# Create a linear regression model
reg = LinearRegression()

# Fit the model to the data
reg.fit(X, y)

# Get the regression coefficients
intercept = reg.intercept_[0]
slope = reg.coef_[0][0]

print(f"Intercept (base salary): {intercept:.2f}")
print(f"Slope (salary increase per year of experience):
{slope:.2f}")
"""
In the code above:
Use LinearRegression() from scikit-learn for a linear
regression model.
The fit method trains the model using our synthetic data.
The intercept_ gives the base salary (y-intercept), and
coef_ provides the increase in salary for each additional
year of experience (slope).

3. Visualize the Regression Line
Let's plot the data points and the regression line.
"""
# Predict values
y_pred = reg.predict(X)
```

```
plt.scatter(X, y)
plt.plot(X, y_pred, color='red')
plt.xlabel("Years of Experience")
plt.ylabel("Salary")
plt.title("Experience vs. Salary with Regression Line")
plt.show()
"""
In the visualization, data points are shown as blue
dots.
The red line is the linear regression model's prediction.

4. Evaluate the Model
Finally, let's compute the RMSE (Root Mean Squared Error)
to evaluate the performance of our model.
"""

from sklearn.metrics import mean_squared_error
rmse = np.sqrt(mean_squared_error(y, y_pred))
print(f"Root Mean Squared Error: {rmse:.2f}")


"""
In this step:
Use the mean_squared_error function in scikit-learn to
compute the MSE.
The square root of the MSE gives us the RMSE, which
indicates the model's prediction error in the same units as
the target variable.
This entire process allows us to understand the
relationship between experience and salary, model it using
linear regression, and evaluate the performance of the
model.
"""
```

Listing 5.1 starts with two `import` statements, followed by formulas for X and y that generate quasi-random value for y based on the values in X. Next, a scatter plot is displayed based on the values for X and y.

The next portion of Listing 5.1 initializes the variable `reg` as an instance of the class `LinearRegression`, and then invokes the `fit()` method to fit the model to the data in the CSV file `death.csv`. Now we can initialize the variable `intercept` and `slope` from the fitted model with this pair of code snippets:

```
intercept = reg.intercept_[0]
slope = reg.coef_[0][0]
```

Launch the code in Listing 5.1, and you will see two graphs displayed. Figure 5.1 shows the data points, and Figure 5.2 shows the data point with the best-fitting line.

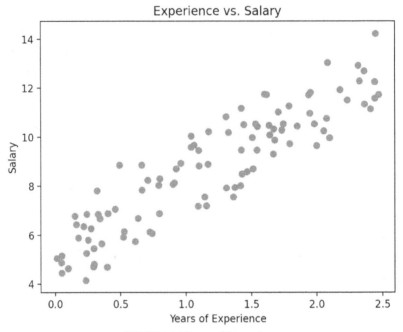

FIGURE 5.1 The set of data points

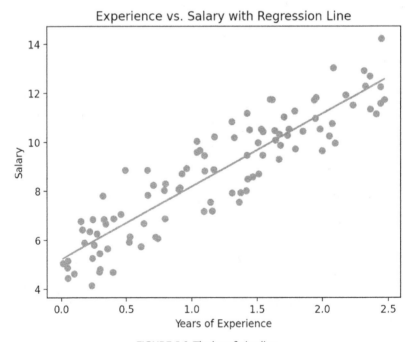

FIGURE 5.2 The best-fitting line

LINEAR REGRESSION WITH A DATASET WITH GPT-4

The example in this section uses linear regression on the `death.csv` dataset that was downloaded from the following Web page:

https://data.world/nrippner/cancer-linear-regression-model-tutorial

For your convenience, Listing 5.2 displays a portion of the contents of the CSV file `death.csv`.

LISTING 5.2: death.csv

```
county,fips,met_objective_of_45_5_1,age_adjusted_death_
rate,lower_95_confidence_interval_for_death_rate,upper_95_
confidence_interval_for_death_rate,average_deaths_per_
year,recent_trend_2,recent_5_year_trend_2_in_death_
rates,lower_95_confidence_interval_for_trend,upper_95_
confidence_interval_for_trend
United States,0,No,46,45.9,46.1,"157,376",falli
ng,-2.4,-2.6,-2.2
"Perry County, Kentucky",21193,No,125.6,108.9,144.2,43,stab
le,-0.6,-2.7,1.6
"Powell County, Kentucky",21197,No,125.3,100.2,155.1,18,sta
ble,1.7,0,3.4
"North Slope Borough, Alaska",2185,
No,124.9,73,194.7,5,**,**,**,**
// details omitted for brevity
"Yakutat City and Borough, Alaska<sup>3</sup>",2282,*,*,*,*
,*,**,**,**,**
"Yukon-Koyukuk Census Area,
Alaska",2290,*,*,*,*,*,**,**,**,**
"Zapata County, Texas",48505,*,*,*,*,*,*,*,*,*,*
"Zavala County, Texas",48507,*,*,*,*,*,*,**,**,**,**
"Ziebach County, South Dakota",46137,*,*,*,*,*,*,**,**,**,**
```

Let's perform linear regression on this dataset using GPT-4, starting with the upload of the death.csv dataset. You can perform this step in ChatGPT by selecting "GPT-4" and then click on the "+" symbol at the bottom of the screen, after which you upload the dataset from your laptop.

At this point we are ready to perform a multi-step sequence of steps to analyze and prepare the death.csv dataset for linear regression, as shown below:

1. Describe the features of the death.csv dataset.
2. Describe the preparation process of the death.csv dataset.
3. Describe the exploratory analysis.
4. Describe the model selection.
5. Describe the model diagnostics.

Each of the steps in the preceding list is discussed in the following subsections. Note the some of the subsections are quite lengthy, so it might be more efficient for you to skim the sections and then return for an in-depth reading of these subsections.

DESCRIPTIONS OF THE FEATURES OF THE DEATH.CSV DATASET

Based on the contents of the provided dataset, here is a detailed description of each feature shown in italics.

1. *county*
   Description: The name of the county or region
   Type: Categorical (Nominal)
   Example Values: "United States," "Perry County, Kentucky", "Powell County, Kentucky"
   Usage: Can be used as an identifier for each data point

2. *fips*
   Description: Federal Information Processing Standards (FIPS) code, a unique identifier for each county in the US
   Type: Numeric (although used as a categorical identifier)
   Example Values: 0 (for the United States as a whole), 21193, 21197
   Usage: Can be used as a unique identifier, especially for joining with other datasets that use FIPS codes

3. *Met_objective_of_45_5_1*
   Description: Indicates whether a specific objective (possibly a target death rate of 45.5) was met
   Type: Categorical (Binary)
   Example Values: "Yes," "No"
   Usage: Can be used to evaluate and compare the performance of different counties against a set standard or objective

4. *age_adjusted_death_rate*
   Description: The death rate adjusted for age to allow for comparison between regions with different age distributions
   Type: Numeric
   Example Values: 46, 125.6, 125.3
   Usage: A key metric for understanding the overall death rate, independent of age distribution.

5. *lower_95_confidence_interval_for_death_rate* & *upper_95_confidence_interval_for_death_rate*
   Description: Lower and upper bounds of the 95% confidence interval for the age-adjusted death rate. Gives an idea of the uncertainty or variability around the estimated death rate.

Type: Numeric
Example Values: For lower: 45.9, 108.9, 100.2; For upper: 46.1, 144.2, 155.1
Usage: Helps in understanding the reliability and range of the estimated death rates

6. *average_deaths_per_year*
Description: The average number of deaths occurring per year
Type: Numeric
Example Values: 157,376, 43, 18
Usage: Gives an absolute measure of the number of deaths, which can be used for further analysis or planning

7. *recent_trend_2*
Description: Indicates the recent trend in deaths
Type: Categorical (Ordinal)
Example Values: "falling," "stable," "**" (likely representing missing or undefined data)
Usage: Provides insight into whether the death rate is increasing, decreasing, or remaining stable over a recent period

8. *recent_5_year_trend_2_in_death_rates*
Description: The change in death rates over a recent five-year period
Type: Numeric
Example Values: -2.4, -0.6, 1.7
Usage: Indicates the rate of change in death rates, which can be useful for forecasting or understanding recent patterns

9. *lower_95_confidence_interval_for_trend & upper_95_confidence_interval_for_trend*
Description: Lower and upper bounds of the 95% confidence interval for the recent five-year trend in death rates
Type: Numeric
Example Values: For lower: -2.6, -2.7, 0; For upper: -2.2, 1.6, 3.4
Usage: Provides a range of estimates for the trend, offering insight into its reliability and variability
These features provide both absolute and relative metrics related to death rates in different counties, allowing for comprehensive analysis, comparison, and understanding of patterns and trends over time.

THE PREPARATION PROCESS OF THE DATASET

To describe the preparation process of the death.csv dataset, we begin by inspecting the contents of the dataset. We check its structure, the first few rows, and the overall statistics. This will give us an idea of what we are working with and what kind of preparation might have been involved.

Let's start by loading and inspecting the dataset, which has the following structure:

Rows: 3141 entries (including one for the United States as a whole)

Columns: 11 columns

The description of each column is shown below:

- *county:* The name of the county (or "United States" for the national average)
- *fips:* Federal Information Processing Standards (FIPS) code for the county
- *met_objective_of_45_5_1:* Indicates whether a certain objective was met (values appear to be "Yes" or "No")
- *age_adjusted_death_rate:* The death rate adjusted for age
- *lower_95_confidence_interval_for_death_rate:* Lower bound of the 95% confidence interval for the death rate
- *upper_95_confidence_interval_for_death_rate:* Upper bound of the 95% confidence interval for the death rate
- *average_deaths_per_year:* Average number of deaths per year
- *recent_trend_2:* Recent trend in deaths
- *recent_5_year_trend_2_in_death_rates:* Five-year trend in death rates
- *lower_95_confidence_interval_for_trend:* Lower bound of the 95% confidence interval for the trend
- *upper_95_confidence_interval_for_trend:* Upper bound of the 95% confidence interval for the trend

Observations:

Most columns are of the object data type, which suggests that there might be nonnumeric values or missing values denoted with special characters (like "**" in the *recent_trend_2* and *recent_5_year_trend_2_in_death_rates* columns). Some numeric values, like in the *average_deaths_per_year* column, are represented with commas, which is why they are treated as the object data type.

Preparation Process:

Based on the dataset structure and the observations, here is a probable preparation process for the death.csv dataset.

1. Data Collection:
2. The data was likely collected from various county level and national databases or health organizations.
3. Data Cleaning:
4. This involves handling missing values. Special characters like "**" could be used to denote missing or unavailable data.
5. Formatting: Numbers might have been formatted to include commas for readability.

Feature Engineering:
Calculation of confidence intervals: The 95% confidence intervals for death rates and trends suggest statistical calculations were performed post data collection.

Age adjustment: The death rate has been adjusted for age, indicating some form of standardization.

Data Transformation: Data could have been transformed or aggregated to represent averages, trends, and other metrics at the county level.

Data Annotation: Columns like *met_objective_of_45_5_1* suggest that certain metrics or objectives were evaluated and annotated in the dataset.

Data Validation: Ensuring the FIPS code matches with the correct county, and there are no duplicates or inconsistencies in the dataset.

To further understand and suggest improvements, we can conduct more in-depth exploratory data analysis (EDA) and quality checks, which are shown in the next section.

THE EXPLORATORY ANALYSIS

Exploratory data analysis (EDA) is an approach to analyzing datasets, often prior to formal modeling or hypothesis testing. The main goal of EDA is to understand the data, its structure, outliers, and patterns, and to identify potential anomalies or peculiarities. Here is a structured description of the EDA process for the death.csv dataset:

1. *Univariate Analysis*
Analyze one variable at a time. For numeric variables, describe the central tendency (mean, median) and dispersion (range, variance, standard deviation). Histograms, box plots, and density plots can be useful. For categorical variables, use bar plots to understand the frequency or proportion of each category.

2. *Bivariate Analysis*
Analyze the relationship between two variables. Use scatter plots for continuous-continuous pairs. Use box plots for categorical-continuous pairs. Use stacked column charts or mosaic plots for categorical-categorical pairs.

3. *Multivariate Analysis*
Analyze more than two variables simultaneously. Use correlation matrices or heatmaps to understand relationships between continuous variables. Use pair plots or 3D scatter plots for a visual representation of relationships.

4. *Checking for Missing Values*

Identify columns with missing values. Analyze patterns of "missingness." Are they missing at random or is there a pattern?

5. *Outlier Detection*

Detect unusual or suspicious values. Use visual methods (e.g., box plots or scatter plots) or statistical methods (e.g., IQR or Z-scores).

6. *Feature Engineering*

Create new variables from existing ones. For example, from the dataset, one could derive a feature indicating if a county's death rate is above or below the national average.

7. *Data Quality Checks*

Ensure that data is consistent, accurate, and reliable. For instance, FIPS codes should be unique to each county.

8. *Correlation Analysis*

This helps us understand how different continuous variables move in relation to each other. Use the Pearson correlation for continuous variables and Cramér's V for categorical variables.

9. *Trend Analysis*

This is especially relevant for the *recent_5_year_trend_2_in_death_rates* feature in our dataset. This analysis helps to show upward or downward trends in data over time

10. *Distribution Analysis*

This allows us to examine the distribution of key metrics (e.g., *age_adjusted_death_rate*). This allows us to check for normality, skewness, and kurtosis.

11. *Geospatial Analysis*

Since the dataset contains county information, it would be possible (with additional geographic data) to visualize metrics on a map, highlighting regions of interest.

12. *Summary Reports*

This allows us to summarize the findings, perhaps in the form of a dashboard or a report, highlighting important insights from the data.

13. *Hypothesis Generation*

Based on the findings, this allows us to generate hypotheses to be tested in subsequent analyses or modeling. After EDA, the analyst should have a deeper understanding of the dataset's characteristics and its potential limitations. It provides insights that can guide the subsequent modeling process and ensures that the assumptions made during modeling are valid.

DETAILED EDA ON THE DEATH.CSV DATASET

Let's conduct a detailed exploratory data analysis (EDA) on the death.csv dataset. The steps we will undertake are as follows:

- Univariate Analysis – To understand individual features
- Bivariate Analysis – To understand the relationships between pairs of features
- Missing Values Analysis – To identify and understand any missing data
- Outlier Detection – To identify potential outliers in the dataset
- Distribution Analysis – To understand the distribution of important metrics

Let's begin with univariate analysis for a deeper understanding of individual features based on the univariate analysis of the numeric features.

1. *age_adjusted_death_rate*

Most counties have an age-adjusted death rate between 20 and 60. There are few counties with very high death rates, which could be considered outliers.

2. *lower_95_confidence_interval_for_death_rate & upper_95_confidence_interval_for_death_rate*

The distributions of the lower and upper 95% confidence intervals for death rate are similar to the distribution of the age-adjusted death rate. This is expected since they provide a range of estimates around the death rate.

3. *recent_5_year_trend_2_in_death_rates*

The five-year trend in death rates seems to be centered around zero, suggesting that for many counties, the death rates have remained stable. There are counties with both increasing and decreasing trends.

4. *lower_95_confidence_interval_for_trend & upper_95_confidence_interval_for_trend:*

These distributions represent the range of estimates for the five-year trend in death rates. They provide context for the variability and reliability of the trend estimates.

Next, let's analyze the categorical features and understand their distributions from the univariate analysis of the categorical features.

1. *met_objective_of_45_5_1:*

A significant number of counties have not met the objective (indicated by "No"), while a smaller portion have met the objective (indicated by "Yes").

2. *recent_trend_2:*

The majority of counties have a "stable" recent trend in deaths. A considerable number of counties have a "falling" trend. Fewer counties have a "rising" trend in deaths. Some entries are marked with "**," which likely indicates missing or undefined data.

Let's use bivariate analysis to explore relationships between pairs of features. We will start by analyzing the correlation between numeric features using a heatmap.

From the correlation heatmap of the numeric features, we find the following information. The *age_adjusted_death_rate* is highly correlated with both *lower_95_confidence_interval_for_death_rate* and *upper_95_confidence_ interval_for_death_rate*. This is expected, as the confidence intervals provide the range of uncertainty around the death rate. Similarly, *recent_5_year_ trend_2_in_death_rates* has a high correlation with *lower_95_confidence_inter- val_for_trend* and *upper_95_confidence_interval_for_trend*. The correlations among other pairs of variables are relatively low.

Next, let's analyze the missing values in the dataset to understand if there is any missing data and decide how to handle it.

1. *recent_5_year_trend_2_in_death_rates, lower_95_confidence_interval_ for_trend, and upper_95_confidence_interval_for_trend:*

All have the same count of missing values, which is 447 (or about 14.23% of the data). This suggests that when the trend data is missing, its corresponding confidence intervals are also missing.

2. *age_adjusted_death_rate, lower_95_confidence_interval_for_death_rate, and upper_95_confidence_interval_for_death_rate:*

All have the same count of missing values, which is 328 (or about 10.44% of the data). This is similar to the trend columns: when the death rate data is missing, its corresponding confidence intervals are also missing.

Next, let's examine outlier detection. We will use box plots to visually identify potential outliers in the numeric columns:

1. *age_adjusted_death_rate:*

There are a few data points above the upper whisker that can be considered as potential outliers. These represent counties with exceptionally high age-adjusted death rates.

2. *lower_95_confidence_interval_for_death_rate & upper_95_confidence_ interval_for_death_rate:*

Both these features show potential outliers above their respective upper whiskers, consistent with the outliers in the age-adjusted death rate.

3. *recent_5_year_trend_2_in_death_rates:*

There are data points both above and below the whiskers, indicating counties with unusually high or low trends in death rates over the recent 5 years.

4. *lower_95_confidence_interval_for_trend* & *upper_95_confidence_interval_for_trend:*

Both these features exhibit potential outliers, consistent with the outliers in the recent five-year trend.

Next, let's analyze the distribution of some key metrics, focusing on their skewness and kurtosis. Skewness provides insights into the symmetry of the distribution, while kurtosis reveals its "tailedness."

1. *age_adjusted_death_rate*

Skewness (0.55): The distribution is moderately right-skewed, meaning there is a tail on the right side. This indicates that there are some counties with exceptionally high death rates.

Kurtosis (1.29): This value suggests a distribution with heavier tails than a normal distribution, indicating the presence of outliers.

2. *lower_95_confidence_interval_for_death_rate* & *upper_95_confidence_interval_for_death_rate*

Both have skewness values indicating a right-skewed distribution, with the upper confidence interval being more skewed. Their kurtosis values suggest heavier tails than those found in a normal distribution.

3. *recent_5_year_trend_2_in_death_rates*

Skewness (-2.35): The distribution is significantly left-skewed, meaning there is a tail on the left side. This indicates that many counties have a decreasing trend in death rates.

Kurtosis (58.03): This high value indicates the presence of extreme outliers or sharp peaks in the distribution.

4. *lower_95_confidence_interval_for_trend* & *upper_95_confidence_interval_for_trend*

Both these features exhibit high skewness and kurtosis values, indicating non-normal distributions with pronounced tails and potential outliers.

These insights from the distribution analysis can guide further statistical analysis, hypothesis testing, and modeling efforts. For the next steps in EDA, we delve deeper into the bivariate and multivariate analyses to understand the relationships between features.

BIVARIATE AND MULTIVARIATE ANALYSES

Let's explore the relationships between features using bivariate and multi-variate analyses.

Bivariate Analysis

- Use scatter plots between continuous variables to visualize relationships.
- Use box plots for categorical-continuous pairs to see how a continuous variable varies across different categories.
- Use crosstabs or stacked bar plots for categorical-categorical pairs to understand the distribution of categories across different groups.

Multivariate Analysis

- Use pair plots to view the relationships between multiple continuous variables simultaneously.
- Use correlation heatmaps to understand the linear relationships between continuous variables.

Let's start with the bivariate analysis. We will create scatter plots between the *age_adjusted_death_rate* and other continuous features to understand their relationships. The scatter plots provide insights into the relationship between *age_adjusted_death_rate* and other continuous features.

1. *age_adjusted_death_rate vs. lower_95_confidence_interval_for_death_rate & age_adjusted_death_rate vs. upper_95_confidence_interval_for_death_rate*

These plots exhibit a strong linear relationship, which is expected since the confidence intervals provide bounds around the age-adjusted death rate.

2. *age_adjusted_death_rate vs. recent_5_year_trend_2_in_death_rates*

The relationship here does not seem to be linear. While many counties have a stable trend around zero, there is a spread of data points across different death rates, indicating that the overall death rate is not necessarily predictive of the recent trend.

3. *age_adjusted_death_rate vs. lower_95_confidence_interval_for_trend & age_adjusted_death_rate vs. upper_95_confidence_interval_for_trend*

These plots show a dispersed pattern, suggesting that the confidence intervals for the trend do not have a straightforward linear relationship with the age-adjusted death rate.

Next, let's analyze the relationship between the categorical feature recent_trend_2 and the continuous feature age_adjusted_death_rate using a box plot. This will help us understand how the age-adjusted death rate varies across different recent trends (rising, falling, stable). The box plot illustrates the distribution of the age_adjusted_death_rate across different recent trends.

1. *Falling*

Counties with a falling trend tend to have higher median death rates, but there is a wide spread, suggesting variability in the extent of the decrease among these counties.

2. *Stable*

Counties with a stable trend have a lower median death rate compared to those with a falling trend. The interquartile range (IQR) is also narrower, indicating less variability among these counties.

3. *Rising*

Counties with a rising trend in death rates show a lower median compared to those with a falling trend but higher than those with a stable trend. The distribution appears more compact with fewer outliers.

4. ** (undefined or missing data)*

This category seems to have a similar distribution to the stable trend, but it is important to investigate and understand the meaning or reason for these undefined entries.

Next, for multivariate analysis, let's create a pair plot for a subset of continuous features to visualize pairwise relationships and distributions. We will focus on *age_adjusted_death_rate, recent_5_year_trend_2_in_death_rates*, and their respective confidence intervals. The pair plot provides an overview of pairwise relationships and individual distributions for the selected features.

1. *Diagonal KDE Plots*

These plots show the distribution of individual features. As observed earlier, *age_adjusted_death_rate* is moderately right-skewed, while the *recent_5_year_trend_2_in_death_rates* is left-skewed.

2. *Off-Diagonal Scatter Plots*

The scatter plots between *age_adjusted_death_rate* and its confidence intervals (both lower and upper) show strong linear relationships, as expected. The relationship between *age_adjusted_death_rate* and *recent_5_year_trend_2_in_death_rates* does not exhibit a clear trend, confirming our earlier observation.

Now, to further explore multivariate relationships, let's create a correlation heatmap using a wider set of continuous features. This will give us insight into linear relationships between these features. The extended correlation heatmap reinforces some of our earlier observations and provides additional insights.

1. *age_adjusted_death_rate and its confidence intervals*

As seen before, there is a high correlation between the age_adjusted_death_rate and its lower and upper 95% confidence intervals. This is expected, as these intervals provide bounds around the primary metric.

2. *recent_5_year_trend_2_in_death_rates and its confidence intervals*

Similarly, the *recent_5_year_trend_2_in_death_rates* also exhibits a high correlation with its respective confidence intervals.

3. *age_adjusted_death_rate and recent_5_year_trend_2_in_death_rates*

The correlation between these two is relatively low, suggesting that the overall death rate is not strongly linearly related to the recent five-year trend in death rates.

Confidence Intervals

The confidence intervals for the death rate and the trend are correlated with each other to some extent, which makes sense since they are derived from the same underlying data. We have completed a comprehensive EDA on the death.csv dataset. We have investigated individual features, analyzed bivariate relationships, and explored multivariate associations. The insights gained from this EDA can inform subsequent modeling, hypothesis testing, and further analyses.

THE MODEL SELECTION PROCESS

The model selection process involves choosing the best machine learning or statistical model for a particular dataset and problem. This process is crucial because the success of your predictions or inferences largely depends on the model you choose. Here is a structured description of the model selection process.

1. *Define the Problem*

Clearly define the objective: Is it a classification, regression, clustering, or another type of problem? Determine the evaluation metric. For instance, accuracy might be suitable for balanced classification problems, but precision, recall, or the F1-score might be more appropriate for imbalanced datasets. For regression problems, you might consider metrics like RMSE or MAE.

2. *Baseline Model*

Start with a simple model to serve as a benchmark. This could be a linear regression for regression problems or a logistic regression for classification tasks. You should have a basic measure of performance to which you can compare more complex models.

3. *Choose Candidate Models*

Based on the problem type and data characteristics, shortlist a set of algorithms that are known to work well for such problems. For example, for structured tabular data, algorithms like decision trees, random forest, gradient boosting machines, and SVMs might be considered. For unstructured data like images, you might consider deep learning models.

4. *Data Preparation*

Different algorithms might require different data preprocessing steps. Normalize or standardize data for algorithms like SVMs or neural networks. Handle categorical variables using encoding techniques like one-hot encoding, especially for algorithms that do not handle categorical data natively. Ensure the data is split into training and validation (and possibly test) sets.

5. *Hyperparameter Tuning*

Almost every algorithm has hyperparameters that need to be set. These can greatly influence performance. Use techniques like grid search, random search, or Bayesian optimization to find the optimal hyperparameters for each candidate model.

6. *Cross-Validation*

To ensure that your model's performance is robust and not overly optimistic, use cross-validation. K-fold cross-validation is a common technique. Cross-validation provides a more generalized performance metric for the model on unseen data.

7. *Model Evaluation*

Evaluate each model using your chosen metric(s) on the validation set. Compare the performance of different models against the baseline and against each other.

8. *Ensembling*

If individual models are not performing well enough, consider combining multiple models. Techniques like bagging, boosting, or stacking can often result in better performance than individual models.

9. *Model Interpretability*

It is not always about getting the highest accuracy; sometimes understanding why a model makes certain decisions is crucial. Depending on the domain (like healthcare or finance), you might prioritize simpler, more interpretable models over black-box models, even if the latter has slightly better performance.

10. *Final Model Selection*

Select the final model based on validation performance, interpretability, and business objectives. Train this model on the combined training and validation set to make final predictions on the test set.

11. *Deployment and Monitoring*

Once the final model is selected and evaluated, it can be deployed in a production environment. Continuously monitor the model's performance in the real world. Over time, as the data evolves, the model might need retraining or fine-tuning.

12. *Feedback Loop*

As the model is used and predictions are collected, this data can be fed back into the training dataset for future model improvements.

The goal of the model selection process is not always to find the model with the highest performance metric. It is to find a model that meets the business objectives, is reliable, interpretable (if needed), and generalizes well to unseen data.

CODE FOR LINEAR REGRESSION WITH THE DEATH.CSV DATASET

Let's implement linear regression using the death.csv dataset. Here is a step-by-step process we will follow:

1. Data Preprocessing: Handle missing values and prepare the data for modeling.
2. Feature Selection: Choose the independent variables (features) that we will use to predict the dependent variable.
3. Data Splitting: Split the dataset into training and testing sets.
4. Model Training: Train a linear regression model on the training set.
5. Model Evaluation: Evaluate the model's performance on the test set.
6. Model Interpretation: Interpret the model's coefficients.

For this demonstration, let's use the *age_adjusted_death_rate* as the dependent variable and *recent_5_year_trend_2_in_death_rates* as the independent variable.

Let's begin with data preprocessing. The linear regression model's performance on the test data is as follows:

Mean Squared Error (MSE): 145.22145.22
R-squared (R^2) Value: 0.11140.1114

The $R2R2$ value suggests that about 11.14% of the variance in the *age_adjusted_death_rate* is explained by the *recent_5_year_trend_2_in_death_rates*. This is not a very high value, indicating that the linear model using just the recent five-year trend might not be sufficient to capture all the variability in the death rates.

Finally, let's proceed to the model interpretation by examining the model's coefficients. The linear regression model can be represented by the equation:
    age_adjusted_death_rate = 1.5506**recent_5_year_trend_2_in_death_rates* + 54.9239

Interpreting the coefficients yields the following:

The coefficient of *recent_5_year_trend_2_in_death_rates* equals 1.5506. For every unit increase in the *recent_5_year_trend_2_in_death_rates*, the *age_adjusted_death_rate* increases by approximately 1.5506 units, keeping all other factors constant.

Intercept (54.9239):

When the *recent_5_year_trend_2_in_death_rates* is zero, the predicted *age_adjusted_death_rate* is approximately 54.9239.

Given the moderate $R2R2$ value, it is essential to consider other features or even more advanced modeling techniques to improve predictive power, if needed. This linear model provides a basic understanding and relationship between the two variables.

Listing 5.3 displays the content of `linreg2_gpt4.py` that illustrates how to perform linear regression using a subset of the rows in the `death.csv` dataset.

LISTING 5.3: linreg2_gpt4.py

```
import pandas as pd
from sklearn.linear_model import LinearRegression
from sklearn.model_selection import train_test_split
from sklearn.metrics import mean_squared_error, r2_score

# the CSV death_clean.csv is described later:
death_df = pd.read_csv('death_clean.csv')

# Step 1: Data Preprocessing
# Drop rows with missing values in the columns of interest
processed_data = death_df.dropna(subset=["age_adjusted_
death_rate", "recent_5_year_trend_2_in_death_rates"])
```

```
# Step 2: Feature Selection
X = processed_data[["recent_5_year_trend_2_in_death_
rates"]]   # Independent variable
y = processed_data["age_adjusted_death_rate"]   # Dependent
variable

# Step 3: Data Splitting
X_train, X_test, y_train, y_test = train_test_split(X, y,
test_size=0.2, random_state=42)

# Step 4: Model Training
linear_reg = LinearRegression()
linear_reg.fit(X_train, y_train)

# Step 5: Model Evaluation
y_pred = linear_reg.predict(X_test)
mse = mean_squared_error(y_test, y_pred)
r2 = r2_score(y_test, y_pred)

# this code snippet added by the author:
print("mse:",mse,"r2:",r2)
```

Listing 5.3 starts with several import statements, followed by initializing the Pandas data frame `death_df` with the contents of the CSV file `death_clean.csv`. Note that this CSV file was created by the author by removing the data points in `death_clean.csv` that contain one or more asterisks.

The next portion of Listing 5.3 initializes the Pandas data frame `processed_data`, which consists of dropping two columns in the `Dataframe` `death_df` with this code snippet:

```
processed_data = death_df.dropna(subset=["age_adjusted_
death_rate", "recent_5_year_trend_2_in_death_rates"])
```

Now that we have a validated dataset, we can initialize the independent variable `X` and the dependent variable `y` with this pair of code snippets:

```
X = processed_data[["recent_5_year_trend_2_in_death_
rates"]]
y = processed_data["age_adjusted_death_rate"]
```

Next, perform a standard train/test split of the dataset whereby 80% of the data is for training and 20% of the dataset is for testing, as performed by the following code snippet:

```
X_train, X_test, y_train, y_test = train_test_split(X, y,
test_size=0.2, random_state=42)
```

The fourth step involves initializing `linear_reg` as an instance of the class `LinearRegression`, after which we can fit this instance to the data. The final portion of Listing 5.3 performs the model evaluation by invoking the `pre-dict()` method of the trained model `linear_reg`. At this point, we can initialize use as the MSE and the R^2 score, respectively, and then print their values. Now launch the code in Listing 5.3, and you will see the following output:

```
mse: 145.2243931078172 r2: 0.11141880352501743
```

DESCRIBE THE MODEL DIAGNOSTICS

Model diagnostics play a crucial role in identifying potential issues with the regression model and ensuring the assumptions underlying linear regression are met. Here are the primary diagnostics and associated checks for linear regression:

1. linearity
2. independence of errors
3. homoscedasticity
4. normality of residuals
5. multicollinearity
6. outliers and leverage points
7. model specification

The *assumption of linearity* means that the relationship between the independent variables and the dependent variable should be linear.

Diagnostic Tools:
Residual vs. fitted plot: If there is a pattern in this plot (like a curve), it suggests non-linearity. Scatter plots of the observed vs. predicted values.

The assumption of the *independence of errors* means that the residuals (errors) should be independent.

Diagnostic Tools:
The Durbin-Watson test detects the presence of autocorrelation (a relationship between values separated from each other by a given time lag) in the residuals.

The *assumption of homoscedasticity* means that the variance of the residuals should remain constant across all levels of the independent variable(s).

Diagnostic Tools:

• Residual vs. Fitted plot: If there is a funnel shape, it suggests heteroscedasticity (non-constant variance). The Breusch-Pagan or White tests test for heteroscedasticity statistically.

The *assumption of normality of residuals* means that the residuals should be approximately normally distributed.

Diagnostic Tools:

- Histogram or Kernel Density Plot: For visual inspection of normality.
- Q-Q (Quantile-Quantile) plot: If residuals lie on the 45-degree reference line, they are approximately normally distributed.
- Shapiro-Wilk test: A formal test for normality.

The *assumption of multicollinearity* means that the independent variables should not be highly correlated with each other.

Diagnostic Tools:

- VIF: A VIF > 10 indicates high multicollinearity.
- Correlation matrix or heatmap: For a visual inspection of correlations between variables.

Detecting outliers and leverage points is important because outliers can overly influence the model, leading to unreliable estimates.

Diagnostic Tools:

- Standardized residuals vs. Leverage plot: Helps identify points that have high leverage on the regression line.
- Cook's Distance: Measures the effect of deleting a given observation.

A correct model specification means that there is no omitted variable bias, and no inclusion of unnecessary variables.

Diagnostic Tools:

- Added Variable (Partial Regression) plots: Helps in checking if a variable adds information to the model.
- RESET (Regression Specification Error Test): Tests for model misspecification.

For our linear regression model using the death.csv dataset, let's conduct some of these diagnostics, starting with checking for linearity, homoscedasticity, and normality of residuals. Based on the diagnostic plots, we have the following:
Residual vs. Fitted Plot:
Linearity: There does not seem to be any clear pattern in the residuals against the fitted values, indicating that the linearity assumption is not strongly violated.
Homoscedasticity: The spread of residuals appears to be relatively uniform across the range of fitted values, suggesting that the homoscedasticity assumption is not strongly violated.
Histogram of Residuals:

The histogram shows the distribution of residuals. While it is not perfectly normal, the distribution does not have extreme deviations from normality.

Q-Q Plot:

The Q-Q plot shows how well the distribution of residuals aligns with a normal distribution. The residuals largely follow the 45-degree reference line, especially in the center. There are some deviations, especially in the tails, indicating some minor deviations from perfect normality.

To further ensure the model's reliability, additional diagnostics like checking for multicollinearity (more relevant for models with multiple predictors), outliers, and high-leverage points should also be considered. For this simple linear model with only one predictor, multicollinearity is not a concern.

DESCRIBE ADDITIONAL MODEL DIAGNOSTICS

After prompting ChatGPT to delve deeper into additional model diagnostics for our linear regression, ChatGPT responded with the text shown after the following list of items:

- Influence plots
- Cook's distance
- VIF (variance inflation factor)
- Condition Number

Influence plots help identify points that have a high influence on the regression equation.

Cook's distance measures the effect of deleting a given observation. Data points with large Cook's distance might be influential.

VIF: While multicollinearity is not a concern for our simple model with one predictor, it is good to be aware of this diagnostic for future reference when you expand the model.

Condition Number: A high condition number can indicate multicollinearity and potential numerical instability in the regression.

Let's start with the influence plots and Cook's distance. An influence plot provides a visual representation of the observations' influence on the regression. The size of the point is proportional to the Cook's distance, and points further to the right have higher leverage. Most observations are clustered toward the left, indicating low leverage. However, some points, especially those with larger sizes, might be influential.

Cook's Distance:

We have identified 73 observations with a Cook's Distance greater than the threshold "4nn4," where "nn" is the number of observations. These are potentially influential points that might unduly affect the model's fit.

The presence of influential observations suggests a couple of potential courses of action:

- Investigate influential points: Before considering removing any data points, it is essential to understand why they might be influential. Are they errors, or do they represent genuine extreme cases?
- Robust regression: If the dataset has influential points or outliers, consider using robust regression methods that down-weight the influence of outliers.

MORE RECOMMENDATIONS FROM GPT-4

Given the results and diagnostics from the linear regression model using the death.csv dataset, here are some recommendations.

1. *Address the Outlier*
Investigate the potential outlier identified during diagnostics. Determine if it is a data error or an actual extreme value. If it is an error, correct or remove it. If it is genuine, you can decide whether to keep it, based on the context and its potential impact on the model.

2. *Expand the Model*
The current model uses only one predictor. Consider adding other relevant predictors from the dataset to improve the explanatory power of the model. When adding more predictors, watch out for multicollinearity and ensure to run diagnostics again.
Alternative Models:
Given the moderate R^2 value, consider using more complex regression models like polynomial regression, ridge or lasso regression, or even non-linear models.
Ensemble methods like random forests or gradient boosting machines might also be worth exploring.

3. *Feature Engineering*
Explore creating new features or transforming existing ones. For instance, nonlinear transformations (e.g., logarithms) might help if certain relationships are not linear.

4. *Handle Missing Values More Strategically*
We dropped rows with missing values for simplicity. Depending on the nature of the missing data, consider imputation techniques to utilize more of the data.

5. *Model Validation*
Ensure robust validation using techniques like k-fold cross-validation. This provides a more reliable estimate of model performance on unseen data.

6. *Domain Knowledge*

Engage domain experts to understand the features better, validate the model's findings, and potentially identify new relevant features.

7. *Model Interpretability*

If the goal is to understand the factors affecting death rates, consider using models like decision trees or SHAP values with ensemble methods for better interpretability.

8. *Regular Updates*

Depending on how the data evolves over time, the model might need regular updates or fine-tuning. Set up a monitoring mechanism.

9. *Data Quality and Collection*

Ensure the quality of the data. If there are systematic errors or biases in data collection, even the best models can produce misleading results.

In conclusion, while the initial linear regression model provides a foundational understanding, there is ample room for improvement and refinement. The best approach would be iterative: refine the model, validate it, interpret results, and adjust as necessary.

SUMMARY

This chapter was your first full chapter of this book containing material that was generated by GPT-4. You saw how GPT-4 described the preparation process of the dataset as well as the exploratory analysis.

Then you saw the detailed EDA on the death.csv dataset, the model selection process, and the actual linear regression code for this dataset.

In addition, you learned about model diagnostics that GPT-4 generated, followed by a list of recommendations that was generated by GPT-4.

## CHAPTER 6

MACHINE LEARNING CLASSIFIERS WITH GPT-4

This chapter contains Python-based code samples from GPT-4 for numerous machine learning classification algorithms.

The first part of this chapter prompts GPT-4 for information regarding machine learning classifiers. This section also contains a high-level description of scikit-learn that is generated by GPT-4.

The second section in this chapter prompts GPT-4 for descriptions of well-known machine learning algorithms, such as kNN, logistic regression, support vector machine (SVM), decision trees, random forests, and Naïve Bayes. This section also contains Python-based code samples for each of these machine learning algorithms.

This chapter includes GPT-4-generated Python code for machine learning models with various algorithms, including kNN, decision trees, random forests, and SVMs. You will also see some content regarding the same algorithms, all of which is generated by GPT-4. First, however, we begin with a discussion about the algorithms; you can then examine the sections that contain the GPT-4-generated Python code.

As you read the material in this chapter, keep in mind that additional comments are occasionally included in order to improve the legibility of the material that GPT-4 has generated. For instance, after sections of text from GPT-4, you might see the following: "NOTE: This concludes the text that was generated by GPT-4."

MACHINE LEARNING (ACCORDING TO GPT-4)

Machine learning (ML) is a subset of artificial intelligence (AI) that focuses on building systems that can learn from and make decisions based on data.

Rather than being explicitly programmed to perform a task, a machine learning algorithm uses statistical techniques to learn patterns in data and make predictions or decisions based on it. The following is a more in-depth discussion.

Important Concepts

- Learning:
- Machine learning involves training an algorithm to recognize patterns using a dataset. The better the quality and quantity of the data, the better an algorithm can learn.
- Model:
- Once an algorithm has learned from data, it forms a model. This model can then be used to make predictions or decisions without being explicitly programmed to perform the task.
- Prediction:
- This involves using the model to determine an output for a new input. For example, in spam detection, the prediction would be whether a new email is spam or not.

Types of Machine Learning

- Supervised Learning:
- The algorithm is trained on a labeled dataset, meaning each example in the dataset is paired with the correct output. The goal is to learn mapping from inputs to outputs.
- Examples: regression, classification
- Unsupervised Learning:
- The algorithm is trained on an unlabeled dataset, trying to learn the underlying structure of the data.
- Examples: clustering, dimensionality reduction
- Semi-supervised Learning:
- This approach uses both labeled and unlabeled data for training. It is often used when acquiring a fully labeled dataset is expensive or time-consuming.
- Reinforcement Learning:
- The algorithm learns by interacting with an environment and receiving feedback in terms of rewards or penalties.
- Example: training a robot to navigate a maze

Applications of Machine Learning

Machine learning has a vast array of applications, including the following:

- Image and Voice Recognition: This is used in facial recognition or voice-activated assistants.
- Medical Diagnosis: Assisting doctors in diagnosing diseases based on symptoms or medical imagery is an important application.

- Financial Forecasting: ML can be used in predicting stock market trends.
- Recommendation Systems: These systems can suggest products, movies, or music based on user preferences.
- Natural Language Processing: NLP is commonly used in chatbots and translation services.
- Autonomous Vehicles: ML allows cars to navigate without human intervention.

Challenges in Machine Learning

- Overfitting: This occurs when a model learns the training data too "closely" and performs poorly on new, unseen data.
- Underfitting: This occurs when a model is too simplistic to capture the underlying structure of the data.
- Bias and Fairness: Ensuring that ML models do not perpetuate or amplify biases present in the data is critical to the usefulness of the application.
- Explainability: This aspect involves making complex models understandable to humans.
- Data Privacy: Protecting user data and ensuring ethical use of ML should be a high priority.

Machine learning is about developing algorithms that can learn from and make decisions based on data. The rise of big data and improvements in computational power have led to significant advancements in ML, making it a critical component of modern technological solutions.

WHAT IS SCIKIT-LEARN?

Scikit-learn, often referred to simply as "sklearn," is a popular open-source machine learning library in Python. It provides simple and efficient tools for data analysis and modeling, making it a favorite choice for both beginners and experts in the field of machine learning.

Features and Capabilities

1. Algorithms: Scikit-learn includes a wide range of supervised and unsupervised learning algorithms, such as:

   - classification: e.g., SVMs, random forests, Naïve Bayes
   - regression: e.g., linear regression, ridge regression, decision trees
   - clustering: e.g., k-means, hierarchical clustering, DBSCAN
   - dimensionality reduction: e.g., PCA (Principal Component Analysis), t-SNE

2. Model Selection and Evaluation: Provides tools to help in splitting datasets, grid search, cross-validation, and various metrics to evaluate the performance of machine learning models

3. Data Preprocessing: Offers functions for preprocessing data, like normalization, standardization, and encoding categorical variables

4. Feature Extraction: Contains utilities for extracting features from images and text (e.g., using the bag-of-words approach)

5. Pipeline: Provides a tool for sequentially applying a list of transforms and a final estimator. Intermediate steps of the pipeline must be transformers (e.g., a scaler or PCA), and the last estimator can be any object (e.g., classifier, regressor)

6. Compatibility: Designed to interoperate with the Python numerical and scientific libraries, NumPy and SciPy

Advantages

- Simplicity: Scikit-learn's API is designed to be consistent and easy to use.
- Comprehensive Documentation: Detailed documentation with examples, making it accessible for beginners
- Performance: Efficient implementations of popular algorithms
- Community Support: Being open-source and popular means a large community of users and contributors, leading to regular updates and quick bug fixes.

Limitations

1. Neural Networks: While scikit-learn does have basic tools for neural networks, it is not specialized for deep learning. Libraries like TensorFlow, Keras, or PyTorch are more suited for deep learning tasks.

2. Scalability: For very large datasets or distributed computing, tools like Apache Spark's MLlib or Dask might be more appropriate.

Typical Usage

Scikit-learn is typically used in traditional machine learning tasks where data fits in memory and deep learning is not required. It is particularly well-suited for prototyping and building end-to-end machine learning pipelines.

In summary, scikit-learn is a versatile and comprehensive machine learning library in Python, and its combination of simplicity and power makes it a popular choice for many data scientists and researchers.

WHAT IS THE KNN ALGORITHM?

The k-nearest neighbors (kNN) algorithm is a simple, intuitive, and non-parametric machine learning algorithm used for both classification and regression tasks. Here is a how it works.

Basic Concept

Given a new, unseen observation, kNN searches the training set for the k training examples that are closest to the observation and returns the output value (class or numeric value) that has the highest representation among those k neighbors.

Steps

1. Choose the number k: Determine the number of neighbors you want to consider. Typically, k is an odd number to prevent tie situations (in case of classification).
2. Distance Metric: Decide on a distance metric to measure the "closeness" of instances. The most common metric is the Euclidean distance, but others like Manhattan, Minkowski, and Hamming distance can also be used depending on the nature of the data.
3. Search: For a new data point, compute the distance to all points in the training set, and identify the k-nearest points.
4. Aggregate

   - For classification: Return the class that appears most frequently among the k neighbors
   - For regression: Return the average (or median) of the output values of the k neighbors

Advantages

- Simple and Intuitive: No assumptions about the data's distribution or the decision boundary
- Versatile: Works for both classification and regression
- Non-parametric: No explicit training phase, and it can handle datasets where the decision boundary is very irregular.

Disadvantages

- Computationally Intensive: It needs to compute the distance to all training samples for each prediction, which can be slow for large datasets.
- Memory Usage: It stores the entire dataset, so memory consumption can be high.

- Sensitive to irrelevant features: The distance metric can be heavily influenced by features that are not important for classification or regression.
- Sensitive to the scale of data: Features with a larger scale can dominate the distance metric, so it is often necessary to normalize or standardize data.

Use Cases

kNN is particularly useful when the following is true:

- The data is labeled.
- The dataset is not too large (to avoid computational inefficiency).
- The decision boundary is very irregular.

Despite its simplicity, kNN can be surprisingly effective, especially when the underlying decision boundary is complex and not easily captured by other linear models. In practice, due to its computational and memory demands, kNN is often used more as a baseline or in smaller datasets.

SELECTING THE VALUE OF K IN THE KNN ALGORITHM

Determining the optimal value of k in the k-nearest neighbors (kNN) algorithm is crucial because this value can significantly influence the model's performance. In particular, the value of k can affect both the bias and variance of the predictions. Here are some points to consider for selecting the best value for k in the kNN algorithm:

- cross-validation
- bias-variance tradeoff
- distance metric
- square root rule
- domain knowledge
- even versus odd k
- computational efficiency
- diversity in the dataset

Cross-Validation

The most common method of determining the optimal k is through cross-validation, especially k-fold cross-validation. First, split the dataset into training and validation sets. For each potential value of k, train the kNN algorithm on the training set and validate on the validation set. Measure the accuracy (or other relevant metrics) for each k on the validation set. Choose the k that yields the best performance on the validation set.

Bias-Variance Tradeoff

A small value of k (e.g., k=1) means that noise in the data will have a higher influence on the result, leading to a model with high variance but low bias. A large k value has a smoothing effect that can reduce variance but increase bias. This might make the algorithm more resistant to outliers but could yield less distinct boundaries between classes.

Distance Metric

The choice of distance metric (e.g., Euclidean, Manhattan, and Minkowski) can influence the optimal k. Experiment with different distance metrics while optimizing k.

Square Root Rule

A commonly suggested heuristic, especially when starting the search for an optimal k, is to set k to the square root of the number of data points in the training dataset. This is not a strict rule but can serve as a starting point.

Domain Knowledge

Sometimes, domain knowledge or the specific context of the problem can guide the choice of k. For example, in a problem where you know pairs or triplets of data points are often relevant together, k=2k=2 or k=3k=3 might be a logical starting point.

Even versus Odd k

It is often recommended to choose an odd number for k to avoid ties, i.e., two classes having the same number of nearest neighbors. However, note that many kNN implementations have tie-breaking mechanisms.

Computational Efficiency

As k increases, the computation might become more intensive (since you are considering more neighbors). However, if k is too small, the model might be overly sensitive to noise in the data.

Diversity in the Dataset

If the dataset has many overlapping classes, a smaller k might be more appropriate. If the classes are more distinct, a larger k can work well.

In practice, try a range of values for k and validate the performance for each value. Visualization tools, such as plots showing validation accuracy against different k values, can be helpful in making a decision.

THE ELBOW METHOD FOR THE KNN ALGORITHM

If you are familiar with the k-means clustering algorithm, you undoubtedly know about the "elbow method" for determining the optimal value for k. The natural issue to consider is whether this method can be used for determining the optimal value for k in the kNN algorithm.

The elbow method is primarily associated with the k-means clustering algorithm, where it is used to determine the optimal number of clusters. In the context of k-means , the "elbow" is a point in a plot of the within-cluster sum of squares (WCSS) against the number of clusters. This point represents a balance between precision (more clusters) and computational efficiency (fewer clusters).

For kNN, the primary goal is classification (or regression), not clustering. The parameter k in kNN represents the number of neighbors to consider when making a prediction, not the number of clusters in the data.

However, the concept of using a plot to identify a point of diminishing returns (an "elbow") can be applied to kNN in the context of hyperparameter tuning.

Validation Error

You can plot the validation error (or accuracy) for a range of k values. As k increases, the model may initially become more accurate as it reduces variance. However, after a certain point, increasing k might introduce more bias, leading to increased error or decreased accuracy.

The "elbow" in this context would be the point at which increasing k no longer results in significant improvements in validation error (or accuracy).

Distance Consideration

The idea of diminishing returns can also be applied to the distance metric in kNN. For instance, one could examine the average or median distances to the kth nearest neighbor for various k values to understand the data's density and distribution.

While the concept of an "elbow" can be applied in the context of kNN hyperparameter tuning, it is essential to differentiate between the purpose of the elbow method in k-means (determining cluster count) versus its potential application in kNN (tuning the neighbor count for optimal prediction).

A MACHINE LEARNING MODEL WITH THE KNN ALGORITHM

This section contains an example of GPT-4 generating a machine learning model using the kNN algorithm and the death.csv dataset. The first half of this section contains the explanation of the steps that GPT-4 performed, along with "markers" that reference the appropriate section in the code, followed by Listing 6.1 that contains the Python-based code that GPT-4 generated.

The first half starts with the following prompt that was given to GPT-4 in order to generate Python code for a machine learning model that uses the kNN algorithm:

"Please generate a machine learning model using the kNN algorithm and the death.csv dataset."

[NOTE: The following text was generated by GPT-4, and some formatting has been applied to improve readability]

The response from GPT-4 is shown below.

Before we proceed with creating a machine learning model using the kNN (k-Nearest Neighbors) algorithm, I'll outline the steps we will follow:

- Load the Data: Read the death.csv dataset.
- Data Preprocessing: Clean and preprocess the dataset to make it suitable for modeling.
- Feature Selection: Choose relevant features that will be used to train the model.
- Train-Test Split: Split the dataset into a training set and a testing set.
- Model Training: Use the kNN algorithm to train the model on the training set.
- Model Testing: Evaluate the model's performance on the testing set.
- Performance Metrics: Calculate metrics like accuracy to understand how well the model is performing.

Let's start by loading the dataset and taking a look at its first few rows.

Now that we have the dataset loaded, let's proceed with the data preprocessing steps:

- Handling Missing Values: We need to ensure there are no missing values or handle them if they exist.
- Encoding Categorical Features: If there are any categorical features, we need to encode them into numerical values for the kNN algorithm.
- Feature Selection: We'll select relevant features for the modeling process.
- Scaling: kNN is sensitive to feature scaling, so it is important to normalize or standardize the dataset.

Let's first handle missing values and check the data types of each column. There are no missing values in the dataset, which is good news. However, upon inspection of the data types, we can see that several columns that should be numeric (like *age_adjusted_death_rate*, *average_deaths_per_year*, etc.) are represented as objects. This suggests that there might be non-numeric characters or symbols in these columns.

To proceed:

I will convert the columns to numeric data types, handling any non-numeric characters.

- Encode categorical features.
- Select relevant features for modeling.
- Normalize the dataset to prepare for the kNN algorithm.

The columns have been successfully converted to appropriate numeric data types.

Next, we need to:

- Encode Categorical Features: Convert categorical features into numerical values.
- Feature Selection: Decide which features to use for modeling.
- Scaling: Normalize the dataset.

For simplicity, let's use the numeric features directly and encode the categorical feature *recent_trend_2* using one-hot encoding. We'll then split the data into training and test sets, scale the features, and proceed with the kNN modeling.

Let's start with encoding the categorical feature and splitting the data.

The data has been successfully preprocessed and split into training and test sets. We now have 2512 samples in the training set and 629 samples in the test set, with 12 features in each.

Next, we will proceed to:

- Model Training: Train a kNN classifier on the training data.
- Model Testing: Predict the target variable on the test data using the trained kNN classifier.
- Performance Metrics: Evaluate the model's performance using accuracy.

Let's start by training the kNN classifier.

It seems we have NaN values in the dataset which are causing issues during the training process. This likely resulted from the conversion of non-numeric characters to NaN.

To handle this, I'll:

- Impute the missing values in the training and test datasets.
- Retrain the kNN classifier.

The kNN classifier achieved an accuracy of approximately 98.09% on the test dataset. This is a high accuracy, indicating that the model was able to predict the target variable *met_objective_of_45_5_1* with a high degree of correctness for the given dataset.

However, it is essential to remember that accuracy is just one metric. Depending on the specific application or problem, other metrics (like precision, recall, or F1-score) might be more relevant. Also, the choice of k in kNN can significantly influence the results. We used the default value of k=5, but a different value might yield different results.

The preceding narrative (starting from the beginning of this section) describes the process that GPT-4 will follow in order to train a machine learning model using the kNN algorithm, along with the death.csv dataset.

The actual Python code that GPT-4 generated is displayed in Listing 6.1, which contains the code for knn_gpt4.py. Note that this filename was manually chosen (not by GPT-4 itself) to reflect the contents of the Python code for this task.

LISTING 6.1: knn_gpt4.py

```python
import pandas as pd

# STEP #1:
# Load the dataset
death_data = pd.read_csv('death.csv')

# Display the first few rows of the dataset
death_data.head()

# STEP #2:
# Checking for missing values
missing_values = death_data.isnull().sum()

# Checking data types
data_types = death_data.dtypes

missing_values, data_types
"""
RESULT

(county                                                0
 fips                                                  0
 met_objective_of_45_5_1                               0
 age_adjusted_death_rate                               0
 lower_95_confidence_interval_for_death_rate           0
 upper_95_confidence_interval_for_death_rate           0
 average_deaths_per_year                               0
 recent_trend_2                                        0
 recent_5_year_trend_2_in_death_rates                  0
 lower_95_confidence_interval_for_trend                0
 upper_95_confidence_interval_for_trend                0
 dtype: int64,
 county                                           object
 fips                                              int64
 met_objective_of_45_5_1                          object
 age_adjusted_death_rate                          object
 lower_95_confidence_interval_for_death_rate      object
 upper_95_confidence_interval_for_death_rate      object
 average_deaths_per_year                          object
 recent_trend_2                                   object
 recent_5_year_trend_2_in_death_rates             object
 lower_95_confidence_interval_for_trend           object
 upper_95_confidence_interval_for_trend           object
 dtype: object)
"""
```

```
# STEP #3:
# Convert columns with numeric information to the
appropriate data type
cols_to_convert = [
    'age_adjusted_death_rate',
    'lower_95_confidence_interval_for_death_rate',
    'upper_95_confidence_interval_for_death_rate',
    'average_deaths_per_year',
    'recent_5_year_trend_2_in_death_rates',
    'lower_95_confidence_interval_for_trend',
    'upper_95_confidence_interval_for_trend'
]

# Replacing non-numeric characters and converting to float
for col in cols_to_convert:
    death_data[col] = death_data[col].str.replace(',', '',
regex=True).str.replace('\*\*', 'NaN', regex=True)
    death_data[col] = pd.to_numeric(death_data[col],
errors='coerce')

# Checking the data types again
death_data.dtypes
"""
RESULT

county                                          object
fips                                             int64
met_objective_of_45_5_1                         object
age_adjusted_death_rate                        float64
lower_95_confidence_interval_for_death_rate    float64
upper_95_confidence_interval_for_death_rate    float64
average_deaths_per_year                        float64
recent_trend_2                                  object
recent_5_year_trend_2_in_death_rates           float64
lower_95_confidence_interval_for_trend         float64
upper_95_confidence_interval_for_trend         float64
dtype: object
"""

# STEP #4:
from sklearn.model_selection import train_test_split
from sklearn.preprocessing import StandardScaler,
OneHotEncoder

# One-hot encoding of the 'recent_trend_2' feature
encoded_features = pd.get_dummies(death_data['recent_
trend_2'], prefix='recent_trend')
death_data = pd.concat([death_data, encoded_features],
axis=1)
death_data.drop('recent_trend_2', axis=1, inplace=True)

# Drop non-numeric and target columns
X = death_data.drop(columns=['county', 'fips', 'met_
objective_of_45_5_1'])
```

```
# Target variable
y = death_data['met_objective_of_45_5_1']

# Splitting the dataset into training and test sets (80%
train, 20% test)
X_train, X_test, y_train, y_test = train_test_split(X, y,
test_size=0.2, random_state=42)

# Scaling the features
scaler = StandardScaler()
X_train_scaled = scaler.fit_transform(X_train)
X_test_scaled = scaler.transform(X_test)

X_train_scaled.shape, X_test_scaled.shape
"""
RESULT
((2512, 12), (629, 12))
"""


# STEP #5:
from sklearn.impute import SimpleImputer

# Imputing missing values using the mean
imputer = SimpleImputer(strategy='mean')
X_train_scaled_imputed = imputer.fit_transform(X_train_
scaled)
X_test_scaled_imputed = imputer.transform(X_test_scaled)

from sklearn.neighbors import KNeighborsClassifier
from sklearn.metrics import accuracy_score

# Initializing the kNN classifier with k=5 (default value)
knn_classifier = KNeighborsClassifier()

# Training the kNN classifier
knn_classifier.fit(X_train_scaled_imputed, y_train)

# Predicting on the test set
y_pred = knn_classifier.predict(X_test_scaled_imputed)

# Calculating accuracy
accuracy = accuracy_score(y_test, y_pred)
accuracy

# STEP #6:
# Training the kNN classifier again
knn_classifier.fit(X_train_scaled_imputed, y_train)

# Predicting on the test set
y_pred = knn_classifier.predict(X_test_scaled_imputed)

# Calculating accuracy
accuracy = accuracy_score(y_test, y_pred)
```

```
print("=> accuracy: ", accuracy)
"""
RESULT
0.9809220985691574
"""
```

The description of the code in Listing 6.1 (which precedes the code listing) illustrates how GPT-4 performs a machine learning task with the kNN algorithm. You can make a comparison between GPT-4-generated Python code in Listing 6.1 and handwritten Python code for solving a machine learning task. Launch the code in Listing 6.1, and you will see the following output:

```
=> accuracy:   0.9809220985691574
```

A MACHINE LEARNING MODEL WITH THE DECISION TREE ALGORITHM

This section contains an example of GPT-4 generating a machine learning model using the kNN algorithm and the death.csv dataset. The first half of this section contains the explanation of the steps that GPT-4 performed, along with "markers" that reference the appropriate section in the code, followed by Listing 6.2 that contains the Python-based code that GPT-4 generated.

The following prompt was supplied to GPT-4 to generate the Python code for a model using a decision tree, followed by a description of the code:

"Please generate a machine learning model using the decision tree algorithm and the death.csv dataset."

The response from ChatGPT is as follows:

I'll outline the steps we will follow to generate a machine learning model using the decision tree algorithm:

- Load the Data: We have already loaded the death.csv dataset earlier.
- Data Preprocessing: We have mostly preprocessed the dataset earlier. We'll continue using the same preprocessed data.
- Model Training: Use the decision tree algorithm to train the model on the training set.
- Model Testing: Evaluate the model's performance on the test set.
- Performance Metrics: Calculate metrics like accuracy to understand how well the model is performing.

[NOTE: GPT-4 generated the following statements due to internal processing errors.]

Let's start by training a decision tree classifier.

I apologize for the inconvenience, but it seems there was a technical issue.

Let's retrain the decision tree classifier and compute its accuracy on the test set.

I apologize for the oversight. I need to re-import the necessary libraries and preprocess the data again since the code execution state was reset.

I'll quickly go through the steps to preprocess the data and then train the decision tree classifier.

I apologize for the inconvenience. Due to the reset state, the dataset needs to be re-uploaded.

Could you kindly re-upload the death.csv dataset so we can proceed with the decision tree algorithm modeling?

Author: "Please proceed."

The response from ChatGPT is as follows:

Thank you for re-uploading the dataset. Let's proceed with preprocessing the data and then training the decision tree classifier.

[NOTE: GPT-4 encountered a sequence of errors as shown below.]

I apologize for the oversight. The error indicates that there are still non-numeric characters in the dataset which we missed in our earlier preprocessing steps.

Let's correct the data preprocessing by handling non-numeric characters and then train the decision tree classifier again.

My apologies for the oversight. I forgot to define the *cols_to_convert* list of columns to process. Let me correct that and proceed with the preprocessing and training of the decision tree classifier.

I'm sorry for the repeated oversight. It seems I made an error in preprocessing the dataset. I'll correct it and ensure the dataset is cleaned properly before training the decision tree classifier.

Let's handle the non-numeric characters and proceed with the model training.

I apologize for the repeated mistakes. The data preprocessing step seems to still encounter string values that are not being appropriately handled.

To ensure this is resolved, I'll take a different approach:

I'll investigate the unique values in each column to identify any non-numeric characters. I'll ensure these non-numeric characters are handled appropriately. Then, I'll proceed with the decision tree classifier training.

It appears there are no columns with non-numeric characters left. This is puzzling because the error suggests otherwise.

I'll take a different approach: I will identify and drop any rows with non-numeric characters in our feature set, then proceed with the decision tree classifier training.

The decision tree classifier achieved an accuracy of 100% on the test dataset. This indicates that the model was able to perfectly predict the target variable *met_objective_of_45_5_1* for the given test dataset.

However, it is crucial to approach such results with caution. A 100% accuracy might indicate that the model has overfitted to the training data, especially with a model like decision trees, which are prone to overfitting.

One way to validate this would be to perform cross-validation or check the model's performance on a different, unseen dataset.

[NOTE: This concludes the text that was generated by GPT-4.]

Listing 6.2 displays the content of `decision_tree_gpt4.py` that illustrates how to create a machine learning model using the decision tree algorithm and the death.csv dataset.

LISTING 6.2: decision_tree_gpt4.py

```python
import pandas as pd

# Load the dataset
death_data = pd.read_csv('death.csv')

# Display the first few rows of the dataset
death_data.head()

# Checking for missing values
missing_values = death_data.isnull().sum()

# Checking data types
data_types = death_data.dtypes

missing_values, data_types
"""
RESULT

(county                                                    0
 fips                                                      0
 met_objective_of_45_5_1                                   0
 age_adjusted_death_rate                                   0
 lower_95_confidence_interval_for_death_rate               0
 upper_95_confidence_interval_for_death_rate               0
 average_deaths_per_year                                   0
 recent_trend_2                                            0
 recent_5_year_trend_2_in_death_rates                      0
 lower_95_confidence_interval_for_trend                    0
 upper_95_confidence_interval_for_trend                    0
 dtype: int64,
 county                                               object
 fips                                                  int64
 met_objective_of_45_5_1                              object
 age_adjusted_death_rate                              object
 lower_95_confidence_interval_for_death_rate          object
 upper_95_confidence_interval_for_death_rate          object
 average_deaths_per_year                              object
 recent_trend_2                                       object
 recent_5_year_trend_2_in_death_rates                 object
 lower_95_confidence_interval_for_trend               object
 upper_95_confidence_interval_for_trend               object
 dtype: object)
"""
```

```
# Convert columns with numeric information to the
appropriate data type
cols_to_convert = [
    'age_adjusted_death_rate',
    'lower_95_confidence_interval_for_death_rate',
    'upper_95_confidence_interval_for_death_rate',
    'average_deaths_per_year',
    'recent_5_year_trend_2_in_death_rates',
    'lower_95_confidence_interval_for_trend',
    'upper_95_confidence_interval_for_trend'
]

# Replacing non-numeric characters and converting to float
for col in cols_to_convert:
    death_data[col] = death_data[col].str.replace(',', '',
regex=True).str.replace('\*\*', 'NaN', regex=True)
    death_data[col] = pd.to_numeric(death_data[col],
errors='coerce')

# Checking the data types again
death_data.dtypes
"""
RESULT

county                                          object
fips                                             int64
met_objective_of_45_5_1                         object
age_adjusted_death_rate                        float64
lower_95_confidence_interval_for_death_rate    float64
upper_95_confidence_interval_for_death_rate    float64
average_deaths_per_year                        float64
recent_trend_2                                  object
recent_5_year_trend_2_in_death_rates           float64
lower_95_confidence_interval_for_trend         float64
upper_95_confidence_interval_for_trend         float64
dtype: object
"""

from sklearn.model_selection import train_test_split
from sklearn.preprocessing import StandardScaler,
OneHotEncoder

# One-hot encoding of the 'recent_trend_2' feature
encoded_features = pd.get_dummies(death_data['recent_
trend_2'], prefix='recent_trend')
death_data = pd.concat([death_data, encoded_features],
axis=1)
death_data.drop('recent_trend_2', axis=1, inplace=True)

# Drop non-numeric and target columns
X = death_data.drop(columns=['county', 'fips', 'met_
objective_of_45_5_1'])
```

```
# Target variable
y = death_data['met_objective_of_45_5_1']

# Splitting the dataset into training and test sets (80%
train, 20% test)
X_train, X_test, y_train, y_test = train_test_split(X, y,
test_size=0.2, random_state=42)

# Scaling the features
scaler = StandardScaler()
X_train_scaled = scaler.fit_transform(X_train)
X_test_scaled = scaler.transform(X_test)


X_train_scaled.shape, X_test_scaled.shape

from sklearn.impute import SimpleImputer

# Imputing missing values using the mean
imputer = SimpleImputer(strategy='mean')
X_train_scaled_imputed = imputer.fit_transform(X_train_
scaled)
X_test_scaled_imputed = imputer.transform(X_test_scaled)
```

*** NEW CODE BLOCK STARTS HERE ***

```
from sklearn.tree import DecisionTreeClassifier
from sklearn.metrics import accuracy_score

# Initializing the Decision Tree classifier
dt_classifier = DecisionTreeClassifier(random_state=42)

# Training the Decision Tree classifier
dt_classifier.fit(X_train_scaled_imputed, y_train)

# Predicting on the test set
y_pred_dt = dt_classifier.predict(X_test_scaled_imputed)

# Calculating accuracy for the Decision Tree classifier
accuracy_dt = accuracy_score(y_test, y_pred_dt)
print("accuracy_dt: ", accuracy_dt)
```

The description of the code in Listing 6.2 (which precedes the code listing) illustrates how GPT-4 performs a machine learning task using a decision tree classifier. The code in Listing 6.2 enables you to make a comparison between GPT-4-generated Python code and handwritten Python code for creating a machine learning model using a decision tree algorithm. Launch the code in Listing 6.2, and you will see the following output:

```
accuracy_dt: 1.0
```

A MACHINE LEARNING MODEL WITH THE RANDOM FOREST ALGORITHM

This section contains an example of GPT-4 generating a machine learning model using the random forest algorithm and the death.csv dataset. The first half of this section contains the explanation of the steps that GPT-4 performed, along with "markers" that reference the appropriate section in the code, followed by Listing 6.3 that contains the Python-based code that GPT-4 generated.

The following prompt was supplied to GPT-4 in order to generate the Python code for a model using a random forest algorithm:

"Please generate a machine learning model using a Random Forest algorithm and the death.csv dataset."

The response from ChatGPT is as follows:

The dataset contains various columns related to death rates in different counties in the United States. Here are the key columns:

county: Name of the county.
fips: FIPS code for the county.
met_objective_of_45_5_1: Indicates if the county met a certain objective (not specified in the header).
age_adjusted_death_rate: Age-adjusted death rate in the county.
lower_95_confidence_interval_for_death_rate: Lower bound of the 95% confidence interval for the death rate.
upper_95_confidence_interval_for_death_rate: Upper bound of the 95% confidence interval for the death rate.
average_deaths_per_year: Average number of deaths per year in the county.
recent_trend_2: Recent trend in death rate.
recent_5_year_trend_2_in_death_rates: Recent 5-year trend in death rates.
lower_95_confidence_interval_for_trend: Lower bound of the 95% confidence interval for the trend.
upper_95_confidence_interval_for_trend: Upper bound of the 95% confidence interval for the trend.

To build a machine learning model using a random forest algorithm, we need to identify the target variable and the features. The target variable could be something like "*age_adjusted_death_rate*" or "*average_deaths_per_year*," and the features would be other columns in the dataset.

Let's proceed to preprocess the data and then build the random forest model. Could you specify which variable you would like to predict, and if there are any specific columns you would like to use or exclude as features?

Author: "Please predict the column variable met_objective_of_45_5_1."

The response from ChatGPT is as follows:

The random forest model was trained to predict the "*met_objective_of_45_5_1*" variable in your dataset. Here are the results of the model evaluation:

- Accuracy: The model achieved an accuracy of approximately 62.8%. This means that it correctly predicted whether the county met the objective in about 62.8% of the cases in the test set.
- Classification Report: The report provides a detailed analysis of the model's performance:
- Precision: It measures the accuracy of positive predictions. For example, when the model predicts that a county met the objective, it is correct about 78% of the time for one of the classes.
- Recall: It measures how many of the actual positive cases the model captures through labeling it as positive. For instance, for one of the classes, the model correctly identifies 74% of all counties that actually met the objective.
- F1-Score: This is a weighted average of precision and recall. For the best-performing class, the F1-score is 0.76, indicating a relatively balanced performance between precision and recall.
- Support: This shows the number of actual occurrences of each class in the specified dataset. For instance, there were 407 instances of one of the classes in the test dataset.

These results suggest that while the model performs reasonably well in predicting the *"met_objective_of_45_5_1"* variable, there is room for improvement, particularly in the classes with lower precision and recall scores. Fine-tuning the model, selecting different features, or even using a different modeling approach could potentially improve performance.

Author to ChatGPT: "Please generate the Python code for a machine learning model using a random forest algorithm and the death.csv dataset."

The response from ChatGPT is as follows:

The random forest model was trained to predict the *"met_objective_of_45_5_1"* variable in your dataset. Here are the results of the model evaluation:

- Accuracy: The model achieved an accuracy of approximately 62.8%. This means that it correctly predicted whether the county met the objective in about 62.8% of the cases in the test set.
- Classification Report: The report provides a detailed analysis of the model's performance:
- Precision: It measures the accuracy of positive predictions. For example, when the model predicts that a county met the objective, it is correct about 78% of the time for one of the classes.
- Recall: It measures how many of the actual positive cases the model captures through labeling it as positive. For instance, for one of the classes, the model correctly identifies 74% of all counties that actually met the objective.

- F1-Score: This is a weighted average of precision and recall. For the best-performing class, the F1-score is 0.76, indicating a relatively balanced performance between precision and recall.
- Support: This shows the number of actual occurrences of each class in the specified dataset. For instance, there were 407 instances of one of the classes in the test dataset.

These results suggest that while the model performs reasonably well in predicting the *"met_objective_of_45_5_1"* variable, there is room for improvement, particularly in the classes with lower precision and recall scores. Fine-tuning the model, selecting different features, or even using a different modeling approach could potentially improve performance.

Author: "Please generate the Python code for a machine learning model using a random forest algorithm and the death.csv dataset."

The response from ChatGPT is as follows:

Certainly! Below is the Python code for creating a machine learning model using the random forest algorithm with the death.csv dataset. This code includes steps for data preprocessing, splitting the dataset into training and testing sets, building the random forest model, and evaluating its performance.

Listing 6.3 displays the content of `random_forest_gpt4.py` that illustrates how to create a machine learning model using a random forest algorithm and the `death.csv` dataset.

LISTING 6.3: *random_forest_gpt4.py*

```
import pandas as pd
from sklearn.model_selection import train_test_split
from sklearn.ensemble import RandomForestClassifier
from sklearn.metrics import classification_report, accuracy_
score
from sklearn.preprocessing import LabelEncoder
import numpy as np

# Load the dataset
data = pd.read_csv('/path/to/death.csv')  # Replace with
the correct file path

# Preprocessing
# Encoding the target variable
le = LabelEncoder()
data['met_objective_of_45_5_1_encoded'] = le.fit_
transform(data['met_objective_of_45_5_1'])

# Selecting features - excluding target variable and non-
numeric columns
features = data.select_dtypes(include=[np.number])

# Dropping any remaining missing values
```

```
features = features.dropna()

# Defining target and feature variables
X = features.drop('met_objective_of_45_5_1_encoded',
axis=1)
y = features['met_objective_of_45_5_1_encoded']

# Splitting the dataset into training and testing sets
X_train, X_test, y_train, y_test = train_test_split(X, y,
test_size=0.2, random_state=42)

# Building the Random Forest model
rf_classifier = RandomForestClassifier(random_state=42)
rf_classifier.fit(X_train, y_train)

# Predicting and evaluating the model
y_pred = rf_classifier.predict(X_test)
accuracy = accuracy_score(y_test, y_pred)
report = classification_report(y_test, y_pred)

# Outputting the results
print("Accuracy:", accuracy)
print("Classification Report:\n", report)
```

Remember to replace '/path/to/death.csv' with the actual
path of your death.csv file. This code assumes that the
target variable you want to predict is 'met_objective_
of_45_5_1', and it uses all numeric columns in the dataset
as features, excluding any columns with non-numeric data.
Adjustments might be necessary based on the specific
requirements of your analysis.
ChatGPT can make mistakes. Consider checking important
information.

Author: "Please explain the Python code that you just generated."

The response from ChatGPT is as follows:
Certainly, I'll walk you through the Python code step by step:

1. **Import Libraries**

   - pandas is used for data manipulation and analysis.
   - sklearn.model_selection's train_test_split function is used to split the
     dataset into training and testing sets.
   - sklearn.ensemble's RandomForestClassifier is the random forest model
     for classification tasks.
   - sklearn.metrics includes functions like classification_report and accu-
     racy_score for evaluating the model's performance.
   - sklearn.preprocessing.LabelEncoder is used to convert categorical text
     data into a model-understandable numerical format.
   - numpy is used for numerical operations.

2. **Load the Dataset**

   - The read_csv function from pandas is used to read the death.csv file. You need to replace "/path/to/death.csv " with the actual path to your dataset.

3. **Preprocessing**

   - The LabelEncoder is used to encode the target variable "*met_objective_of_45_5_1*" into numerical format since random forest in sklearn requires numerical input.
   - The dataset is then filtered to include only numeric columns since the model cannot process non-numeric data directly.

4. **Handling Missing Values**

   - Any remaining missing values in the dataset are dropped to ensure the model receives clean data.

5. **Defining Target and Feature Variables**

   - X (features) is assigned all columns except the target variable ("*met_objective_of_45_5_1_encoded*").
   - y (target) is the encoded as the "*met_objective_of_45_5_1*" column.

6. **Splitting the Dataset**

   - The dataset is split into training (80%) and testing (20%) sets using train_test_split. The random_state is set for reproducibility of results.

7. **Building the Random Forest Model**

   - A RandomForestClassifier object is created and trained on the training data (X_train and y_train).

8. **Predicting and Evaluating the Model**

   - The model is used to make predictions on the test set (X_test).
   - The predictions are then evaluated using accuracy_score (to measure the overall accuracy) and classification_report (to see precision, recall, f1-score, and support for each class).

9. **Outputting the Results**

   - Finally, the accuracy and classification report are printed out to see how well the model performed.

This code provides a basic framework for a machine learning task using a random forest classifier. Depending on the specifics of your dataset and the problem at hand, additional steps like more sophisticated data cleaning, feature engineering, or hyperparameter tuning of the model might be necessary for optimal results.

Launch the code in Listing 6.3, and you will see the following output:

```
Accuracy: 0.6279809220985691
Classification Report:
              precision    recall  f1-score   support

           0       0.34      0.34      0.34        65
           1       0.78      0.74      0.76       407
           2       0.40      0.45      0.42       157

    accuracy                           0.63       629
   macro avg       0.51      0.51      0.51       629
weighted avg       0.64      0.63      0.63       629
```

A MACHINE LEARNING MODEL WITH THE SVM ALGORITHM

This section contains an example of GPT-4 generating a machine learning model using the SVM algorithm and the death.csv dataset. The first half of this section contains the explanation of the steps that GPT-4 performed, along with "markers" that reference the appropriate section in the code, followed by Listing 6.4 that contains the Python-based code that GPT-4 generated.

The following prompt was supplied to GPT-4 in order to generate the Python code for a model using an SVM algorithm: "Please generate the Python code for a machine learning model using an SVM algorithm and the death.csv dataset, and also provide an explanation of the Python code."

The response from ChatGPT is as follows:

Certainly! Below is the Python code for creating a machine learning model using the SVM algorithm with the death.csv dataset. After the code, I'll provide an explanation.

Listing 6.4 displays the content of svm_gpt4.py that illustrates how to create a machine learning model using an SVM algorithm and the death.csv dataset.

LISTING 6.4: svm_gpt4.py

```python
import pandas as pd
from sklearn.model_selection import train_test_split
from sklearn.svm import SVC
from sklearn.metrics import classification_report, accuracy_
score
from sklearn.preprocessing import LabelEncoder,
StandardScaler
import numpy as np
```

```
# Load the dataset
data = pd.read_csv('death.csv')  # Replace with the correct
file path

# Preprocessing
# Encoding the target variable
le = LabelEncoder()
data['met_objective_of_45_5_1_encoded'] = le.fit_
transform(data['met_objective_of_45_5_1'])

# Selecting features - excluding target variable and non-
numeric columns
features = data.select_dtypes(include=[np.number])

# Dropping any remaining missing values
features = features.dropna()

# Defining target and feature variables
X = features.drop('met_objective_of_45_5_1_encoded',
axis=1)
y = features['met_objective_of_45_5_1_encoded']

# Scaling the features (important for SVM)
scaler = StandardScaler()
X_scaled = scaler.fit_transform(X)

# Splitting the dataset into training and testing sets
X_train, X_test, y_train, y_test = train_test_split(X_
scaled, y, test_size=0.2, random_state=42)

# Building the SVM model
svm_classifier = SVC(random_state=42)
svm_classifier.fit(X_train, y_train)

# Predicting and evaluating the model
y_pred = svm_classifier.predict(X_test)
accuracy = accuracy_score(y_test, y_pred)
report = classification_report(y_test, y_pred)

# Outputting the results
print("Accuracy:", accuracy)
print("Classification Report:\n", report)
```

Explanation of the Code

1. Import Libraries:
2. The same libraries are used as in the random forest model, with the addition of sklearn.svm.SVC, which is the SVM classifier, and sklearn.preprocessing.StandardScaler for feature scaling.
3. Load the Dataset:

4. The dataset is loaded from a CSV file. You need to replace "/path/to/death.csv" with the actual file path.

5. Preprocessing:

6. The target variable (*"met_objective_of_45_5_1"*) is encoded into a numerical format using LabelEncoder.

7. Non-numeric columns are excluded, and any missing values are dropped.

8. Feature Scaling:

9. StandardScaler is applied to the features. This is an important step for the SVM as it is sensitive to the scale of the input features.

10. Define Target and Features:

11. X is the set of features, and y is the target variable.

12. Splitting the Dataset:

13. The dataset is divided into training and testing sets.

14. Building the SVM Model:

15. An SVM classifier (SVC) is instantiated and trained on the training data.

16. Model Prediction and Evaluation:

17. The model makes predictions on the test set, and its performance is evaluated using accuracy and a classification report.

18. Output Results:

19. The accuracy and classification report are printed to assess the model's performance.

This code provides a basic implementation of an SVM model for classification. As with any machine learning model, further tuning and validation might be necessary to optimize its performance for your specific dataset.

Launch the code in Listing 6.3, and you will see the following output:

```
Accuracy: 0.6470588235294118
Classification Report:
                precision    recall  f1-score   support

            0       0.00      0.00      0.00        65
            1       0.65      1.00      0.79       407
            2       0.00      0.00      0.00       157

     accuracy                           0.65       629
    macro avg       0.22      0.33      0.26       629
 weighted avg       0.42      0.65      0.51       629
```

[NOTE: This concludes the text and output that was generated by GPT-4.]

THE LOGISTIC REGRESSION ALGORITHM

Logistic regression is a statistical method and machine learning algorithm used to model and analyze datasets in which the outcome is categorical. While its name includes "regression," it is primarily used for binary classification tasks (i.e., when the output can take on two possible outcomes). It can also be extended to handle multiclass classification.

Basic Concept

Logistic regression models the probability that a given instance belongs to a particular category. It predicts the log odds of the probability of the event occurring, and the transformation of this log odds gives the probability.

Mathematical Representation

For binary classification (with labels 0 and 1), the probability $P(Y=1)P(Y=1)$ is modeled as follows:

$$P(Y=1) = 11 + e - z$$
$$P(Y=1) = 1 + e - z1$$

where:
e is the base of natural logarithms.
z is a linear combination of predictors: $z = \beta 0 + \beta 1 X1 + \beta 2 X2 + \ldots$

Steps

1. Linear Transformation: Compute a weighted sum of the input features (plus a bias term).
2. Logistic Transformation: Pass the result from step 1 through the logistic (sigmoid) function to get the probability $P(Y=1)P(Y=1)$.
3. Decision Threshold: Convert the probability into a binary outcome (0 or 1) using a threshold, commonly 0.5.

Parameter Estimation

The coefficients (parameters) of the logistic regression model are typically estimated using Maximum Likelihood Estimation (MLE). The goal is to find the set of parameters that maximize the likelihood of the observed data.

Advantages

- Interpretability: Coefficients can be interpreted in terms of odds ratios, making it easy to explain the influence of predictors.
- Efficiency: It does not require too many computational resources
- Outputs Probabilities: It provides a probabilistic framework which can be useful for understanding the confidence of predictions

Disadvantages

- Assumes Linearity: It assumes a linear decision boundary, which might not capture more complex relationships without feature engineering.
- Not Suitable for Complex Relationships: For highly non-linear relationships, other algorithms like decision trees or neural networks might be more appropriate.
- Vulnerable to Overfitting: With a large number of features, it can overfit, especially when features are correlated.

Use Cases

Logistic regression is widely used in fields like medicine (disease diagnosis), finance (credit approval), marketing (customer churn prediction), and many other domains where the outcome is binary.

Extensions

1. Multinomial Logistic Regression: Used when the target variable has more than two categories
2. Regularized Logistic Regression: Incorporates L1 (Lasso) or L2 (Ridge) regularization to prevent overfitting

Logistic regression is a foundational algorithm for binary classification tasks, providing both good interpretability and a probabilistic framework for predictions.

THE NAÏVE BAYES ALGORITHM

Naïve Bayes is a probabilistic machine learning algorithm based on the Bayes' theorem, with an assumption of independence among predictors (hence the "naïve" label). Despite its simplicity and the naive assumption, the algorithm is remarkably effective for many tasks, particularly in text classification scenarios like spam filtering or sentiment analysis.

Bayes' theorem provides a way to calculate the probability of a hypothesis based on prior knowledge. It is formulated as follows:

$P(A|B) = P(B|A) \times P(A)/P(B)$

where
$P(A|B)$ is the posterior probability of hypothesis A given the data B.
$P(A)$ is the prior probability of A.
$P(B|A)$ is the likelihood, the probability of data B given hypothesis A.
$P(B)$ is the evidence, the probability of data B.

Naïve Bayes for Classification

For a classification problem with a response variable YY and predictors X1,X2,...,XnX1,X2,...,Xn, the Naïve Bayes classifier estimates the conditional probability:

P(Y=k|X1,X2,...,Xn)
P(Y=k|X1,X2,...,Xn)

Given the independence assumption, this can be simplified to the following:

P(Y=k|X1,X2,...,Xn)∝P(Y=k)×∏i=1nP(Xi|Y=k)
P(Y=k|X1,X2,...,Xn)∝P(Y=k)×i=1∏nP(Xi|Y=k)

The class k with the highest posterior probability is the prediction for a given input.

Types of Naïve Bayes

1. Gaussian Naïve Bayes: Assumes that continuous features follow a Gaussian (normal) distribution
2. Multinomial Naïve Bayes: Suitable for discrete data. Commonly used in text classification where data is typically represented as word counts or term frequencies
3. Bernoulli Naïve Bayes: Useful for binary/Boolean features

Advantages

- Efficiency: Requires a small amount of training data to estimate the necessary parameters
- Simplicity: Easy to understand and implement
- Good performance: Especially in text classification tasks
- Scalability: Can handle large datasets and high-dimensional feature spaces

Disadvantages

- Independence Assumption: The assumption of predictor independence is often violated in real-world applications, which can impact performance.
- Data Distribution: The model's performance can suffer if the distributional assumptions (e.g., Gaussian) do not align with the actual data distribution.

Use Cases
Naïve Bayes is particularly popular in the following:

1. Text Classification: Such as spam detection, sentiment analysis, and categorizing news articles
2. Recommendation Systems: Like suggesting news articles or music
3. Face Recognition: As part of a larger system

Naïve Bayes is a versatile and computationally efficient classification algorithm. Its strength lies in its simplicity, probabilistic nature, and surprisingly robust performance in many scenarios, especially when the dimensionality of the data is high.

THE SVM ALGORITHM

The SVM is a supervised machine learning algorithm primarily used for classification tasks, though it can also be used for regression. It is known for its robustness and ability to handle high-dimensional data. The main objective of the SVM is to find the optimal hyperplane that best divides the dataset into classes.

Basic Concept
For a two-class problem, imagine plotting your data points in a multi-dimensional space. SVM tries to find a hyperplane (a line in 2D, a plane in 3D, and so on) that best separates the two classes. The optimal hyperplane is the one that has the maximum margin, which is the maximum distance between data points of both classes.

Important Components

1. Support Vectors: These are the data points that lie closest to the hyperplane and effectively define it. They are the data points that would alter the position of the hyperplane if they were removed.
2. Margin: It is the distance between the nearest data point (of any class) and the hyperplane. The objective of SVM is to maximize this margin.
3. Hyperplane: This is the decision boundary that separates the classes. In a two-dimensional space, it is a line.

Types

1. Linear SVM: Used for linearly separable data. It finds a hyperplane that best separates the two classes.
2. Non-linear SVM (Kernel SVM): When data is not linearly separable, SVM uses a trick called the "kernel trick" to project the data into a higher-dimensional space where it is linearly separable. Common kernels include polynomial, radial basis function (RBF), and sigmoid.

Advantages

- Effective in High Dimensions: It works well even when the number of features is greater than the number of samples.
- Robust: It maximizes the margin, making it robust to outliers.
- Versatility: The kernel trick can adapt the algorithm to non-linear data.

Disadvantages

- Not Suitable for Large Datasets: Due to its computational complexity, it might not be the best choice for very large datasets.
- Sensitive to Noise: A small number of mislabeled examples can dramatically decrease performance.
- Choice of Kernel: The performance can be sensitive to the choice of the kernel and its parameters.

Use Cases
SVMs are used in a variety of applications.

1. Text Classification: Due to its ability to handle high-dimensional data, SVMs are often used for text categorization.
2. Image Recognition: As part of image classification pipelines
3. Bioinformatics: For protein classification and cancer classification
4. Handwriting Recognition: To recognize handwritten characters

Support Vector Machines offer a powerful method for classification tasks, especially when the data has many features or when the classes are not linearly separable. Proper tuning, especially when using kernel SVMs, is crucial for achieving the best performance.

THE DECISION TREE ALGORITHM

A *decision tree* is a flowchart-like, tree-structured algorithm used for both classification and regression tasks in machine learning. It breaks down a dataset into smaller and smaller subsets while incrementally developing an associated decision tree in parallel.

Basic Concept
The decision tree algorithm tries to solve the problem by using tree representation. Each internal node of the tree corresponds to a feature, and each leaf node corresponds to a response or class label.

Important Components

1. Decision Nodes: Represented by squares, these nodes contain a decision or test on a single attribute.

2. Branches: Represent the outcome of a test and connect nodes
3. Leaf Nodes: Terminal nodes that predict the outcome

Algorithm

1. Selection of Attribute: The attribute to be placed at a decision node is selected based on a metric (such as information gain or the Gini impurity). The goal is to select the attribute that provides the best split.
2. Branch Creation: For each possible value of the selected attribute, a branch is created.
3. Recursive Splitting: Steps 1 and 2 are then repeated for each branch, using the subset of data associated with that branch.
4. Termination: The recursion stops when one of the stopping conditions is met, such as the maximum tree depth is reached, the minimum node size is reached, or if the node contains data from a single class.

Types

1. Classification Trees: Used when the response variable is categorical. The outcome is a class label.
2. Regression Trees: Used when the response is numeric or continuous. The outcome is a real value.

Metrics for Splitting

1. Information Gain: Measures how much information a feature gives us about the class. It is based on entropy.
2. Gini Impurity: Measures the disorder of a set of elements. It is used by the CART (Classification and Regression Trees) algorithm for classification tasks.
3. Variance Reduction: Used by CART for regression trees

Advantages

• Interpretability: Trees can be visualized and are easy to understand, even by non-experts.
• Minimal Data Preparation: It does not require normalization or dummy variables
• Handles both Continuous and Categorical Variables: It can be used for both classification and regression tasks.
• Non-parametric: It makes no assumptions about the distribution and the classifier structure.

Disadvantages

- Overfitting: Without proper tuning, trees can memorize the training data, leading to overfitting.
- Instability: Small changes in data can result in a completely different tree.
- Optimization: Finding the optimal tree for a set of data is NP-hard. Hence, heuristics like the greedy algorithm are used, which can sometimes result in sub-optimal trees.

Use Cases

Decision trees are versatile and can be used in a variety of applications, including the following:

1. Medical Diagnosis: Based on symptoms, predict the likelihood of a disease
2. Credit Risk Analysis: Decide whether to approve or deny a loan
3. Marketing: Identify potential customers for a marketing campaign

Extensions

1. Random Forest: Ensemble of decision trees, providing better predictive performance by reducing overfitting
2. Gradient Boosted Trees: Sequentially builds decision trees where each tree corrects the errors of its predecessor

Decision trees offer an intuitive and visual approach to decision-making processes. Their simplicity and ease of interpretation make them a popular choice in various domains, but care must be taken to handle their limitations.

THE RANDOM FOREST ALGORITHM

Random forest is an ensemble learning method primarily used for classification and regression tasks. It operates by constructing multiple decision trees during training and outputs the class that is the mode (for classification) or mean (for regression) of the classes produced by individual trees.

Basic Concept

1. Bootstrapping: Random Forest starts by taking multiple bootstrap samples (random samples with replacement) from the dataset. This introduces variability and ensures that each tree in the forest is trained on a slightly different subset of data.
2. Feature Randomness: For each split in the decision tree, only a random subset of features is considered. This further ensures the diversity of trees in the forest, making the ensemble less correlated and more robust.

3. Aggregation:

- For classification, each tree in the forest "votes" for a class, and the class with the most votes is the random forest's prediction.
- For regression, the average prediction of all the trees is the final prediction.

Advantages

- High Accuracy: It combines multiple trees to produce a high-accuracy classifier.
- Overfitting Control: The ensemble nature and randomness introduced in tree building help control overfitting.
- Handles Large Data: It efficiently handles datasets with a larger number of features and observations.
- Feature Importance: It provides insights into the importance of different features in making predictions.
- Versatility: It can be used for both classification and regression tasks.
- Handles Missing Values: It can handle datasets with missing values.

Disadvantages

- Complexity: It is more computationally intensive than a single decision tree.
- Interpretability: While individual trees are interpretable, a forest might not be as intuitive to understand.
- Slower Prediction: Making predictions requires aggregating across all trees in the forest, which can be slower than other algorithms.

Hyperparameters

Some key hyperparameters to consider when tuning a random forest include the following:

1. Number of Trees: The number of trees in the forest
2. Maximum Depth: The maximum depth of each tree
3. Minimum Samples Split: The minimum number of samples required to split an internal node
4. Minimum Samples Leaf: The minimum number of samples required to be at a leaf node

Use Cases

Random forests are versatile and find applications in various domains, including the following:

- banking: credit risk analysis
- medicine: disease identification
- e-commerce: recommendation systems
- remote sensing: satellite image classification

The random forest is a powerful and flexible algorithm that builds upon the decision tree's strengths while addressing some of its weaknesses. By aggregating the results of multiple, diverse trees, it achieves high accuracy and robustness against overfitting. It is especially valuable in scenarios where you need a quick baseline model or when interpretability is not the primary concern.

SUMMARY

This chapter is packed with a lot of material, and it's your second full chapter with material for classifiers that was generated by GPT-4. You got a brief introduction to scikit-learn, followed by a discussion of the kNN algorithm.

Next, you learned about cross-validation, bias-variance tradeoffs, and distance metrics. In addition, you learned about the elbow method for selecting the optimal value of k in the kNN algorithm.

Furthermore, you saw code samples generated by GPT-4 involving the kNN algorithm, the decision tree algorithm, the SVM algorithm, and the logistic regression algorithm.

The final portion of this chapter contained a high-level description, generated by GPT-4, of the following algorithms: logistic regression, naive bayes, SVG, decision tree, and random forest.

## CHAPTER 7

MACHINE LEARNING CLUSTERING WITH GPT-4

This chapter is the third chapter containing Python code samples that were generated by GPT-4, which includes Python code for three popular machine learning clustering tasks.

The first part of this chapter introduces you to clustering in machine learning, followed by a list of ten clustering algorithms. This section also describes the advantages and disadvantages of the k-means, hierarchical clustering, and DBSCAN algorithms.

The second part of this chapter contains three Python-based code samples for the k-means, hierarchical clustering, and DBSCAN algorithms using a synthetic dataset. All the code samples were generated by supplying a suitable prompt to GPT-4.

WHAT IS CLUSTERING?

Clustering is an essential concept in machine learning, particularly in unsupervised learning. *Clustering* is the task of partitioning a dataset into groups, known as clusters, such that items in the same group are more similar to each other than to those in other groups.

Important Points

- Type of Learning: Clustering is a form of unsupervised learning. This means you do not need labeled data to work with clustering algorithms. Instead, the goal is to discover hidden patterns in the data.
- Objective: The primary objective is to segregate groups with similar traits and assign them into clusters.

Applications

- Market Segmentation: Grouping customers based on purchase history
- Social Network Analysis: Identifying communities within the network
- Search Result Grouping: Grouping similar documents or Web pages in search results
- Image Segmentation: Dividing an image into regions based on pixel similarities
- Anomaly Detection: Detecting unusual patterns that do not conform to expected behavior (outliers)

Metrics

- Within-cluster Sum of Squares (WCSS): This measures the squared average distance of all the points within a cluster to the center of that cluster.
- Silhouette Score: This measures how close each point in one cluster is to the points in the neighboring clusters.
- Davies-Bouldin Index: This is a measure of the average similarity between each cluster and its most similar cluster, where similarity is the ratio of within-cluster distances to between-cluster distances. Lower values are better.

Popular Clustering Algorithms

- K-means: This partitions data into kk distinct, non-overlapping subsets (or clusters). It does this by minimizing the sum of the squared distances between data and the corresponding cluster centroid.
- Hierarchical Clustering: This produces a set of nested clusters organized as a hierarchical tree. This type of clustering can be visualized as a dendrogram (a tree-like diagram) that showcases the sequence of clusters formed.
- DBSCAN (Density-Based Spatial Clustering of Applications with Noise): This creates clusters based on the density of data points. It can find arbitrarily-shaped clusters and is useful for data with noise and outliers.
- Gaussian Mixture Models (GMMs): These models assume that data is generated from a mixture of several Gaussian distributions. GMM tries to identify these Gaussian distributions.
- Agglomerative Clustering: Similar to hierarchical clustering, but this tends to be more scalable. It starts with each item as a single cluster and merges them into larger ones.

Challenges

- Number of Clusters: One of the challenges in clustering is determining the number of clusters the algorithm should segment the data into. For k-means, a popular technique is the "elbow method."

- Shape and Size of Clusters: Some algorithms assume clusters to be spherical and equally-sized, which might not always be the case.
- Feature Scaling: Clustering algorithms, especially distance-based methods like k-means, are sensitive to feature scaling. You should scale features so they have similar magnitudes.
- High Dimensionality: Clustering in high-dimensional spaces can be problematic, which is referred to as the "curse of dimensionality." Techniques like PCA (Principal Component Analysis) can be used to reduce dimensionality.

Clustering provides insights into the distribution, categorization, and structure of data. It is a powerful tool for data analysis, anomaly detection, and preprocessing steps like data reduction.

TEN CLUSTERING ALGORITHMS

This section contains a list of ten clustering algorithms in machine learning, along with their advantages and disadvantages:

- k-means clustering
- hierarchical clustering
- DBSCAN (Density-Based Spatial Clustering of Applications with Noise)
- agglomerative clustering
- mean shift clustering
- Gaussian Mixture Model (GMM)
- affinity propagation
- spectral clustering
- agglomerative clustering
- OPTICS (Ordering Points To Identify the Clustering Structure)

K-means Clustering
Advantages

- simple and easy to implement
- works well for clusters that are spherical and equally-sized
- fast for a large number of variables

Disadvantages

- It assumes clusters are spherical and equally-sized, which may not always be the case.
- The number of clusters kk has to be specified beforehand.
- Sensitive to initialization, as different initial centroids can result in different clusters.

Hierarchical Clustering
Advantages

- It does not require the number of clusters to be specified.
- It provides a dendrogram, which can be useful for understanding the data hierarchy.

Disadvantages

- It is more computationally expensive than k-means.
- It is not scalable for very large datasets.

DBSCAN (Density-Based Spatial Clustering of Applications with Noise)
Advantages

- can find arbitrarily-shaped clusters
- does not require the number of clusters to be specified
- can identify noise/outliers

Disadvantages

- may struggle with clusters of varying densities
- Not always deterministic: border points that are reachable from multiple clusters can be part of either cluster.

Agglomerative Clustering
Advantages

- suitable for smaller datasets
- does not require the number of clusters to be specified (though often specified in practice)

Disadvantages

- not scalable for very large datasets

Mean Shift Clustering
Advantages

- does not assume any prior knowledge on the number of clusters
- can find arbitrarily-shaped clusters

Disadvantages

- computationally more expensive
- The bandwidth parameter needs to be carefully chosen.

Gaussian Mixture Model (GMM)
Advantages

• assumes each cluster follows a Gaussian distribution
• can model elliptical clusters

Disadvantages

• more computationally intensive than k-means
• needs to estimate more parameters

Affinity Propagation
Advantages

• automatically determines the number of clusters
• uses all data points as potential exemplars

Disadvantages

• can be slow and requires more memory for large datasets
• might produce a large number of clusters

Spectral Clustering
Advantages

• can capture complex cluster structures
• can be used to identify non-convex clusters

Disadvantages

• can be computationally expensive for large datasets
• number of clusters must be specified beforehand

Agglomerative Clustering
Advantages

• provides a hierarchical approach, resulting in a tree of clusters
• suitable for smaller datasets

Disadvantages

• not suitable for large datasets
• The number of clusters needs to be specified.

OPTICS (Ordering Points To Identify the Clustering Structure)
Advantages

- does not require the number of clusters to be specified
- can identify clusters of varying densities

Disadvantages

- more computationally intensive than simpler algorithms like k-means

Each of these clustering algorithms has its own set of assumptions and is suitable for different types of data and requirements. The choice of algorithm often depends on the size, dimensionality, and nature of the data, as well as the specific problem context.

The three of the most popular clustering algorithms in machine learning are the first three algorithms in the list of the preceding section. Each of these algorithms are described in subsequent sections, along with Python-based code samples.

METRICS FOR CLUSTERING ALGORITHMS

This section contains a list of metrics that you can use for evaluating clustering algorithms. Clustering algorithm evaluation is essential to determine how well the algorithm is performing. Here is a list of metrics commonly used for evaluating clustering algorithms, along with their advantages and disadvantages:

- Silhouette Score
- Calinski-Harabasz Index
- Davies-Bouldin Index
- Dunn Index
- Adjusted Rand Index (ARI)
- Normalized Mutual Information (NMI)
- Fowlkes-Mallows Index
- purity
- cohesion
- separation

Silhouette Score
Advantages

- measures how similar an object is to its cluster compared to other clusters
- values range from -1 to 1, with a high value indicating good clustering

Disadvantages

- does not work well with non-convex clusters or clusters of varying densities
- computational cost can be high for large datasets

Davies-Bouldin Index
Advantages

- measures the average similarity between each cluster and its most similar cluster
- A lower value indicates better clustering.

Disadvantages

- It assumes that clusters are convex and isotropic, which is not always the case.

Calinski-Harabasz Index
Advantages

- computes the ratio of the between-cluster dispersion mean and the within-cluster dispersion
- A higher value indicates better clustering.

Disadvantages

- It assumes that clusters are convex and isotropic.

Dunn Index
Advantages

- considers the ratio between the minimal inter-cluster distance and maximal intra-cluster distance
- A higher Dunn index indicates better clustering.

Disadvantages

- computationally expensive

Adjusted Rand Index (ARI)
Advantages

- measures the similarity of two clusterings
- adjusted for chance, providing a more reliable score

Disadvantages

• requires knowledge of the ground truth

Normalized Mutual Information (NMI)
Advantages

• measures the mutual information between two clusterings
• normalized to be in the range [0, 1]

Disadvantages

• requires knowledge of the ground truth

Fowlkes-Mallows Index
Advantages

• measures the geometric mean of precision and recall
• values range from 0 to 1, with 1 indicating perfect clustering

Disadvantages
requires knowledge of the ground truth

Purity
Advantages

• measures the extent to which clusters contain a single class
• simple to understand and compute

Disadvantages

• requires knowledge of the ground truth
• does not account for cluster size

Cohesion
Advantages

• measures how closely related are instances within the same cluster

Disadvantages

• sensitive to the number of clusters

Separation
Advantages

• measures how distinct or well-separated a cluster is from other clusters

Disadvantages

• sensitive to the number of clusters

When evaluating clustering algorithms, it is crucial to consider the nature of the data and the specific use case. Depending on the context, certain metrics may be more appropriate than others. It is also beneficial to use multiple metrics to get a comprehensive understanding of the clustering performance.

K-MEANS CLUSTERING

Advantages

• Simplicity: The algorithm is straightforward and easy to implement.
• Efficiency: It is computationally fast, especially with optimization variants like the Elkan algorithm.
• Scalability: K-means scales well to large datasets, especially when using MiniBatch k-means.
• Popular: Due to its simplicity and applicability, it is widely used in practice.

Disadvantages

• Number of Clusters: You need to specify the number of clusters k beforehand, which is not always feasible.
• Spherical Assumption: It assumes that clusters are spherical and equally-sized. It may perform poorly with elongated or irregularly-shaped clusters.
• Initialization Sensitivity: The algorithm's results can vary based on initial centroid placement. Though techniques like k-means++ help, convergence to a local minimum can still be an issue.
• Sensitive to Outliers: Outliers can heavily influence the position of centroids.
• Feature Scaling: It is sensitive to feature scaling. Features need to be scaled for the algorithm to work properly.

HIERARCHICAL CLUSTERING

Advantages

• Dendrograms: Hierarchical clustering produces a dendrogram, which can be a useful tool for understanding the hierarchical structure of data and for visualization.
• No Need to Specify k: Unlike k-Means, you do not need to specify the number of clusters beforehand.
• Flexibility: It can produce a diverse range of cluster structures, making it suitable for various applications.

- Deterministic: Always produces the same clustering results given the same input and parameters.

Disadvantages

- Computational Complexity: The standard algorithm has a high computational complexity, making it less suitable for large datasets.
- Sensitivity: It can be sensitive to noise and outliers.
- Difficulty in Choosing the Right Level: Deciding the level in the hierarchy to cut and form clusters can be tricky.

DBSCAN (DENSITY-BASED SPATIAL CLUSTERING OF APPLICATIONS WITH NOISE)

Advantages

- No Need to Specify Number of Clusters: DBSCAN automatically determines the number of clusters based on the data.
- Shape Flexibility: It can find arbitrarily-shaped clusters, which is a significant advantage over k-means.
- Noise Handling: It can identify and handle noise and outliers.
- No Assumption of Cluster Structure: It does not assume clusters to be spherical or of any specific shape.

Disadvantages

- Difficulty with Clusters of Varying Densities: It struggles when clusters have significantly different densities.
- Border Points: Points that are reachable from more than one cluster can be assigned to the wrong cluster.
- Parameter Sensitivity: It requires setting parameters (like the radius of neighborhoods and the minimum number of points) which can heavily influence the results.

While these are three of the most popular clustering algorithms, the best algorithm often depends on the specific dataset and the problem requirements. It is common practice to try multiple algorithms and evaluate which one works best for the given scenario.

Now that you have a basic understanding of clustering in machine learning, let's look at a machine learning model that is based on the k-means algorithm, which is the topic of the next section.

WHAT IS THE K-MEANS ALGORITHM?

The *k-means algorithm* is one of the most widely used clustering methods due to its simplicity and efficiency.

K-means Clustering Overview

K-means is a partitioning method that divides a dataset into k distinct, non-overlapping subsets (or clusters). The goal of the k-means algorithm is to find groups in the data, with the number of groups represented by the variable k.

Algorithm

- Initialization: Randomly choose k data points (seeds) to be the initial centroids.
- Assignment: Assign each data point to the closest centroid. All the points assigned to a centroid constitute a cluster.
- Update: Calculate the new mean (centroid) of each cluster.
- Iterate: Repeat Steps 2 and 3 until the centroids do not change significantly, or a set number of iterations is reached.

Important Concepts

- Centroid: The center of a cluster. In k-Means, the centroid is the mean of all points in the cluster.
- WCSS (Within-cluster Sum of Squares): It measures the squared average distance of all the points within a cluster to the center of that cluster. The objective of k-Means is to minimize this metric.

Determining the Value of k

One challenge with k-means is selecting the appropriate number of clusters k. A common technique is the "elbow method."

1. Compute the clustering algorithm for different values of k (e.g., k from 1 to 10).
2. For each k, calculate the total WCSS.
3. Plot the curve of WCSS vs. the number of clusters k.
4. The location of a bend (the "elbow") in the plot is generally considered an indicator of the appropriate number of clusters.

Strengths

- simple and easy to implement
- efficient in terms of computational cost
- scales well to large datasets

Limitations

- It assumes that clusters are spherical and equally-sized, which might not always be the case.
- The number of clusters k has to be set beforehand.
- It is sensitive to the initialization of centroids. This issue is often addressed by running the algorithm multiple times with different initializations and choosing the best result.
- It might converge to a local optimum. This is why it is common to run the whole process multiple times with different starting conditions.
- It is sensitive to feature scaling.

Variants

- k-means++: This variant aims to address the random initialization weakness of k-means by specifying a procedure to initialize the centroids before proceeding with the standard k-means optimization iterations.

K-means is a foundational clustering algorithm that has been widely used in various applications. While it is powerful and scalable, careful preprocessing of data and consideration of its assumptions are essential to get meaningful cluster assignments.

WHAT IS THE HIERARCHICAL CLUSTERING ALGORITHM?

The *hierarchical clustering algorithm* is a type of clustering algorithm that builds a hierarchy of clusters by either a bottom-up or top-down approach. Hierarchical clustering builds a tree of clusters. This tree, called a *dendrogram*, helps in visualizing the sequence in which clusters were merged or split.

There are two primary strategies for hierarchical clustering:

1. Agglomerative (Bottom-Up): This is the most common strategy. It starts by treating each object as a singleton cluster. Pairs of clusters are successively merged until all clusters have been merged into one big cluster containing all objects.
2. Divisive (Top-Down): It starts with all objects in one single cluster. In successive steps, the cluster is split into smaller clusters, until each object has its own singleton cluster.

Agglomerative Hierarchical Clustering Algorithm
Here, we will focus on the more commonly used agglomerative hierarchical clustering.

1. Initialization: Treat each data point as a single cluster, leading to nn clusters for nn data points.

2. Agglomeration

   - Find the pair of clusters that are closest to each other.
   - Merge these two clusters into a single cluster.
   - Update the distance matrix (used to store distances between clusters).
   - Repeat the process until only a single cluster remains.

3. Completion: The result of the aforementioned process is a tree-like diagram called a dendrogram. The dendrogram represents the order in which clusters were merged.

Distance Metric
The choice of the distance metric is crucial in hierarchical clustering.

- Euclidean Distance: Ordinary straight-line distance between two points in Euclidean space
- Manhattan Distance: Sum of the absolute differences of their coordinates
- Cosine Similarity: Measures the cosine of the angle between two non-zero vectors

Linkage Criteria
When two clusters SS and TT are combined into a larger cluster, the choice of how to define the distance between clusters is determined by the linkage criterion:

- Single Linkage: The distance between two clusters is defined as the shortest distance between two points in each cluster.
- Complete Linkage: The distance between two clusters is defined as the maximum distance between any two points in the clusters.
- Average Linkage: The distance between two clusters is defined as the average distance between each point in one cluster to every point in the other cluster.
- Ward's Method: This method minimizes the variance of the distances between the clusters being merged.

Advantages

- Dendrogram: provides a deep insight into the hierarchical structure of data
- No Need to Specify Number of Clusters: Unlike k-means, you do not need to specify the number of clusters beforehand.
- Flexibility: can produce a diverse range of cluster structures, making it suitable for various applications

Disadvantages

- Computational Complexity: not scalable for very large datasets
- Irreversible: Once a decision is made to combine two clusters, it cannot be undone.
- Sensitivity to Noise and Outliers: Noisy data can lead to clusters being merged incorrectly.
- Choice of Linkage: Different linkage methods can produce different hierarchical structures. Choosing the right linkage method is crucial.

Hierarchical clustering is particularly useful when the hierarchical structure in the data is of interest. It is useful for smaller datasets and when a dendrogram is beneficial for analysis or presentation. However, for large datasets or when computational efficiency is a concern, other clustering methods, like k-means or DBSCAN, might be more appropriate.

WHAT IS THE DBSCAN ALGORITHM?

The *Density-Based Spatial Clustering of Applications with Noise* (DBSCAN) is a prominent clustering algorithm known for its capability to detect clusters of arbitrary shapes and its insensitivity to the ordering of input data.

Principle

DBSCAN groups together data points that are close to each other based on a distance measurement (usually Euclidean distance) and a minimum number of data points. It also marks as outliers the points that are in low-density regions.

Steps

1. Random Point Selection: Start with an arbitrary data point that has not been visited.
2. Neighborhood Check: Retrieve the neighborhood of this point (all points within a predefined distance εε).
3. Expand Cluster:

   - If there are a sufficient number of neighbors (greater than a threshold minPtsminPts), mark the current point as a core point and form a cluster.
   - Add all reachable data points (directly and indirectly) within the distance εε to this cluster.
   - Repeat the process for each unvisited point in the cluster.

4. Mark Noise: If a point does not belong to any cluster and does not have enough neighbors, mark it as noise or an outlier.
5. Iteration: Repeat the process until all points are either assigned to a cluster or marked as noise.

Important Concepts

- Core Point: A data point is a core point if it has more than minPtsminPts points within $\varepsilon\varepsilon$ distance.
- Border Point: A data point is a border point if it has fewer than minPtsminPts within $\varepsilon\varepsilon$ distance but lies within the $\varepsilon\varepsilon$ distance of a core point.
- Noise/Outlier: A data point is noise if it is neither a core point nor a border point.
- Directly Density Reachable: A point PP is directly density reachable from point QQ if PP is within $\varepsilon\varepsilon$ distance from QQ and QQ is a core point.
- Density Reachable: Point PP is density reachable from QQ if there is a sequence of points P1,...,PnP1,...,Pn where P1=QP1=Q and Pn=PPn=P such that Pi+1Pi+1 is directly density reachable from PiPi.

Advantages

- Arbitrary Shape Clusters: Unlike kk-Means, DBSCAN can find clusters of arbitrary shapes, not just spherical.
- Noise Handling: It can effectively handle noise and outliers.
- No Need to Specify Number of Clusters: The algorithm does not require the number of clusters to be specified beforehand.

Disadvantages

- Parameter Sensitivity: The results can vary based on the distance threshold $\varepsilon\varepsilon$ and minPtsminPts. Selecting appropriate values can be challenging.
- Varying Densities: DBSCAN can struggle when clusters have significantly different densities.
- High-Dimensional Data: The algorithm's effectiveness diminishes with an increase in the dimensionality of the data.

DBSCAN is a powerful algorithm, especially when the clusters are of varying shapes and there is a need to distinguish outliers. It is particularly effective for spatial data and data with noise. However, parameter tuning and understanding the nature of the data are crucial for obtaining optimal results with DBSCAN.

A MACHINE LEARNING MODEL WITH THE K-MEANS ALGORITHM

This section contains an example of GPT-4 generating a machine learning model using the k-means algorithm and a synthetic dataset. The first half of this section contains the explanation of the steps that GPT-4 performed, followed by Listing 7.1, which contains the Python-based code that GPT-4 generated.

Here is an outline of what we will be doing:

1. Generate a dataset: We will create a synthetic dataset with clusters using Scikit-learn's make_blobs function.
2. Visualize the dataset: We will plot the dataset to see the clusters.
3. k-means clustering: We will use the k-means algorithm to identify clusters.
4. Visualize clusters: We will plot the dataset again, but this time colored by the clusters identified by k-means.

Let's generate the synthetic dataset and visualize it. Here is the generated dataset with three clusters. The colors represent the actual clusters (as this is a synthetic dataset, we know the true cluster assignments).

Next, we will use the k-means algorithm to identify clusters in this dataset. We will set kk (the number of clusters) to 3, as that is the number of centers we used to generate the dataset. After clustering, we will visualize the results.

The visualization shows the results of the k-means clustering. The data points are colored according to the clusters identified by the k-means algorithm. The red "X" markers represent the cluster centers determined by k-means.

As observed, the k-means algorithm has successfully identified the clusters in the synthetic dataset.

Listing 7.1 displays the content of kMeans_GPT4.py that illustrates how to create a machine learning model using the k-means algorithm and the death. csv dataset.

LISTING 7.1: kMeans_GPT4.py

```
from sklearn.datasets import make_blobs
import matplotlib.pyplot as plt

# Generate a synthetic dataset with 3 clusters
X, y = make_blobs(n_samples=300, centers=3, random_
state=42, cluster_std=2.0)

# Visualizing the dataset
plt.figure(figsize=(8, 6))
plt.scatter(X[:, 0], X[:, 1], c=y, s=50, cmap='viridis')
plt.title("Generated Dataset with 3 Clusters")
plt.xlabel("Feature 1")
plt.ylabel("Feature 2")
plt.show()
```

```
# Re-importing necessary libraries due to the reset
from sklearn.datasets import make_blobs
import matplotlib.pyplot as plt

# Generating the synthetic dataset again
X, y = make_blobs(n_samples=300, centers=3, random_
state=42, cluster_std=2.0)

# Visualizing the dataset
plt.figure(figsize=(8, 6))
plt.scatter(X[:, 0], X[:, 1], c=y, s=50, cmap='viridis')
plt.title("Generated Dataset with 3 Clusters")
plt.xlabel("Feature 1")
plt.ylabel("Feature 2")
plt.show()

from sklearn.cluster import KMeans

# Applying kMeans clustering
kmeans = KMeans(n_clusters=3, random_state=42)
kmeans_labels = kmeans.fit_predict(X)

# Visualizing the identified clusters
plt.figure(figsize=(8, 6))
plt.scatter(X[:, 0], X[:, 1], c=kmeans_labels, s=50,
cmap='viridis')
plt.scatter(kmeans.cluster_centers_[:, 0], kmeans.cluster_
centers_[:, 1], s=200, c='red', marker='X', label='Cluster
Centers')
plt.title("kMeans Clustering Results")
plt.xlabel("Feature 1")
plt.ylabel("Feature 2")
plt.legend()
plt.show()
```

Listing 7.1 starts with several import statements, followed by the invocation of make_blobs() to create a synthetic dataset. The next code block generates and displays a scatter plot from the data in the generated dataset via this code snippet:

```
plt.scatter(X[:, 0], X[:, 1], c=y, s=50, cmap='viridis')
```

The next portion of Listing 7.1 is actually redundant: the pair of import statements that occurred previously in the code are imported again. Moreover, the same scatter plot is generated, which is also redundant.

The next portion of Listing 7.1 initializes the variable kmeans as an instance of the class KMeans that was imported from sklearn.cluster. Next, the variable kmeans_labels is initialized with the result of invoking the fit_predict() method of the kmeans variable. Another scatter plot is generated in the next code block, which displays additional information about the center of each cluster via this pair of code snippets:

```
plt.scatter(X[:, 0], X[:, 1], c=kmeans_labels, s=50,
cmap='viridis')
plt.scatter(kmeans.cluster_centers_[:, 0], kmeans.cluster_
centers_[:, 1], s=200, c='red', marker='X', label='Cluster
Centers')
```

Launch the code in Listing 7.1, and you will see two images generated. Figure 7.1 displays three clusters, and Figure 7.2 displays the three clusters with their centroids shown in red.

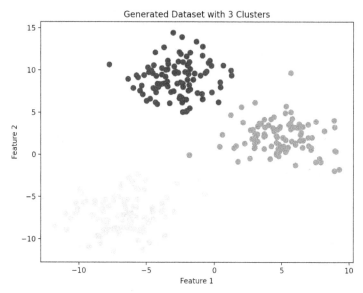

FIGURE 7.1 Three clusters

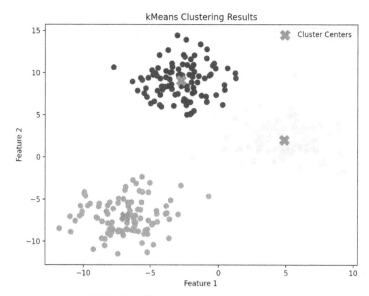

FIGURE 7.2 Three clusters and their centroids

A MACHINE LEARNING MODEL WITH THE HIERARCHICAL CLUSTERING ALGORITHM

This section contains an example of GPT-4 generating a machine learning model using the hierarchical clustering algorithm and a synthetic dataset. The first half of this section contains the explanation of the steps that GPT-4 performed, followed by Listing 7.2, which contains the Python-based code that GPT-4 generated.

Let's go through the steps to apply the hierarchical clustering algorithm on a dataset:

1. Generate a synthetic dataset: We will create a synthetic dataset with clusters using Scikit-learn's make_blobs function.
2. Visualize the dataset: Plot the dataset to see the clusters.
3. Compute the linkage matrix: Using the linkage function from SciPy, which will capture the hierarchical relationship between points.
4. Dendrogram visualization: Display a dendrogram to visualize how clusters are merged step by step.
5. Cutting the dendrogram: To decide the number of clusters, we will cut the dendrogram and retrieve the cluster labels.
6. Visualize the clusters: We will plot the dataset colored by the clusters identified by hierarchical clustering.

Let's proceed again by generating the synthetic dataset and then applying the hierarchical clustering algorithm on it.

Here is the generated dataset with three clusters.

Next, we will compute the linkage matrix using the linkage function from the SciPy library. This matrix will capture the hierarchical relationship between the data points. We will then visualize this relationship using a dendrogram.

Here is the dendrogram produced by the hierarchical clustering. Each vertical line represents a merging of two clusters. The height of the vertical line indicates the distance at which the merging occurred. As you move from the bottom to the top of the dendrogram, clusters are successively merged until only one large cluster remains.

To decide the number of clusters for our dataset, we will cut the dendrogram. A common practice is to choose a distance threshold and draw a horizontal line at that distance. The number of vertical lines the horizontal line intersects is the number of clusters.

For this demonstration, we will cut the dendrogram to retrieve three clusters (since we initially generated the data with three clusters). We will then visualize the clusters.

Here is the result of the hierarchical clustering algorithm on the synthetic dataset. The data points are colored according to the clusters identified by cutting the dendrogram.

The algorithm has successfully identified and grouped the data points into three distinct clusters, which aligns well with the way the synthetic data was generated.

Listing 7.2 displays the content of hierarchical_clustering_GPT4.py that illustrates how to create a machine learning model using the hierarchical clustering algorithm and the death.csv dataset.

LISTING 7.2: hierarchical_clustering_GPT4.py

```
# Importing necessary libraries
from sklearn.datasets import make_blobs
import matplotlib.pyplot as plt
import numpy as np
from scipy.cluster.hierarchy import dendrogram, linkage,
fcluster

# Generating the synthetic dataset again
X_hc, y_hc = make_blobs(n_samples=150, centers=3, random_
state=42, cluster_std=2.0)

# Visualizing the dataset
plt.figure(figsize=(8, 6))
plt.scatter(X_hc[:, 0], X_hc[:, 1], c=y_hc, s=50,
cmap='viridis')
plt.title("Generated Dataset with 3 Clusters")
plt.xlabel("Feature 1")
plt.ylabel("Feature 2")
plt.show()

# Computing the linkage matrix
Z = linkage(X_hc, 'ward')  # Using the 'ward' method as the
linkage criteria

# Displaying the dendrogram
plt.figure(figsize=(10, 7))
dendrogram(Z)
plt.title("Dendrogram for Hierarchical Clustering")
plt.xlabel("Data Points")
plt.ylabel("Euclidean Distances")
plt.show()
```

Listing 7.2 starts with several import statements, followed by the invocation of make_blobs() to create a synthetic dataset. The next code block generates and displays a scatter plot from the data in the generated dataset via this code snippet:

```
plt.scatter(X[:, 0], X[:, 1], c=y, s=50, cmap='viridis')
```

The next portion of Listing 7.2 initializes the variable z by invoking the linkage() method to perform hierarchical/agglomerative clustering, followed by a block of code the invokes dendrogram(Z) to display the dendrogram.

For more detailed information, consult the sklearn documentation regarding the `linkage()` method:

https://docs.scipy.org/doc/scipy/reference/generated/scipy.cluster.hierarchy.linkage.html#scipy.cluster.hierarchy.linkage

Launch the code in Listing 7.2, and you will see three images generated. Figure 7.3 displays three clusters, and Figure 7.4 displays a dendrogram (which is a tree-like structure) that visualizes the three clusters displayed in Figure 7.3.

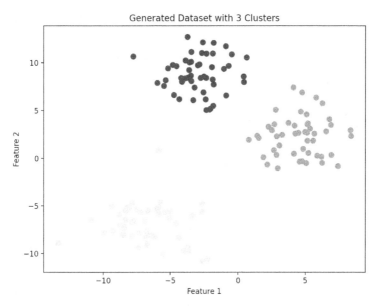

FIGURE 7.3 Three clusters

A MACHINE LEARNING MODEL WITH THE DBSCAN ALGORITHM

This section contains an example of GPT-4 generating a machine learning model using the DBSCAN algorithm and a synthetic dataset. The first half of this section contains the explanation of the steps that GPT-4 performed, followed by Listing 7.3 that contains the Python-based code that GPT-4 generated.

The process for creating an ML model using the DBSCAN algorithm involves the following steps:

1. Generate a synthetic dataset: We will reuse the dataset we created earlier with blobs.
2. Visualize the dataset: To understand the cluster distribution
3. Apply DBSCAN: Use the DBSCAN algorithm to identify clusters in the dataset.
4. Visualize the results: Plot the dataset, colored by the clusters identified by DBSCAN.

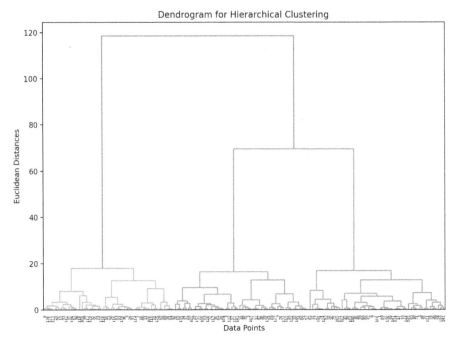

FIGURE 7.4 A dendrogram

Let's start by visualizing the previously generated synthetic dataset.

Here is the generated dataset that we will be clustering using the DBSCAN algorithm.

Now, let's apply the DBSCAN algorithm to identify clusters.

Here are the results of the DBSCAN algorithm on the synthetic dataset. The data points are colored based on the clusters identified by DBSCAN.

DBSCAN has successfully identified the clusters in the dataset. Note that DBSCAN may label some points as noise (often labeled as "-1"). In this visualization, it seems that all points have been assigned to clusters, indicating no noise in this particular instance.

Listing 7.3 displays the content of DBSCAN_GPT4.py that illustrates how to create a machine learning model using the DBSCAN algorithm and the death. csv dataset.

LISTING 7.3: DBSCAN_GPT4.py

```
# Importing necessary libraries
from sklearn.datasets import make_blobs
import matplotlib.pyplot as plt
import numpy as np
from scipy.cluster.hierarchy import dendrogram, linkage,
fcluster
```

```
# Generating the synthetic dataset again
X_hc, y_hc = make_blobs(n_samples=150, centers=3, random_
state=42, cluster_std=2.0)

# Visualizing the previously generated dataset
plt.figure(figsize=(8, 6))
plt.scatter(X_hc[:, 0], X_hc[:, 1], c=y_hc, s=50,
cmap='viridis')
plt.title("Generated Dataset")
plt.xlabel("Feature 1")
plt.ylabel("Feature 2")
plt.show()

from sklearn.cluster import DBSCAN

# Applying DBSCAN clustering
dbscan = DBSCAN(eps=2.5, min_samples=5)
dbscan_labels = dbscan.fit_predict(X_hc)

# Visualizing the clusters identified by DBSCAN
plt.figure(figsize=(8, 6))
plt.scatter(X_hc[:, 0], X_hc[:, 1], c=dbscan_labels, s=50,
cmap='viridis')
plt.title("DBSCAN Clustering Results")
plt.xlabel("Feature 1")
plt.ylabel("Feature 2")
plt.show()
```

Listing 7.3 starts with several import statements, followed by the invocation of make_blobs() to create a synthetic dataset. The next code block generates and displays a scatter plot from the data in the generated dataset.

The next portion of Listing 7.3 initializes the variable dbscan as an instance of the class DBSCAN that was imported from sklearn.cluster. Notice that the variable dbscan_labels is initialized with the result of invoking the fit_predict() method of the variable dbscan. The content of dbscan_labels is a list of cluster labels, where "noisy" samples are assigned the label "-1." In addition, the parameter eps specifies the maximum distance between two samples for one to be considered as in the neighborhood of the other.

The final portion of Listing 7.3 creates a scatter plot that displays the clusters that DBSCAN has identified in the dataset. Launch the code in Listing 7.3, and you will see two images generated. Figure 7.5 displays three clusters, and Figure 7.6 displays the three clusters with cluster labels.

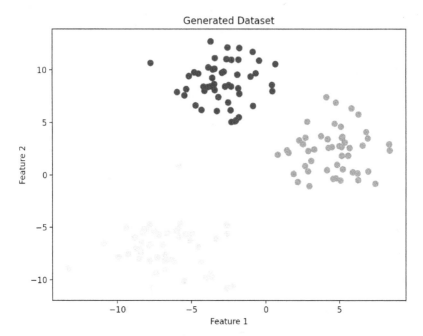

FIGURE 7.5 Generated dataset

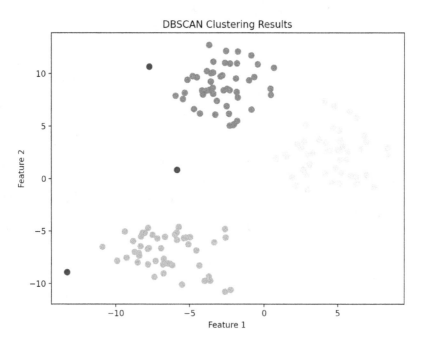

FIGURE 7.6 Three clusters with cluster labels

SUMMARY

This chapter is your third full chapter with material for clustering that was generated by GPT-4. After a brief overview of clustering, you saw a list of ten clustering algorithms, along with their advantages and disadvantages. In addition, you learned about metric for clustering algorithms.

Finally, you saw Python code samples that were generated by GPT-4 for the kMeans, Hierarchical Clustering, and the DBSCAN clustering algorithms.

Next you saw a Python-based code sample for the k-means algorithm, which is one of the popular clustering algorithms in machine learning. Then you learned about the hierarchical clustering algorithm, followed by a Python-based code sample that uses this algorithm. In addition, you saw a Python-based code sample for the DBSCAN algorithm, which is yet another popular clustering algorithms in machine learning.

## CHAPTER 8

CHATGPT AND DATA VISUALIZATION

This chapter contains examples of using ChatGPT and GPT-4 to perform data visualization, such as charts and graphs that are based on datasets (e.g., the Titanic dataset). ChatGPT generated all the code samples via the Advanced Data Analysis plugin. ChatGPT also generated some of the accompanying text for the Python-based code samples.

The first part of this chapter describes the process of uploading a dataset in ChatGPT and then providing prompts for tasks such as explaining the features in a given dataset, generating visualizations, and downloading the curated dataset. You will also learn how to prompt ChatGPT to create and train a machine learning model.

The second part of this chapter contains examples of data visualization with Matplotlib, where the code samples were generated with ChatGPT. The third part of this chapter contains examples of data visualization with Seaborn, where the code samples were generated with ChatGPT.

Before you read the material in this chapter, please keep in mind that some formatting has been applied to the AI content that GPT-4 has generated in this chapter as well as Chapters 5, 6, and 7. However, the additional formatting has been kept to a minimum so that you will become familiar with the style of GPT-4.

WORKING WITH CHARTS AND GRAPHS

If you have already worked with charts and graphs, then you already know that every chart type has its unique strengths and is best suited for specific kinds of data and analysis. The choice of chart often depends on the nature of the data and the specific insights one wants to derive. This section contains multiple subsections that provide information about an assortment of charts and graphs, as shown below:

- bar charts
- pie charts
- line graphs
- heat map
- histograms
- box plots
- Pareto charts
- radar charts
- treemaps
- waterfall charts
- scatter plots

Most of the charts and graphs in the preceding bullet list are discussed in the following subsections.

Bar Charts

Bar charts represent data with rectangular bars. The lengths of the bars are proportional to the values they represent. They can be vertical (column charts) or horizontal. An example of usage involves comparing the sales of different products in a store.

Some advantages of bar charts are listed below:

- easily interpretable and widely recognized
- can compare individual or multiple data series
- effective for displaying data that spans several categories

Some disadvantages of bar charts are listed below:

- not ideal for showing patterns or trends over time
- can become cluttered when comparing too many categories

Pie Charts

Pie charts represent data in a circular format, with individual sections (slices) showing categories' proportion to the whole. An example of usage involves representing the market share of different companies in an industry.

Some advantages of pie charts are listed below:

- simple visualization that shows part-to-whole relationships
- clearly indicate proportions
- effective when there are a limited number of categories

Some disadvantages of pie charts are listed below:

- not efficient for comparing individual categories
- can become ineffective and difficult to interpret with too many slices
- do not show absolute values, only proportions

Line Graphs

Line graphs display data points connected by straight lines. They are used primarily to visualize values over a continuous interval or time period. An example of usage involves tracking a company's revenue growth over several years.

Some advantages of line graphs are listed below:

- effective for displaying trends over time
- can compare multiple data series on one graph
- clear visualization of data points and intervals

Some disadvantages of line graphs are listed below:

- not suitable for showing part-to-whole relationships
- can become cluttered when displaying too many data series
- require a meaningful order of data points

Heat Maps

A heat map represents data in a matrix format, where individual values are depicted as colors. The color intensity usually represents the magnitude of the value. An example of usage involves visualizing visitor activity on different parts of a Web page.

Some advantages of heat maps are listed below:

- quickly identify patterns, correlations, and areas of concentration
- use color effectively to convey information about magnitudes

Some disadvantages of heat maps are listed below:

- not suitable for detailed numerical analysis
- Color choices are crucial; poor choices can lead to misinterpretation.

Histograms

A histogram is a graphical representation of the distribution of a dataset. It is an estimate of the probability distribution of a continuous variable. An example of usage involves showing the distribution of the ages in a population.

Some advantages of histograms are listed below:

- provide a visual interpretation of numerical data by indicating the number of data points that lie within a range of values
- can help identify data distribution patterns

Some disadvantages of histograms are listed below:

- do not show exact values
- number and width of bins can influence perception

Box Plots

Box plots, or box and whisker plots, represent a summary of a dataset using quartiles. The "box" shows the interquartile range, while the "whiskers" indicate variability outside the upper and lower quartiles. An example of usage involves comparing sales performances across different teams.

Some advantages of box plots are listed below:

- quickly visualize data spread and skewness
- identify outliers

Some disadvantages of box plots are listed below:

- not suitable for detailed distribution analysis
- do not show the frequency distribution of data

Pareto Charts

Pareto charts combine a bar chart and a line graph to represent the cumulative frequency of occurrences. It identifies the most significant factors in a dataset. An example of usage involves identifying which product defects occur most frequently.

Some advantages of Pareto charts are listed below:

- efficiently highlight the most important factors in large datasets
- aid in prioritizing efforts

Some disadvantages of Pareto charts are listed below:

- limited to datasets where ranking and prioritization are relevant
- not suitable for showing relationships between data points

Radar Charts

Radar charts are a graphical method of displaying data in a 2D chart of three or more quantitative variables. The data points are plotted on axes that start from the center. An example of usage involves comparing the performance metrics of products.

Some advantages of radar charts are listed below:

- can compare multiple quantitative variables
- provide a visual overview of the data

Some disadvantages of radar charts are listed below:

- can become cluttered when comparing too many datasets
- difficult to interpret with similar values

Treemaps

Treemaps display hierarchical data as nested rectangles. Each branch of the hierarchy is represented by colored rectangles. An example of usage involves visualizing storage usage on a computer.

Some advantages of tree maps are listed below:

- efficient use of space
- can represent multiple dimensions using size and color

Some disadvantages of tree maps are listed below:

- not suitable for datasets with large hierarchies
- can become difficult to interpret

Waterfall Charts

Waterfall charts represent the cumulative effect of sequentially occurring positive or negative values. An example of usage involves visualizing how profit or revenue is affected by various factors.

Some advantages of waterfall charts are listed below:

- clearly visualize positive and negative sequential changes
- help in understanding the gradual transition from one data point to another

Some disadvantages of waterfall charts are listed below:

- limited to situations where understanding sequential changes is necessary
- can become confusing with too many data points

LINE PLOTS WITH MATPLOTLIB

The following prompt was supplied to GPT-4 to generate Python code for a simple line plot: "Please generate Python code to plot a simple line graph in order to visualize a trend."

Listing 8.1 displays the content of `line_plots.py` that ChatGPT generated to render a line plot using Matplotlib.

LISTING 8.1: line_plot.py

```python
import matplotlib.pyplot as plt

def plot_line(x, y, title, x_label, y_label):
    plt.plot(x, y)
    plt.title(title)
    plt.xlabel(x_label)
    plt.ylabel(y_label)
    plt.grid(True)
    plt.show()

# Usage
x = [1, 2, 3, 4, 5]
y = [2, 4, 1, 3, 5]
plot_line(x, y, 'Sample Line Graph', 'X-Axis', 'Y-Axis')
```

Listing 8.1 starts with an `import` statement and then defines the function `plot_line()` that renders a line plot. Matplotlib has the `plot()` function that provides a straightforward way to create line graphs. In this function, we visualize a trend across the x and y axes.

The next portion of code initializes the Python lists x and y and then invokes `plot_line()` with three strings that are the values for the title, the horizontal axis, and the vertical axis. Figure 8.1 displays the output from launching the code in Listing 8.1.

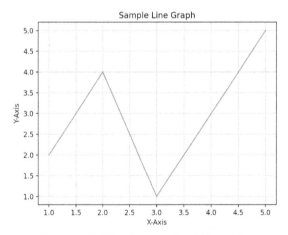

FIGURE 8.1 A line plot created with Matplotlib

PIE CHARTS USING MATPLOTLIB

Pie charts are ideal for displaying proportional data among categories. The pie function from Matplotlib provides an easy way to achieve this. The following prompt was supplied to GPT-4 to generate Python code for a pie chart: "Please generate Python code to display a simple pie chart."

Listing 8.2 displays the content of `pie_chart1.py` that ChatGPT generated to render a line using Matplotlib.

LISTING 8.2: pie_chart1.py

```
import matplotlib.pyplot as plt

def plot_pie(labels, sizes, title):
    plt.pie(sizes, labels=labels, autopct='%1.1f%%',
startangle=140)
    plt.title(title)
    plt.axis('equal')  # Equal aspect ratio ensures the pie
is drawn as a circle.
    plt.show()

# Usage
labels = ['A', 'B', 'C']
sizes = [215, 130, 245]
plot_pie(labels, sizes, 'Sample Pie Chart')
```

Listing 8.2 starts in a similar fashion as Listing 8.1, except that the `plot_pie()` function for generating a pie chart is generated. The next portion of Listing 8.2 initializes the Python lists' labels and sizes. The function `plot_pie()` is invoked with these lists, as well as a string that is displayed as the title of the pie chart. Figure 8.2 displays the pie chart that is rendered by launching the code in Listing 8.2.

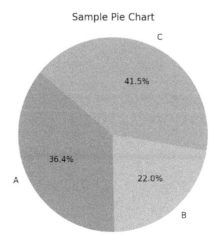

FIGURE 8.2 A pie chart created with Matplotlib

BOX AND WHISKER PLOTS USING MATPLOTLIB

Box plots, or box and whisker plots, provide a summary of the distribution of data, highlighting the central tendency, variability, and presence of outliers. They can be particularly useful for comparing distributions across different groups. They can display the distribution of the data based on the minimum, first quartile, median, third quartile, and maximum.

The following prompt was supplied to GPT-4 to generate Python code for a box plot: "Please generate Python code to render a box plot."

Listing 8.3 displays the content of `boxplot1.py` that ChatGPT generated to render a box plot using Seaborn.

LISTING 8.3: boxplot1.py

```python
import matplotlib.pyplot as plt
import seaborn as sns

import matplotlib.pyplot as plt

def plot_box(data, column):
    plt.boxplot(data[column])
    plt.show()

# Usage
data = sns.load_dataset("iris")
plot_box(data, "sepal_length")
```

Listing 8.3 contains three import statements followed by the `plot_box()` function that generated a box plot. The next portion of Listing 8.3 initializes the variable `data` with the contents of the Seaborn built-in `iris` dataset, and then invokes `plot_box()` with data and a string that specifies the feature (column) to use when rendering a box plot. Figure 8.3 displays the box plot that is rendered by launching the code in Listing 8.3.

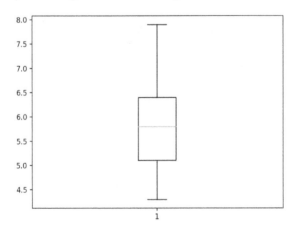

FIGURE 8.3 A box plot created with Matplotlib

TIME SERIES VISUALIZATION WITH MATPLOTLIB

Time series data, where observations are taken at regular time intervals, can be visualized using line plots. This enables analysts to discern trends, patterns, and anomalies. The following prompt was supplied to GPT-4 to generate Python code for time series data: "Please generate Python code to render time series data."

Listing 8.4 displays the content of time_series.py that ChatGPT generated to render a time series using Matplotlib.

LISTING 8.4: time_series.py

```
import matplotlib.pyplot as plt

import pandas as pd

def plot_time_series(dates, values, title):
    plt.figure(figsize=(10, 5))
    plt.plot(dates, values)
    plt.title(title)
    plt.xlabel('Date')
    plt.ylabel('Value')
    plt.tight_layout()
    plt.show()

# Usage
dates = pd.date_range(start="2021-01-01", periods=10,
freq='D')
values = [x**1.5 for x in range(10)]
plot_time_series(dates, values, 'Sample Time Series Data')
```

Figure 8.4 displays the time series that is rendered by launching the code in Listing 8.4.

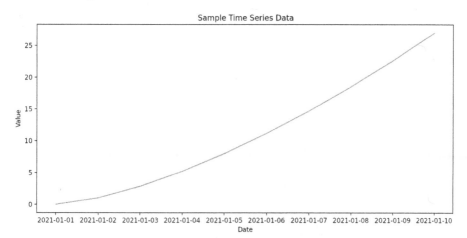

FIGURE 8.4 A time series created with Matplotlib

STACKED BAR CHARTS WITH MATPLOTLIB

Stacked bar charts allow for the representation of subgroups in each category, giving a sense of the total size across categories and the subgroup distributions within them. The following prompt was supplied to GPT-4 to generate Python code for a stacked bar chart: "Please generate Python code to display a stacked bar chart."

Listing 8.5 displays the content of stacked_bar_charts.py that ChatGPT generated to render stacked bar charts using Matplotlib.

LISTING 8.5: stacked_bar_charts.py

```python
import matplotlib.pyplot as plt
import numpy as np

def plot_stacked_bar(data, labels, categories):
    cum_size = np.zeros(len(categories))

    for i, label in enumerate(labels):
        plt.bar(categories, data[label], bottom=cum_size,
label=label)
        cum_size += data[label]

    plt.legend()
    plt.show()

# Usage
data = {
    'A': [10, 15, 20],
    'B': [5, 10, 5]
}
labels = ['A', 'B']
categories = ['Category 1', 'Category 2', 'Category 3']
plot_stacked_bar(data, labels, categories)
```

Figure 8.5 displays the stacked bar charts that are rendered by launching the code in Listing 8.5.

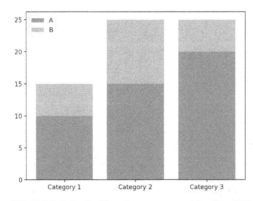

FIGURE 8.5 Stacked bar charts generated by ChatGPT

DONUT CHARTS USING MATPLOTLIB

Donut charts are a variation of pie charts. The hollow center can be used for additional annotations or just to provide a different aesthetic. They represent data proportionally among categories, and are similar to a pie chart but with a hollow center. The following prompt was supplied to GPT-4 to generate Python code for a donut chart: "Please generate Python code to plot a donut chart."

Listing 8.6 displays the content of donut_charts.py that ChatGPT generated to render a donut chart using Matplotlib.

LISTING 8.6: donut_charts.py

```python
import matplotlib.pyplot as plt

def plot_donut_chart(sizes, labels, title, hole_size=0.3):
    fig, ax = plt.subplots()
    ax.pie(sizes, labels=labels, autopct='%1.1f%%',
startangle=90, wedgeprops=dict(width=hole_size))
    ax.axis('equal')
    plt.title(title)
    plt.show()

# Usage
labels = ['A', 'B', 'C']
sizes = [215, 130, 245]
plot_donut_chart(sizes, labels,''Sample Donut Char'')
```

Figure 8.6 displays the donut chart that is rendered by launching the code in Listing 8.6.

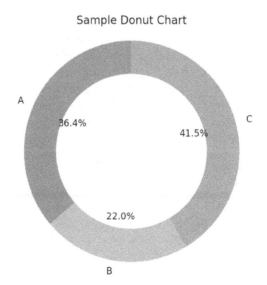

Sample Donut Chart

FIGURE 8.6 A donut chart created using Matplotlib

3D SURFACE PLOTS WITH MATPLOTLIB

Three-dimensional (3D) surface plots are used for visualizing functions with two variables. They can reveal intricate patterns and relationships in the data. The following prompt was supplied to GPT-4 to generate Python code for a 3D surface: "Please generate Python code to plot a 3D surface."

Listing 8.7 displays the content of 3d_surface.py that ChatGPT generated to render a 3D surface using mpl_toolkits.

Incidentally, if you encounter issues with mpl_toolkits, please read the following post, which contains useful information:

*https://stackoverflow.com/questions/37661119/python-mpl-toolkits-
installation-issue*

LISTING 8.7: 3d_surface.py

```
import matplotlib.pyplot as plt
import numpy as np

def plot_3d_surface(x, y, z):
    fig = plt.figure()
    ax = fig.add_subplot(111, projection='3')
    ax.plot_surface(x, y, z, cmap='viridi')
    plt.show()

# Usage
x = np.linspace(-5, 5, 50)
y = np.linspace(-5, 5, 50)
x, y = np.meshgrid(x, y)
z = np.sin(np.sqrt(x**2 + y**2))
plot_3d_surface(x, y, z)
```

Listing 8.7 starts with two import statements, followed by the plot_3d_surface() function that renders a 3D plot. The second half of Listing 8.7 initializes the variables x and y via the NumPy function linspace() that partitions an interval into a set of equally-sized subintervals.

For example, the code snippet np.linspace(-5, 5, 50) divides the interval [-5,5] into 50 equally spaced points, which means that there are 49 intervals of equal width. You can persuade yourself that this is true by replacing 50 with 3: the result is the left endpoint -5, the midpoint, and the right endpoint 5, which creates 2 (=3-1) intervals.

The next code snippet updates x and y with the result of invoking the meshgrid() function in NumPy, after which z is defined as the trigonometric sine function applied to the number that equals the distance of the point (x, y) from the origin. Although the latter number is monotonically increasing as the point (x, y) shifts away from the origin, and z is the sine of that distance, which is a periodic function: as a result, you will see a rolling wave-like effect.

The final code snippet in Listing 8.7 invokes the function `plot_3d_surface()` with the values contained in the variables x, y, and z. Launch the code in Listing 8.7, and you will see the 3D surface that is displayed in Figure 8.7.

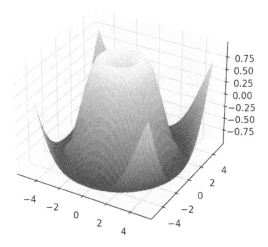

FIGURE 8.7 A 3D surface created with Matplotlib

RADIAL (OR SPIDER) CHARTS WITH MATPLOTLIB

Radial (or spider) charts are used to visualize multivariate data in the form of a two-dimensional chart of three or more quantitative variables. Each variable is represented on a separate axis that starts from the center of the chart. The following prompt was supplied to GPT-4 to generate Python code for a radial chart: "Please generate Python code to display a radial chart."

Listing 8.8 displays the content of `radial_charts.py` that ChatGPT generated to render radial charts using Matplotlib.

LISTING 8.8: radial_charts.py

```
import matplotlib.pyplot as plt
import numpy as np

def plot_spider_chart(values, categories, title):
    angles = np.linspace(0, 2 * np.pi, len(categories),
endpoint=False).tolist()
    values += values[:1]
    angles += angles[:1]

    fig, ax = plt.subplots(figsize=(6, 6), subplot_
kw=dict(polar=True))
    ax.fill(angles, values, color='blue', alpha=0.25)
    ax.set_yticklabels([])
```

```
# the following snippet causes an error:
# ax.set_xticks(angles)
# the following snippet is correct:
ax.set_xticks(angles[:-1]) # Exclude the last angle
since it's cyclic

ax.set_xticklabels(categories)

plt.title(title, size=20, color="blue", y=1.1)
plt.show()
```

```
# Usage
categories = ["A", "B", "C", "D"]
values = [50, 30, 60, 40]
plot_spider_chart(values, categories, 'Sample Spider
Chart')
```

Listing 8.8 starts with two `import` statements, followed by the Python function `plot_spider_chart()` function that renders a radial chart. The second portion of Listing 8.8 initializes the variables `categories` and `values` as two Python lists and then invokes the function `plot_spider_chart()` with the variables `categories`, `values`, and a text string for the title of the plot. Figure 8.8 displays the radial chart that is rendered by launching the code in Listing 8.8.

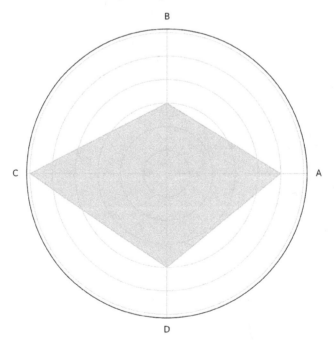

FIGURE 8.8 Radial chart created with Seaborn

There is one more detail that will help you with debugging the code that ChatGPT generates for you. Let's look at the code block in bold in Listing 8.8:

```
# the following snippet causes an error:
# ax.set_xticks(angles)
# the following snippet is correct:
ax.set_xticks(angles[:-1]) # Exclude the last angle since
it's cyclic
```

If you reverse the order of the two code snippets, the code will not work correctly. Here is the "conversation" with ChatGPT to ask for a solution.

Author: "I uploaded radial_charts.py that contains code that you wrote for me. However, this code results in this error: ValueError: The number of FixedLocator locations (5), usually from a call to set_ticks, does not match the number of ticklabels (4). Can you provide a solution?"

The response from ChatGPT is as follows:

Thank you for providing the radial_charts.py file. Let's start by reading its content to understand the structure and context of the code. After that, I'll analyze the potential causes of the mentioned error and offer a solution.

The provided radial_charts.py file contains a function, plot_spider_chart, which is designed to plot a spider (or radar) chart using given values and categories.

Based on the error you reported and the code's structure, the issue likely arises from the mismatch between the number of tick locations (set by ax.set_xticks(angles)) and the number of tick labels (set by ax.set_xticklabels(categories)).

To address this, I'll ensure that the number of tick locations matches the number of tick labels. Let's proceed to make this adjustment and provide a corrected version of the function.

Author: "This works correctly now! Thank you for your help!"

The response from ChatGPT is as follows:

You are welcome! I'm glad to hear it is working as expected now. If you have any more questions or need further assistance in the future, do not hesitate to reach out. Happy coding!

MATPLOTLIB'S CONTOUR PLOTS

Contour plots help visualize three-dimensional data in two dimensions using contour lines. Each contour line represents points of equal value. The following prompt was supplied to GPT-4 to generate Python code for a contour plot: "Please generate Python code to plot a contour plot."

Listing 8.9 displays the content of `contour_lines.py` that ChatGPT generated to render contour lines using Matplotlib.

LISTING 8.9: contour_lines.py

```python
import matplotlib.pyplot as plt
import numpy as np

def plot_contour(x, y, z):
    plt.contourf(x, y, z, 20, cmap='viridis')
    plt.colorbar()
    plt.show()

# Usage
x = np.linspace(-5, 5, 50)
y = np.linspace(-5, 5, 50)
x, y = np.meshgrid(x, y)
z = np.sin(np.sqrt(x**2 + y**2))
plot_contour(x, y, z)
```

Listing 8.9 contains two import statements and then the function `plot_contour()` is defined that renders the contour lines for the code sample. Note that the second part of Listing 8.9 is virtually identical to the code in the second half of Listing 8.7. Figure 8.9 displays the contour plot that is rendered by launching the code in Listing 8.9.

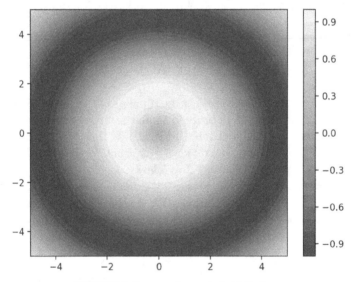

FIGURE 8.9 Contour plot created with Seaborn

STREAMPLOTS FOR VECTOR FIELDS

Streamplots are used for displaying vector fields, like wind patterns. They provide a snapshot of the flow trajectories and can be color-coded for scalar data, and the ability to visualize a vector field as streamlines. The following prompt was supplied to GPT-4 to generate Python code for a vector field: "Please generate Python code to display a vector field."

Listing 8.10 displays the content of `stream_plot.py` that ChatGPT generated to render a stream plot using Seaborn.

LISTING 8.10: stream_plot.py

```
import matplotlib.pyplot as plt
import seaborn as sns
import numpy as np

def plot_streamplot(x, y, u, v):
    plt.streamplot(x, y, u, v, density=1)
    plt.show()

# Usage
x = np.linspace(-5, 5, 10)
y = np.linspace(-5, 5, 10)

# this causes an error:
#y, x = np.meshgrid(y, x)
# this works correctly:
x, y = np.meshgrid(x, y)

u = -1 - x**2 + y
v = 1 + x - y**2
plot_streamplot(x, y, u, v)
```

Figure 8.10 displays the streamplot that is rendered by launching the code in Listing 8.10.

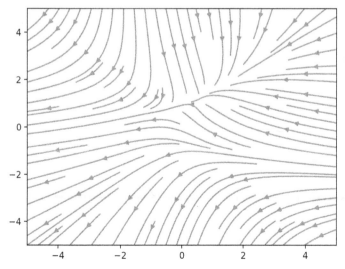

FIGURE 8.10 Streamplot created with Seaborn

The initial code in Listing 8.10 from ChatGPT did not work correctly, so I asked ChatGPT to provide a solution during the following "dialog" with ChatGPT.

Author: "I uploaded stream_plot.py that contains code that you wrote for me. This code results in the following error: ValueError: The rows of 'x' must be equal. Can you provide a solution?"

The response from ChatGPT is as follows:

The shapes of the arrays x, y, u, and v are all (10,10), which means they are consistent in terms of dimensions. The error message "ValueError: The rows of 'x' must be equal" suggests that there might be an issue with the values within the rows of the x array, rather than its shape.

The line y, x = np.meshgrid(y, x) swaps the original x and y arrays. This might be causing inconsistencies in the rows of the x array.

To address the error, I'll modify the meshgrid creation and ensure the x and y arrays are correctly initialized. Let's make the necessary adjustments.

Author: "This works! Thanks for your help!"

The response from ChatGPT is as follows:

You are welcome! I'm glad to hear it is working as expected now. If you have any more questions or need further assistance in the future, do not hesitate to reach out. Happy coding!

QUIVER PLOTS FOR VECTOR FIELDS

Quiver plots are useful for representing vector fields, showing both the direction and magnitude of vectors. For instance, they can be utilized in physics to show electric fields or fluid flow directions. The following prompt was supplied to GPT-4 to generate Python code for a quiver plot: "Please generate Python code to plot a quiver plot."

Listing 8.11 displays the content of quiver_plot.py that ChatGPT generated to render a quiver plot using Matplotlib.

LISTING 8.11: quiver_plot.py

```
import matplotlib.pyplot as plt
import numpy as np

def plot_quiver(x, y, u, v):
    plt.quiver(x, y, u, v, scale=20)
    plt.show()

# Usage
x, y = np.meshgrid(np.arange(0, 2 * np.pi, .2),
np.arange(0, 2 * np.pi, .2))
u = np.sin(x)
v = np.cos(y)
plot_quiver(x, y, u, v)
```

Figure 8.11 displays the quiver plot that is rendered by launching the code in Listing 8.11.

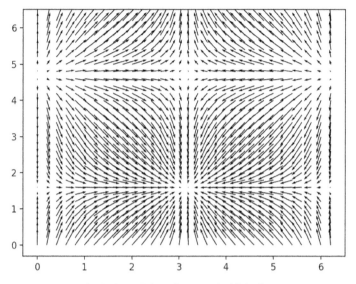

FIGURE 8.11 Quiver plot created with Seaborn

POLAR PLOTS

Polar plots (or radial plots) are suitable for displaying multivariate data in a two-dimensional chart where the variables are represented on axes starting from the same point. They are useful for viewing patterns based on angles and magnitudes. The following prompt was supplied to GPT-4 to generate Python code for a polar plot: "Please generate Python code to display a polar plot."

Listing 8.12 displays the content of `polar_plots.py` that ChatGPT generated to render stacked polar plots using Seaborn and generated by ChatGPT.

LISTING 8.12: polar_plots.py

```
import matplotlib.pyplot as plt
import numpy as np

def plot_polar(theta, radii, title=""):
    plt.figure(figsize=(8, 4))
    ax = plt.subplot(111, projection='polar')
    ax.plot(theta, radii)
    ax.set_title(title)
    plt.show()
# Usage
theta = np.linspace(0, 2 * np.pi, 100)
radii = np.abs(np.sin(theta) * 2)
plot_polar(theta, radii, "Sample Polar Plot")
```

Figure 8.12 displays the polar plot that is rendered by launching the code in Listing 8.12.

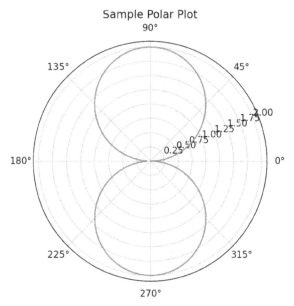

FIGURE 8.12 A polar plot created with Matplotlib

BAR CHARTS WITH SEABORN

Seaborn provides a higher-level interface for Matplotlib, making the creation of stylish plots more accessible. This bar plot helps visualize data across different categories. The following prompt was supplied to GPT-4 to generate Python code for a bar chart: "Please generate Python code to render a bar chart."

Note: Seaborn works best when integrated with Pandas.

Listing 8.13 displays the content of `bar_chart1.py` that ChatGPT generated to a bar chart using Seaborn.

LISTING 8.13: bar_chart1.py

```
import matplotlib.pyplot as plt
import seaborn as sns
import pandas as pd

def plot_bar(data, x_col, y_col):
    sns.barplot(x=x_col, y=y_col, data=data)
    plt.show()

# Usage
data = pd.DataFrame({
```

```
    'Category': ['A', 'B', 'C'],
    'Values': [10, 20, 15]
})
plot_bar(data, 'Category', 'Values')
```

Listing 8.13 starts with three `import` statements, followed by the function `plot_bar()` that renders the bar chart. The second half of Listing 8.13 initializes the Pandas data frame `data` and then invokes `plot_bar()` with data and a string for labeling the horizontal axis and another string for labeling the vertical axis. Figure 8.13 displays the bar chart that is rendered by launching the code in Listing 8.13.

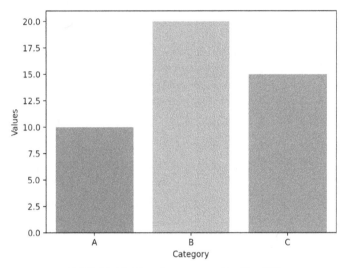

FIGURE 8.13 A bar chart generated by ChatGPT

SCATTER PLOTS WITH REGRESSION LINES USING SEABORN

Scatter plots display data points and utilize a regression line to help reveal relationships. The following prompt was supplied to GPT-4 to generate Python code for a regression line: "Please generate Python code to plot a regression line."

Listing 8.14 displays the content of `scatter_plot.py` that ChatGPT generated to render a scatter chart using Seaborn.

LISTING 8.14: scatter_plot.py

```
import matplotlib.pyplot as plt
import pandas as pd
import seaborn as sns
```

```
def plot_scatter_with_regression(data, x_col, y_col):
    sns.regplot(x=x_col, y=y_col, data=data)
    plt.show()

# Usage
data = pd.DataFrame({
    'X_Values': [10, 20, 30, 40, 50],
    'Y_Values': [15, 25, 35, 45, 55]
})
plot_scatter_with_regression(data, 'X_Values', 'Y_Values')
```

Scatter plots are useful for visualizing relationships between two variables. Seaborn has a `regplot()` function that not only plots the data points but also fits a regression line.

Listing 8.14 starts with three `import` statements and the `plot_scatter_with_regression()` function that renders the scatter plot. The second half of Listing 8.13 initializes the Pandas data frame `data` and then invokes `plot_scattter_with_regression()` with the variable `data`. Figure 8.14 displays the scatter plot that is rendered by launching the code in Listing 8.14.

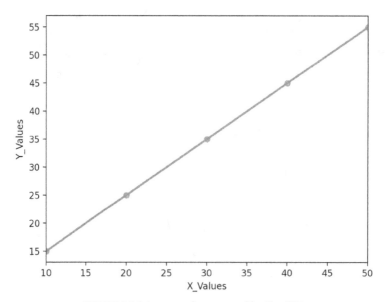

FIGURE 8.14 A scatter plot generated by ChatGPT

HEATMAPS FOR CORRELATION MATRICES WITH SEABORN

Heatmaps are powerful for representing matrices of data, with colors indicating magnitudes. A common use case is visualizing correlation matrices, which help in revealing relationships among different variables. The following prompt was supplied to GPT-4 to generate Python code for a simple line plot: "Please generate Python code to plot a heat map."

Listing 8.15 displays the content of `heatmap1.py` that ChatGPT generated to render a line using Matplotlib.

LISTING 8.15: heatmap1.py

```python
import matplotlib.pyplot as plt
import pandas as pd
import seaborn as sns

def plot_heatmap(data):
    correlation_matrix = data.corr()
    sns.heatmap(correlation_matrix, annot=True,
cmap='coolwarm')
    plt.show()

# Usage
data = pd.DataFrame({
    'A': [1, 2, 3, 4, 5],
    'B': [5, 4, 3, 2, 1],
    'C': [2, 3, 4, 5, 6]
})
plot_heatmap(data)
```

Listing 8.15 starts with three `import` statements and the `plot_heatmap()` function that renders the heat map. The second half of Listing 8.15 initializes the Pandas data frame `data` and then invokes `plot_heatmap()` with the variable `data`. Figure 8.15 displays the heat map that is rendered by launching the code in Listing 8.15.

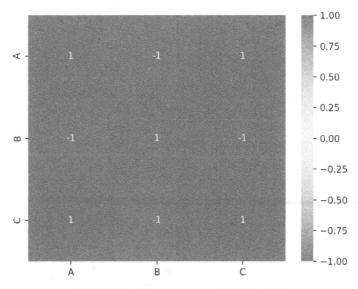

FIGURE 8.15 A heat map created with Matplotlib

HISTOGRAMS WITH SEABORN

Histograms are powerful tools for visualizing the distribution of data. Seaborn's `histplot()` function provides a way to easily generate histograms with additional features like the kernel density estimation. The following prompt was supplied to GPT-4 to generate Python code for a histogram: "Please generate Python code to plot a histogram."

Listing 8.16 displays the content of `histogram1.py` that ChatGPT generated to render a histogram using Seaborn.

LISTING 8.16: histogram1.py

```python
import matplotlib.pyplot as plt
import seaborn as sns

def plot_histogram(data, column, bins=10):
    sns.histplot(data[column], bins=bins)
    plt.show()

# Usage
data = sns.load_dataset("iris")
plot_histogram(data, "sepal_length")
```

Listing 8.16 starts with two `import` statements and the `plot_histogram()` function that renders the histogram. The second half of Listing 8.16 initializes the Pandas data frame `data` with the contents of the Seaborn built-in dataset `iris`, and then invokes `plot_histogram()` with the variable `data`. Figure 8.16 displays the heat map for the `iris` dataset that is rendered by launching the code in Listing 8.16.

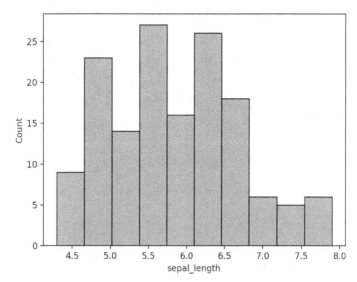

FIGURE 8.16 A histogram generated by ChatGPT

VIOLIN PLOTS WITH SEABORN

Violin plots offer a deeper understanding of the distribution of data. They combine the characteristics of box plots and histograms, showing the probability density of the data at different values. You can combine aspects of box plots and histograms to provide richer descriptions of data distributions. The following prompt was supplied to GPT-4 to generate Python code for a violin plot: "Please generate Python code to plot a violin plot."

Listing 8.17 displays the content of `violin_plots.py` that ChatGPT generated to render a violin plot using Seaborn.

LISTING 8.17: violin_plots.py

```
import seaborn as sns

def plot_violin(data, x_col, y_col):
    sns.violinplot(x=x_col, y=y_col, data=data)
    plt.show()

# Usage
data = sns.load_dataset("iris")
plot_violin(data, "species", "sepal_length")
```

Listing 8.17 starts with one `import` statement and the `plot_violin()` function that renders the violin plot. The second half of Listing 8.17 initializes the Pandas data frame `data` with the contents of the Seaborn built-in dataset `iris`. It invokes `plot_violin()` with the variable `data`. Figure 8.17 displays the violin plot that is rendered by launching the code in Listing 8.17.

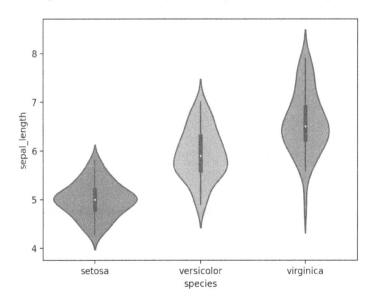

FIGURE 8.17 A violin plot created with Seaborn

PAIR PLOTS USING SEABORN

When dealing with datasets having multiple features, it is often helpful to visualize the pairwise relationships between features. Seaborn has a `pairplot()` function that generates a matrix of scatter plots, allowing for the exploration of such relationships. The following prompt was supplied to GPT-4 to generate Python code for a pair plot: "Please generate Python code to display a pair plot."

Listing 8.18 displays the content of `pair_plots.py` that ChatGPT generated to render a line using Matplotlib.

LISTING 8.18: pair_plots.py

```
import matplotlib.pyplot as plt
import seaborn as sns

def plot_pairplot(data):
    sns.pairplot(data)
    plt.show()

# Usage
data = sns.load_dataset("iris")
plot_pairplot(data)
```

Listing 8.18 starts with two `import` statements and the `plot_pairplot()` function that renders the pair plot. The second part of Listing 8.18 initializes the Pandas data frame `data` with the contents of the Seaborn built-in dataset `iris`, and then invokes `plot_pair()` with the variable `data`. Figure 8.18 displays the pair plot that is rendered by launching the code in Listing 8.18.

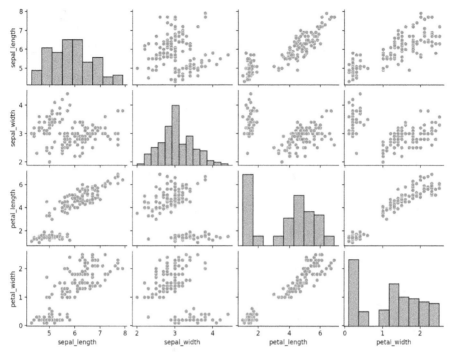

FIGURE 8.18 A pair plot created with Matplotlib

FACET GRIDS WITH SEABORN

Facet grids are a way to visualize the data distribution across several subplots based on a categorical variable. Each facet (subplot) represents a category. The following prompt was supplied to GPT-4 to generate Python code for facet grids: "Please generate Python code to plot facet grids."

Listing 8.19 displays the content of `facet_grids.py` that ChatGPT generated to create and render multiple plots segmented by categories.

LISTING 8.19: facet_grids.py

```
import matplotlib.pyplot as plt
import seaborn as sns

def plot_facetgrid(data, x_col, y_col, facet_col):
    g = sns.FacetGrid(data, col=facet_col)
    g.map(sns.scatterplot, x_col, y_col)
    g.add_legend()
    plt.show()

# Usage
data = sns.load_dataset("iris")
plot_facetgrid(data, "sepal_length", "sepal_width",
"species")
```

Listing 8.19 starts with two `import` statements and the `plot_facet-grid()` function that renders the facets. The second part of Listing 8.19 initializes the Pandas data frame `data` with the contents of the Seaborn built-in dataset `iris`, and then invokes `plot_pair()` with the variable `data`. Figure 8.19 displays the facet grids that is rendered by launching the code in Listing 8.19.

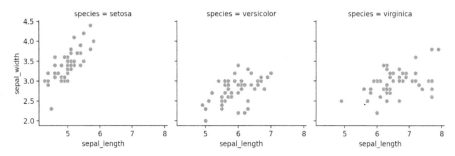

FIGURE 8.19 Facet grids created with Seaborn

HIERARCHICAL CLUSTERING

Seaborn's `clustermap` is a 2D matrix dataset representation where both rows and columns are hierarchically clustered. This allows patterns to emerge from complex datasets. Visualize hierarchically clustered relationships in a heatmap format. The following prompt was supplied to GPT-4 to generate Python code for hierarchical clustering: "Please generate Python code to display hierarchical clustering."

LISTING 8.20: cluster_map.py

```
import matplotlib.pyplot as plt
import seaborn as sns

def plot_clustermap(data):
    sns.clustermap(data, method='average', cmap='coolwarm')
    plt.show()

# Usage
data = sns.load_dataset("iris").drop("species", axis=1)
plot_clustermap(data)
```

Listing 8.20 starts with two `import` statements and the `plot_cluster-map()` function that renders the cluster map. The second part of Listing 8.20 initializes the Pandas data frame `data` with the contents of the Seaborn built-in dataset `iris`, and then invokes `plot_pair()` with the variable `data`. Figure 8.20 displays the cluster map that is rendered by launching the code in Listing 8.20.

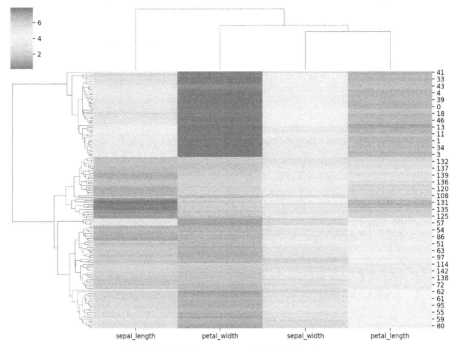

FIGURE 8.20 Cluster map created with Seaborn

SWARM PLOTS

A swarm plot positions each data point on the categorical axis with minimal overlap, giving a better representation of the distribution of values. It creates a categorical scatter plot with non-overlapping points. The following prompt was supplied to GPT-4 to generate Python code for a swarm plot: "Please generate Python code to plot a swarm plot."

Listing 8.21 displays the content of `swarm_plot.py` that ChatGPT generated to render contour lines using Seaborn.

LISTING 8.21: swarm_plot.py

```
import matplotlib.pyplot as plt
import seaborn as sns

def plot_swarm(data, x_col, y_col):
    sns.swarmplot(x=x_col, y=y_col, data=data)
    plt.show()

# Usage
data = sns.load_dataset("iris")
plot_swarm(data, "species", "sepal_length")
```

Listing 8.21 starts with two `import` statements and the `plot_swarm()` function that renders the swarm plot. The second part of Listing 8.21 initializes the Pandas data frame `data` with the contents of the Seaborn built-in dataset `iris`, and then invokes `plot_swarm()` with the variable `data`. Figure 8.21 displays the swarm plot that is rendered by launching the code in Listing 8.21.

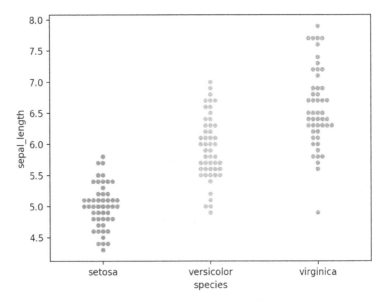

FIGURE 8.21 A swarm plot created with Seaborn

JOINT PLOTS FOR BIVARIATE DATA

Seaborn's `jointplot` displays a relationship between two variables. It combines scatter plots, regression plots, and even hexbin plots with histograms. It displays a relationship between two variables, along with their individual distributions. The following prompt was supplied to GPT-4 to generate Python code for a swarm plot for bivariate data: "Please generate Python code to plot a swarm plot for bivariate data."

Listing 8.22 displays the content of `joint_plot.py` that ChatGPT generated to render a joint plot using Seaborn.

LISTING 8.22: joint_plot.py

```
import matplotlib.pyplot as plt
import seaborn as sns

def plot_jointplot(data, x_col, y_col, kind='scatter'):
    sns.jointplot(x=x_col, y=y_col, data=data, kind=kind)
    plt.show()
```

```
# Usage
data = sns.load_dataset("iris")
plot_jointplot(data, "sepal_length", "sepal_width", "hex")
```

Listing 8.22 starts with two import statements and the plot_joint() function that renders the joint plot. The second part of Listing 8.22 initializes the Pandas data frame data with the contents of the Seaborn built-in dataset iris, and then invokes plot_pair() with the variable data. Figure 8.22 displays the joint plot that is rendered by launching the code in Listing 8.22.

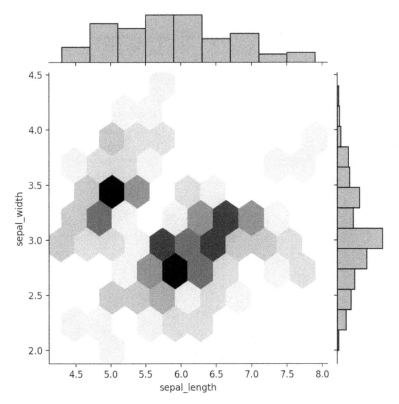

FIGURE 8.22 A joint plot created with Seaborn

POINT PLOTS FOR FACTORIZED VIEWS

Point plots can be useful to highlight the differences between points, especially when categorized by factors (like gender, in the usage example). The lines connecting the points can help emphasize any trends. Emphasize the comparison between points with lines. The following prompt was supplied to GPT-4 to generate Python code for a point plot: "Please generate Python code to display a point plot."

Listing 8.23 displays the content of `point_plot.py` that ChatGPT generated to render a point plot using Seaborn.

LISTING 8.23: point_plot.py

```
import matplotlib.pyplot as plt
import seaborn as sns

def plot_pointplot(data, x_col, y_col, hue=None):
    sns.pointplot(x=x_col, y=y_col, hue=hue, data=data)
    plt.show()

# Usage
data = sns.load_dataset("tips")
plot_pointplot(data, "day", "total_bill", "sex")
```

Listing 8.23 starts with two `import` statements and the `plot_point-plot()` function that renders the point plot. The second part of Listing 8.23 initializes the Pandas data frame `data` with the contents of the Seaborn built-in dataset `tips`, and then invokes `plot_pointplot()` with the variable `data`. Figure 8.23 displays the point plot that is rendered by launching the code in Listing 8.23.

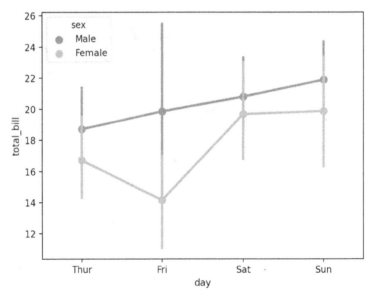

FIGURE 8.23 A point plot created with Seaborn

SEABORN'S KDE PLOTS FOR DENSITY ESTIMATIONS

Kernel Density Estimation (KDE) plots visualize the probability density of a continuous variable. They can be thought of as smoothed histograms and are particularly useful when wanting to discern the underlying distribution of a dataset. The following prompt was supplied to GPT-4 to generate Python code for a KDE plot: "Please generate Python code to render a KDE plot."

Listing 8.24 displays the content of `kde_plot.py` that ChatGPT generated to render a KDE plot using Seaborn.

LISTING 8.24: kde_plot.py

```
import matplotlib.pyplot as plt
import seaborn as sns

def plot_kde(data, column):
    sns.kdeplot(data[column], shade=True)
    plt.show()

# Usage
data = sns.load_dataset("iris")
plot_kde(data, "sepal_length")
```

Listing 8.24 starts with two `import` statements and the `plot_kde()` function that renders the KDE plot. The second part of Listing 8.23 initializes the Pandas data frame `data` with the contents of the Seaborn built-in dataset `iris`, and then invokes `plot_kde()` with the variable `data`. Figure 8.24 displays the point plot that is rendered by launching the code in Listing 8.24.

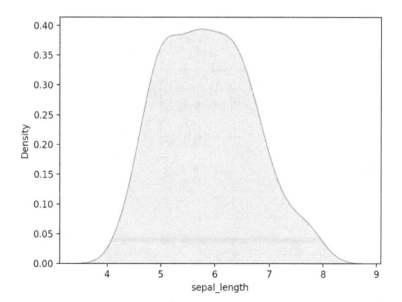

FIGURE 8.24 A KDE plot created with Seaborn

SEABORN'S RIDGE PLOTS

Ridge plots are essentially a series of KDE plots displayed on top of one another, allowing for the comparison of distributions across categories. They display overlaid distribution plots, which is useful for visualizing distribution changes across categories. The following prompt was supplied to GPT-4 to generate Python code for a ridge plot: "Please generate Python code to plot a ridge plot."

Listing 8.25 displays the content of `ridge_plot.py` that ChatGPT generated to render the ridge plot using Seaborn.

LISTING 8.25: ridge_plot.py

```
import matplotlib.pyplot as plt
import seaborn as sns

def plot_ridge(data, x_col, category_col):
    g = sns.FacetGrid(data, row=category_col, hue=category_
col, aspect=5)
    g.map(sns.kdeplot, x_col, clip_on=False, shade=True,
alpha=1, lw=1.5, bw_method=0.2)
    g.map(sns.kdeplot, x_col, clip_on=False, color="w",
lw=1, bw_method=0.2)
    g.map(plt.axhline, y=0, lw=2, clip_on=False)
    plt.show()

# Usage
data = sns.load_dataset("diamonds")
subset_data = data[data['cut'].isin(['Ideal', 'Fair',
'Good'])]
plot_ridge(subset_data, "price", "cut")
```

Listing 8.25 starts with two `import` statements and the `plot_ridge()` function that renders the ridge plot. The second part of Listing 8.25 initializes the Pandas data frame `data` with the contents of the Seaborn built-in dataset `diamonds`, and then invokes `plot_ridge()` with the variable `data`. Figure 8.25 displays the ridge plot that is rendered by launching the code in Listing 8.25.

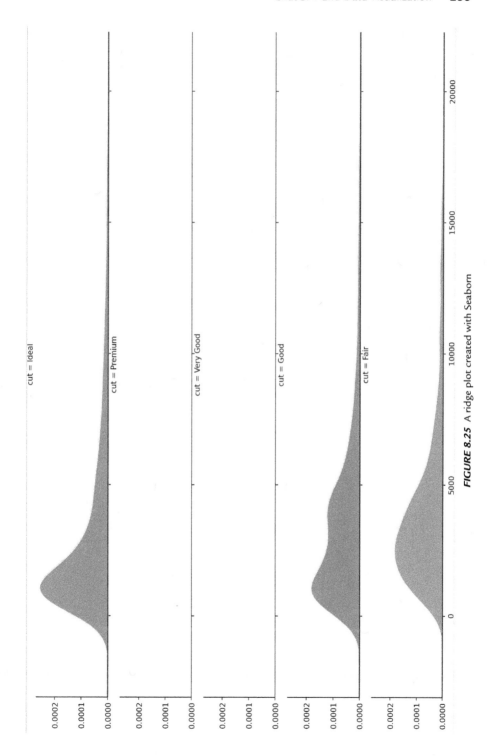

FIGURE 8.25 A ridge plot created with Seaborn

SUMMARY

This chapter contains Python-based solutions generated by ChatGPT for a variety of tasks. You learned about various types of charts and graphs, when to use them, and the advantages and disadvantages of each type of chart and graph.

You learned about data visualization using a popular open-source Python-based library called Matplotlib that can render numerous types charts and graphs.

You also learned how to render histograms, violin plots, and time series visualizations. By mastering these techniques, one can craft compelling narratives from data, aiding in decision-making and insights generation. A well-crafted visualization is worth a thousand rows of raw data.

INDEX